RECONCILIATION

RECONCILIATION

A STUDY OF PAUL'S THEOLOGY

Revised Edition,
with a new Appendix.

Ralph P. Martin

formerly Professor of New
Testament, Fuller Theological
Seminary, Pasadena, California;
Professor in the Biblical Studies
faculty, The University of
Sheffield, England

Academie
Books Grand Rapids,
Michigan
Zondervan Publishing House

Reconciliation: A Study of Paul's Theology
Copyright © 1989 by Ralph P. Martin
Previously published (1981) in the United Kingdom by Marshall, Morgan, and
Scott, London, and in the United States by John Knox Press, Atlanta, under the
series title, New Foundations Theological Library.

ACADEMIE BOOKS is an imprint of Zondervan Publishing House,
1415 Lake Drive, S.E., Grand Rapids, Michigan 49506.

Library of Congress Cataloging in Publication Data

Martin, Ralph P.
    Reconciliation : a study of Paul's theology / Ralph P. Martin.
      p.   cm.
    Reprint. Originally published: Atlanta : John Knox Press, c1981.
    Bibliography: p.
    Includes indexes.
    ISBN 0-310-28811-8
    1. Bible.   N.T.   Epistles of Paul—Theology.   2. Reconciliation—
Biblical teaching.   I. Title.
   [BS2655.R29M37   1989]
   230'.092'4—dc19   88-34367
                                               CIP

Printed in the United States of America

89 90 91 92 93 94 / AK / 10 9 8 7 6 5 4 3 2 1

To
My students,
past, present and future

CONTENTS

ABBREVIATIONS

ET   English Translation

NEB   New English Bible, 1970

RSV   Revised Standard Version, 1952

SE   *Studia Evangelica*, ed. F.L. Cross in the series *TU* (see below)

Strack-   *Kommentar zum Neuen Testament aus Talmud und Midrasch*, I-IV.
Billerbeck Munich. 1956 ed.

TDNT   *Theological Dictionary of the New Testament*, vols. 1-9, edd. G. Kittel
            and G. Friedrich, ET by G.W. Bromiley, Grand Rapids,
            1964-1974

TU   *Texte und Untersuchungen*, Berlin

PREFACE

In recent times students of Paul's theology have been well served with a steady flow of titles, each offering a comprehensive survey of the apostle's teaching. Books by D. E. H. Whiteley, G. Bornkamm, H. J. Schoeps, E. W. Hunt, G. Eichholz, L. E. Keck, H. Ridderbos, and F. F. Bruce are available to assist readers in their understanding of the scope and meaning of Paul's thought on many themes.

The present book does not pretend to be in that class. It does not aspire to give a full coverage of Pauline theology. Instead it has tried to identify, isolate and discuss a single theme, reconciliation in its different uses by Paul and his followers. The suggestion is made that this one term is sufficiently broad as an 'umbrella' idea to accommodate the leading aspects of Paul's main thinking, but no attempt has been made to work out this thesis.

Accepting as basically correct the statements about reconciliation offered in the standard works on the subject (for example, V. Taylor, *Forgiveness and Reconciliation*), I have chosen to do something that is not normally possible in a book on Paul's theology. The excellent treatments referred to above have to be content with a generalising summary of a lot of texts; the limited scope of this book with its focus on a single theme of manageable proportion permits an exegetical enquiry at some depth into the literary form, background, meaning and application — what is called today 'the horizon' — of a few key passages. This exercise will tax the reader's attention and maybe his or her patience, but the effort, I trust, will be judged worthwhile and found to be rewarding. The time is ripe for a closer look at certain biblical texts than is possible in the still-serviceable handbooks. Yet I have sought to keep the discussion as clear as I can and as generally intelligible as is possible in line with the avowed intention of the series, which is to provide 'books primarily . . . for students in universities, theological colleges and seminaries, ministers in pastoral charge and informed laypeople'.

I am grateful for various kinds of help in preparing this book not least the secretarial expertise provided by Mrs. Pamela Stewart and Ms. Wendy Bernhard in the Graduate Studies office, and the proof-reading and comments of graduate students, Daniel G. Reid and Lynn A. Losie, and my faculty colleague, Donald A. Hagner.

The call for the book to be reprinted has given me the opportunity to review the course of the argument put forth and to reconsider some positions adopted. No alteration to the text, save to make a few minor corrections, appears since I believe the book is still a self-contained and (I hope) readable exposition of a central theme in Paul's theology. I remain convinced that reconciliation provides a hermeneutical key to the apostle's understanding of what he meant by gospel in its ultimate formulation.

Not all readers will be persuaded, I am sure. The Appendix, however, does contain some new material by way of response to criticisms and queries.

Ralph P. Martin
Pasadena California
Sheffield, England
1988

CHAPTER ONE

PAUL'S THEOLOGY:
A PROPOSAL

THE NEED

The enterprise of seeking the 'leading theme' or 'centre' of the New Testament message is one that has occupied recent study. After a survey of current options — such as 'justification by faith', 'salvation history', Christ mysticism or an existential call to 'decision' — a contemporary writer concedes 'the multiplex and multiform' character of New Testament theology and recognizes the limitations of all suggested proposals. He offers no solution apart from stating the obvious, namely that 'Jesus Christ is the center of the New Testament', and announcing as a largely unproven assertion that 'there is a unity within the NT writings'.[1]

But to detect the universality of Christ's influence throughout the pluralistic New Testament literature is no satisfying answer to the quest because that discovery is a truism; it merely remarks that Jesus Christ was perceived and proclaimed as the good news of God in the face of diverse human need and desire.

Other contemporary studies hardly advance the discussion any further than a recognition that there is diversity as well as unity within the corpus of writings called the New Testament.[2] Sometimes the distinctives are believed to be so patent and important that scholars have turned away from the idea of 'the New Testament kerygma'; they prefer to speak more boldly of many 'kerygmata' (in the plural) in rivalry or even in competition with one another. More temperately other modern writers, conceding that 'conceptual unity' is a misnomer, agree that the various biblical books are in mutual 'creative tension'.

We may pose the question, What emerges from that creative tension to provide a synthetic formulation of the Christian message that will be true to as much of the New Testament data as a human construction can frame? To put a sharp focus on the issue, Is it possible to suggest a formulation that meets several criteria?

In two essays, appearing in *The Expository Times*, vol. 91 (1979–80), the present writer has sought to set these questions in a wider frame of reference by calling attention to the history of New Testament theology and by offering a groundplan of what have become the following pages. In particular he has kept in mind the tests of a model for Pauline theology that would seek to be as comprehensive as possible.

Those tests relate to the following matters. First, any statement of the centre of Paul's theology should set the sovereign design of God in his initiative and grace at the heart of the matter. Paul's witness is consistent here, namely that the entire enterprise of saving action originates with God whose love shines most brightly in all that he has accomplished for global and personal recovery.

Then, the Pauline message that touches both the cosmic and the human predicament finds its pulsating heartbeat in the cross and victory of Jesus Christ, making Paul's theology essentially one of a 'theology of the cross' (*theologia crucis*).[3] The 'cross' has become for Paul both an effectual symbol of divine grace to sinners and a clarion call to commitment in a life that is cruciform in shape and diaconal in its expression. No statement of Paul's atonement teaching that does not lead to the call of 'dying to live' (heard in 2 Cor. 4:7–12, for instance) can be regarded as adequate.

Thirdly, one of the major problems with the popular model of salvation history is the difficulty it finds in moving with compelling rationale from historical 'is'-ness to ethical 'ought'-ness. How does the death of Christ long ago affect my attitude to life today? How does his rising from death to newness impinge on my future? Any proposed model must grasp the nettle of these questions.

Above all, we are faced with the perennial task of relating Paul's theological work with what we find in the gospels. The relation between Jesus and Paul presents a still unsolved conundrum, classically stated by R. Bultmann, How did the proclaimer of the kingdom of God become the proclaimed of the apostolic preaching? To analyse that question and plot of the course of the debate is obviously not within our purview, nor indeed our competence.[4] But it remains that Paul's gospel has to be set within a developing Christian tradition that equally made room for the canonical gospels as deposits of corporate faith and experience.

As an ancillary matter, all we know of 'Paul's proclamation' was meant to be just that — a proclamation. We are on the quest for a *centrum Paulinum* that is coherent and communicable as much to the pastor and evangelist as to the academic teacher and student of primitive Christianity. Perhaps it is a case of being more important to the former group since it is they who have the task, both as a challenge and a privilege, of conveying to others in their own idiom and against their own cultural background the quintessence of what Paul regarded as his missionary and pastoral message. Moreover, the sweep of Paul's thought is much broader than is sometimes thought to be the case, especially in some parts of evangelical Protestantism. There are dimensions that certainly include the personal, but are large enough to be described as embracing the cosmos and its future, the church as a world-wide family, and the network of social relationships in which men and women stand.

A PROPOSAL

Peter Stuhlmacher has recently summoned us to reopen the issue of 'a synthetic biblical theology'. His short list of criteria is somewhat different from that above; and he asks that the proposal be consonant with Israel's heritage as God's people under the old covenant; the church's canon as our datum beginning; a theology of consent, and an openness to transcendence, by which we understand him to mean a recognition of the primacy of God and his grace.

Although his language and requirements may differ from what is given earlier, he is clear that

> the formation of the New Testament tradition [will have] the proclamation of Jesus Christ as Messianic Reconciler [as] its genuinely theological and critical center.[5]

In several pieces of writing Stuhlmacher has elaborated this theme, and the present writer is grateful for the stimulus of his insights. Yet one's debt lies more in another direction. In proposing that it is *the theme of reconciliation* that is offered as expressing the centre of Paul's thought and ministry he goes back to what he first heard from Professor T. W. Manson in class lectures at Manchester thirty years ago. Manson said:

> Reconciliation is thus the keyword of Paul's Gospel so far as its working out in Christ is concerned. The driving-force

behind the Gospel is the love of God. The *modus operandi* is reconciliation.[6]

To be sure, others such as Johannes Weiss (to whom T. W. Manson was often beholden) had stated this before him, as others like Herman Ridderbos have said the same in more recent times.[7] But it came as a truth with enduring appeal and deepening meaning to one student when his teacher expressed it so memorably. That impression has remained ineffaceable, and the present small book is one feeble effort to repay an obligation to the memory of a great teacher.

The tide of New Testament study flows on relentlessly. Over the past few decades new interests in Pauline studies have come into prominence, and the subsequent pages have tried to reflect these. It may be helpful to set down some features that may show how this book is being written in 1979 and not 1949 when Professor Manson's lectures were delivered.

a. Our appreciation of the unity and diversity has been inescapable ever since W. Bauer's *Orthodoxy and Heresy in Earliest Christianity* (ET 1971) made its impact. One way in which we are conscious more than ever of the manifold variety of New Testament religious thought, life and expression is the recognition that for Paul as for the gospel writers their credal and confessional materials had a pre-history in the tradition of the church before them, and their use of such existing forms was not simply one of borrowing and use. They entered into active dialogue and debate with these statements, sometimes by way of adaptation and sometimes by a correction of them. The present writer finds no problem in assenting, as he does, to a hearty belief in the authority of scripture when that belief is honest enough to admit concerning the documents: 'they are to be interpreted according to their context and purpose.' From all we can learn of the composing of Paul's letters it seems clear that 'context' and 'purpose' alike included an ongoing interaction with ideas and positions that the apostle found inadequate and misleading. Much of the central chapters to follow will illustrate this feature of 'tradition and redaction'.

b. The use of the imagery called a 'trajectory' (derivable from the work of H. Koester and J. M. Robinson) has been illuminating, though not beyond criticism. If it suggests the movement of an idea that is pre-set and inevitable, obviously it can be faulted. But even missiles are liable to mid-course correction and are exposed to unforeseen forces. An ideological trajectory should make allowance for similar deviations in its flight path.

The way a concept such as reconciliation moves through early Christianity in response to various historical, social and theological pressures has become clear in the preparing of this study. This is a warning not to take the word as having a uniform, static meaning. Its nuance must be decided by the context in which it is found, as we can see by comparing the texts in 2 Corinthians, Romans 11 and Ephesians 2.

c. A great deal of interest has been centred in the last few years on the liturgical origin, setting and significance of the New Testament texts. Proposals to see whole books such as 1 Peter and John's Gospel in a liturgical context have been made. A stronger case may be offered when it comes to paragraphs and isolated verses where fragments of hymns, credal statements, baptismal reminders and eucharistic structures have been exposed to view.

A main factor in this latest phase of research has been the application of the principles of form criticism to the epistles as well as to the gospels, often with revealing and positive results. We are ready for a new and less prejudiced look at the gains we owe to form-critical methods, as some recent studies have hinted. It is hoped that this treatment of some hymnic and confessional passages in Paul may lead to that end.

d. 'Reconciliation', the present author believes, can be presented as an interpretative key to Paul's theology; and if we are pressed to suggest a simple term that summarizes his message, the word reconciliation will be the 'chief theme' or 'centre' of his missionary and pastoral thought and practice. But 'reconciliation' is a word with a wide range of meanings.[8]

In a study like this, one is tempted to turn aside to comment on the present relevance of reconciliation to the concerns of the ecumenical church, to social and racial issues in western society today, to ecological matters, to the vexed geopolitical challenges such as world peace and justice, as well as to more properly defined theological interests that embrace teasing and controversial subjects like universalism, liberation theology and the new humanity. Faced with such an agenda the student of the New Testament may be only too thankful that his or her task is much simpler and more straightforward. Any observations the writer would be tempted to make would be the lucubrations of a naive amateur! So the temptation is wisely resisted.

What has emerged, however, is the clarification of a single principle that runs through Paul's teaching in this matter. There is a distinct shift, which only our exegesis can validate if it is true, from treating reconciliation as the operation of impersonal forces or other-worldly processes (as in gnosticism) to Paul's firm anchoring of its operation in the realm of personal relationships both Godward and as involving men and women in society.

Once again, the writer has to cast up his debts and pay tribute to what he read first in J. B. Lightfoot whose sentence may well stand as the epitome of Paul's treatment of reconciliation:[9]

> Though the Gospel is capable of doctrinal exposition, though it is eminently fertile in moral results, yet its substance is neither a dogmatic system nor an ethical code, but a Person and a Life.

In the following pages Part One will contain chapters that survey some suggestions of Paul's 'centre', and move on to consider the background of his gospel and, in particular, the framework of his cosmic christology, his thought-world in the Jewish apocalyptic conflict between good and evil, and his understanding of man as both alienated and disconsolate in a threatening world. In Part Two the sections of Paul's undisputed letters that deal with reconciliation will be subjected to exegetical enquiry and his teaching assessed. Part Three will look in some detail at the special case — in a new contextual setting — presented in the document called 'Ephesians', while a concluding section will seek to establish lines of connection between the Jesus of the Gospel tradition and the apostle to the nations. A Postscript will gather up the previous discussion in a summary statement and suggest some practical bearing for the ministry of the church today.

PART I

THE BACKGROUND TO PAUL'S GOSPEL

CHAPTER TWO

WAYS OF INTERPRETING PAUL

INTRODUCING THE MAN

'It has long been a matter of controversy among New Testament scholars how best we should interpret the theology of Paul.'[1] If this statement of W. D. Davies was true when he first penned it in 1948, the last three decades or so have seen no resolving of the matter. Paul still poses a series of tantalising questions to the would-be interpreter who seeks to understand him in his historical and cultural setting.

We begin with what are indisputable facts. This man was born and raised as a Jew; he lived his adult life in a Graeco-Roman environment and, in a dramatic turnaround of direction, he became a Christian. In this simple statement we have unconsciously placed our finger on the three spheres of existence in which this man of antiquity lived out his days and by which his thinking and living were shaped and moulded.

JEWISH HERITAGE

Both Paul's own autobiography (in Phil. 3:5; cf. Gal. 1:13-14; 2 Cor. 11:22) and the record in Acts 23:6; 26:5 agree in establishing that Saul of Tarsus began his religious life and career as a Pharisee, that is, as an adherent to a rigorous way of understanding and doing the will of Israel's God. This training which nurtured him from his childhood — since it appears that his family background was Pharisaic as well — must have left an indelible impression on him. True, there is some dispute over the exact circumstances which surrounded his early days. The data in Acts 22:3; 26:5 may be read in more than one way, and it is uncertain if Paul is tracing his boyhood training to his life in Jerusalem as a student of the rabbi Gamaliel or to Tarsus, the Cilician city of his birth (Acts 21:39). We shall return to this matter later. What appears clear is that for Saul, whether in Tarsus or Jerusalem, the ancestral traditions of his Jewish faith and practice were indescribably precious and influential. Only on this assumption can we make sense of his words, which his Galatian opponents could easily have checked and contradicted if they had chosen to do so, to the effect that 'I advanced in Judaism beyond many of my own age among my own people, so extremely zealous was I for the traditions of my fathers' (Gal. 1:14).

Those 'Jewish traditions' were given sharper focus in first-century Pharisaism. Again a more detailed discussion of the nature of Pharisaism in Paul's day will come later; here we simply remark on the central elements that would have been dominant in Saul's upbringing. First, the confession of God as one goes back to the deuteronomic credo, 'Hear, O Israel, Yahweh our God is one' (Deut. 6:4). This affirmation became embodied in the synagogue liturgy as the *shema*, a term derived from the opening verb, 'hear'. It marked the characteristic ethos and piety of Judaism in a way few religious watchwords do, so much so that rabbi Akiba died a martyr's death with this limpid attestation of faith ('God is one') on his lips (Berakoth 61*b*).[2]

Paul no less remained committed to Jewish monotheism throughout his life, and whatever adjustments and modifications were required in the light of new truth that dawned with the revelation of Jesus as Israel's Messiah and the head of the universe, he seems never to have compromised — at least to his own satisfaction — this fundamental tenet drawn from his ancestral past. See Galatians 3:20 ('God is one') and 1 Corinthians 8:5-6 ('For us there is one God').

Second, God has graciously made his will and purpose known in his law, Torah. Pharisaic Judaism held this divine revelation in high esteem, since it had been granted to Moses and transmitted to Joshua, and then to the elders of Israel and so on to the 'great synagogue' (Aboth 1:1). The Torah, embodying both the written law of God entrusted to Moses and its oral interpretation committed to the men of the Jewish religious authority from the time of Ezra onwards, became so highly prized that it was given a quasi-independent status. It is not always clear how the rabbinic language is to be understood. The praise of Torah is often excessive and couched in figurative writing. But there is no denying the power of some touching illustrations the rabbis used to express their veneration of God's revelation in his law.

As reported in Exodus Rabbah 33:1, God is likened to a king

whose only daughter is to be given away in marriage to another king. The father is naturally distressed at having to part with his only child. So he devised a plan. Let the couple agree to provide a bedroom for the king that 'I may dwell with you, for I cannot let my daughter go'. In the same way said the Holy One (blessed be he) to Israel: 'I have given you the law, but I cannot be separated from it'. The description of the law as God's daughter is frequent among the rabbis, and is a tribute to the sense of privilege that Israel felt in being granted such a boon. Paul echoes similar sentiments in less dramatic language in Romans 7:12: 'the law is holy, and the commandment is holy and just and good' (cf. v. 14: 'the law is spiritual') as one aspect of his understanding of God's law.

Thirdly, it is not surprising that since Torah is one of the chief pillars on which the world stands (Aboth 1:2), it should be regarded as a 'precious instrument' — in a phrase drawn also from the rabbinic writings — signifying God's choice of Israel as his elect people. The nation is twice blessed by God: on the one side, Israel is claimed as Yahweh's special people bound to him by covenant deed and tie, and on the other the people are told that God loves them. The token of that love is seen tangibly in the gift of Torah, which is a sign of Israel's privilege and destiny as a unique people (Aboth 3:14-17, referring to Deut. 14:1 'You are the children of the Lord your God'). Paul gratefully acknowledges this special relationship in which Israel stood and, for all his fierce denunciation of Israel's hardness and blindness (Rom. 9:31-32; 10:2-3, 21; 11:25, 28; 1 Thess. 2:14-16) that resisted his gospel's appeal, he never disowned Israel as beyond hope nor did he dissociate himself from his compatriots and their heritage. The moving language of Romans 9:1-5; 10:1 is eloquent in showing that Paul as a Christian did not renounce his Jewish past, even if his attempted striving for acceptance with God on the basis of 'legal righteousness' with its concomitant claim to 'boasting' is firmly rejected as 'refuse' (Phil. 3:7-9).

GRAECO-ROMAN ENVIRONMENT

Paul's career as a Christian missionary brought him into direct touch with the contemporary world of Graeco-Roman civilisation. He was no stranger to that society. Even if we grant plausibility to the view that Saul's formative years as an adolescent were spent in Jerusalem among his own people and

under the tutelage of rabbi Gamaliel, the liberal Jewish teacher
of the school of Hillel, it remains true that Judaism even in
Jerusalem was no protective cocoon shielding pious Jews from
outside influences. Recent studies have shown that Palestinian
Judaism was exposed to cultural and religious influences from
the surrounding Gentile world. So much so that it becomes
possible to assert that '"Palestinian" Judaism. . .shared in the
"religious *koinē*" of its Hellenistic oriental environment' because
'Jewish Palestine was no hermetically sealed island in the sea of
Hellenistic oriental syncretism'.[3] To be sure, the religion of
Torah still held paramountcy and the rabbis warned against
cultural assimilation. But after nearly four centuries of hellenistic rule Palestine could not be sheltered completely from Greek
influence.

So Paul was at home in the larger world of his day. The
possible effect on his mind and spirit of life in Tarsus, a city of
diverse cultural backgrounds and reflecting both western and
oriental trends, has been debated. Certainly it was a highly
civilised and sophisticated centre of Greek learning as well as a
city that preserved the ethos of the Jewish Dispersion. Hence
Paul's use of Greek betrays both an education in the piety of the
Greek Bible, the Septuagint, and also a broader acquaintance
with popular Greek culture. He used rhetorical forms in his
writings, such as the stoic diatribe, as part of his debating style.
He drew illustrations from the Graeco-Roman games and
athletic contests. He employed ideas, such as adoption proce-
dures (Gal. 4:1-7) and practices of contemporary society relating
to the release of slaves (also in Gal. 4:5, 9), to enforce the message
of his religious teaching.

But Paul's rootage in his Graeco-Roman milieu went much
deeper. It has recently been demonstrated that he was as much
at home with the social elite of hellenistic cities such as Corinth
and Ephesus as in the ranks of the synagogues of the Jewish
Diaspora.[4] The notion of Paul the letter-writer who used the
common style and vocabulary of the papyri, the so-called *koinē*, is
not quite accurate. His reading of the Greek Bible seems clearly
to have oriented his Christian vocabulary, but in style and
epistolary construction and argument Paul can command a wide
acquaintance with contemporary literary culture and finesse.
He owed far more to his immediate background in the world of
Graeco-Roman civilisation than is popularly thought. The older
verdicts of Gilbert Murray ('He is certainly one of the great

figures in Greek literature') and U. von Wilamowitz-Moellendorff who described him as 'a classic of Hellenism' have been strikingly endorsed in more recent times.[5]

Not the least of his advantages were his social qualifications seen in several ways. He belonged to a privileged group of hellenistic Jewish families to whom Roman citizenship had been accorded (Acts 22:28). This privilege along with the standing he enjoyed in the republican society of his homeland (Acts 21:39) offered 'a combination shared with only a very small minority of persons in the eastern Mediterranean. This fact is demonstrated when it suited him by moving freely in the best circles of that society', comments E. A. Judge[6] citing the evidence of Paul's social contacts at Athens (Acts 17:34), Corinth (Acts 18:8) and Ephesus (Acts 19:31) with possible access to the civic leader at Malta (Acts 28:7).

CHRISTIAN INFLUENCES

The transition by which Saul of Tarsus became a Christian may be credited as exerting the most far-reaching influence on him. What is usually called his conversion marked the change-over from his 'old' life to a new orientation and calling. The nature of that 'conversion' will be considered shortly. For the present it will be sufficient to notice that Paul entered an already existing Christian community.

He warmly pays tribute to the existence of this fellowship in Romans 16. Of Andronicus and Junia(s) he writes: 'They were in Christ before me' (v. 7). Paul's debt to his predecessors in the early Christian communities is one of the firmest conclusions established in recent study. The case for Paul's having taken over and used traditional Christian materials has not been more cogently or attractively stated than by A. M. Hunter. His thesis may be stated thus:

> [Paul] was to an extent we have never fully realized [in 1940 at least, when Hunter's book appeared in its first edition] indebted to the Christianity which existed before and along-side of him. There is much in St. Paul's theology and thinking that is common and apostolic.[7]

To prove his point Professor Hunter directed us to the pre-Pauline or 'twilight' period between Pentecost and the years in which Paul's letters were written. He demonstrated that it is wrong to think of the apostle as a sort of spiritual Columbus or, with a change of metaphor, 'as a lone pioneer blazing, single-handed, the trail of early Christianity'. Admittedly Paul *was* chosen and called to his apostolic ministry, but not in spendid isolation from the rest of his fellow-Christians who were 'in Christ' before him. At conversion there was the church at Damascus ready to receive him, if cautiously at the first; he had contacts with the churches in Jerusalem and Judaea (Acts 9:26-28; Gal. 1:18-24) and greetings sent to the recipients of his sixteenth chapter of Romans represent a great host of men and women already Christian before he came on to the scene. From all these sources he 'received' much of the apostolic teaching he was content to acknowledge as common property and a shared possession (1 Cor. 15:11) and then to 'hand on' (another technical term for the transmitting of a body of instruction, a *paradosis*) this teaching to his converts (1 Cor. 15:1ff.; 1 Thess. 2:13; 4:1; 2 Thess. 3:6; Col. 2:6).

The demonstration of a pre-Pauline tradition known to and valued by Paul before he communicated it to others is conducted on a wide front as the letters are combed for evidence. Much of the data lies not on the surface (as the allusions to the existence of traditions might lead us to expect) but just beneath. The excavations have been made with the tools of stylistic analysis, form criticism, and an evaluation of the content (*Sachkritik*) to see those places where Paul used ideas already current and which he often adapted and modified as he took them over. The results are very impressive.

There are fragments of early Christian creeds (1 Cor. 15:3ff., for example, as well as the short statements embodied in Rom. 10:9-10; 1 Cor. 12:3; Col. 2:6; 1 Thess. 1:9f.) which Paul learned from the churches in Jerusalem and Damascus. Early hymns are quoted by Paul, sometimes to enforce an admonition in his pastoral counselling (Phil. 2:1-11; here 2:6-11 is the quoted hymnic passage which celebrates Christ's road from the Father's presence to his present enthronement by way of the cross. The exaltation gave him the title 'Lord' which is the basis of Paul's ethical appeal in v. 5), and sometimes to repel a threat to Christ's person (Col. 1:15-20). There are baptismal hymns in the Pastoral letters (2 Tim. 2:11-13) and in Ephesians (5:14). Paul appealed to 'sayings of the Lord' that are sometimes parallel with the gospel records (1 Cor. 9:14 = Luke 10:7‖Matt. 10:10), yet often are seen as independent, unattached statements such as

1 Thessalonians 5:21 that early Christian writers regard as one of the unwritten sayings of Jesus; and there are 'words of the Lord' that came presumably from pre-Pauline prophets in the congregation (e.g. 1 Thess. 4:15ff.).

Collections of Old Testament texts were made in the early period and set to good use in debate and discussion with the Jews. Paul evidently treasured this inheritance and put it to telling effect in his synagogue sermons according to the record in Acts and Romans chapters 1-3 where some of these 'discussion sermons' are incorporated. The rich heritage was already there for Paul to enter, as we see from his prefaces to such places as Romans 6:3 ('Do you not know?') and 1 Corinthians 11:23ff. Above all, christological thinking was busy and productive before Paul appeared, and his use of credal formulations such as Romans 1:3f.; 3:24-26 and Philippians 2:6-11 shows that he took over gratefully the teaching on Christ's person and saving work even though he had to supplement and correct it to bring it into line with his convictions.

The gains of this type of study are considerable. First, if Paul already had christological teaching to build on and that teaching offered clear beliefs in Jesus as 'Son of God' and 'Lord' of the universe, M. Hengel's observation[8] is borne out that the two decades of AD 30-50 (i.e. the pre-Pauline era) were more decisive in innovative and ultimately determinative christology than the next seven centuries. In particular the emphasis on Jesus' pre-temporal existence (Phil. 2:6), his being 'sent' as divine son (Rom. 1:3-4, 9) and his atoning death (Rom. 8:3, 29, 32) was already fixed and influential before Paul's preaching began. Second, Paul is shown thereby to be no innovator or arch-corrupter of an alleged 'simple' gospel of Jesus, which he spoiled. The way is more readily open to trace lines of continuity between Jesus and Paul through the *Urgemeinde* or original community, however much both teachings differ in the terminology and idiom that is attributed to them. To this matter we shall return. Here it is enough to note that Paul is more an interpreter of Christ on the basis of church tradition than an inventor, though we need always to keep in view the 'extra' dimension of his theology that came uniquely with his conversion and made him an unrivalled interpreter of Christ's action as he had known it first-hand.

Third, by this exercise in literary research and textual analysis we are offered a window through which to see the terrain of 'early' Christianity in its formative years of initial growth and development. Paul's letters came twenty years or so after Jesus' death as a historical event. To have access to that 'tunnel' period is inestimably precious; and this type of study makes our understanding less unsure.

So Paul was 'a skilled master builder' (1 Cor. 3:10) who, under God, reared the great edifice of what we know as 'Pauline theology'; but he did it by using stones already quarried and hewn into shape, however rough and angular, by his predecessors.

APPROACHES TO OUR UNDERSTANDING OF PAUL

E. P. Sanders has recently written the following short paragraph to alert us to the importance of beginning at the right place in our interpreting of Paul's thought:

> The related questions of the starting point for seeing Paul's religious thought accurately and of the centre of his thinking are among the most difficult in Pauline studies. . . . The choice of the starting point is usually decisive in determining the adequacy of the description, and for this reason it is important to choose the starting point with care and to begin where Paul began.[9]

This insight is especially powerful as we come to pass under review the various possibilities in the field. Whether Sanders's own solution is fully adequate or not is hardly the point here — and we must address that issue later; what is vital is to recognise the importance of seeking to understand Paul on his own terms and with respect to what it is that distinguished him as a Christian apostle from what he may have been before his conversion-call.

The chief categories that have been used to interpret Paul may now be reviewed.

I. PALESTINIAN JUDAISM

There is a line of interpretation from Albert Schweitzer to W. D. Davies that wishes to regard Paul the missionary apostle as a person who basically remained within the framework of the Pharisaic faith in which he had been cradled and trained. The evidence that he was a Pharisee within the ancestral religion of Judaism has already been mentioned; and it has been powerfully assessed by W. C. van Unnik in the interests of a view that Paul in his pre-Christian days had been exclusively brought up and educated in Jerusalem as a student of the rabbi Gamaliel.[10] In Acts 22:3 the phrase 'I was brought up *in this city*' is interpreted to refer to Jerusalem where Saul as a pupil of Gamaliel was thoroughly trained in every point of the ancestral law. It is true that Acts 21:39 might suggest that Tarsus is the city in question. But although van Unnik's syntactical argument to do with the position of the participle — that in Luke's usage such parts of speech precede the words to which they are related — is open to doubt, as N. Turner has shown,[11] it still remains more likely from the sense of the passage that 'born in Tarsus' is to be separated from 'brought up in this city' where he was later educated at the school of Gamaliel. The scales which may be fairly evenly balanced at Acts 22:3 are tipped in favour of van Unnik's position in the light of Acts 26:4, which reads:

> My manner of life from my youth, spent from the beginning among my own nation and at Jerusalem, is known by all the Jews.

The issue is to enquire what is meant by the term 'nation' (*ethnos*), whether it refers to Gentiles in Tarsus or Jews in Jerusalem. Also what is the force of the copula 'and' (*te*): does it mark a distinction between Paul's early contact with his birthplace in Tarsus among his own people there and his later life in Jerusalem, with an interval separating that later experience from 'the situation of childhood days before he went for his education to Jerusalem' (Turner)? The key to the answer, however, lies in the final phrase of the verse. Whatever Paul is alluding to is believed to be known to *all the Jews*, and since Paul was speaking then in Jerusalem the inference is that it is Jerusalem Jews who are in mind. Otherwise how could they be expected to know — what Paul assumes — that he had lived in Jerusalem from an early age, if it was true that he came to the holy city from Tarsus only in late adolescence? So the conjunction must be taken in the sense, 'yes, indeed', and the words 'at Jerusalem' define what is meant by 'among my own nation'.

To conclude that Saul of Tarsus was exposed in the formative years of his adolescence to cultural and religious influences in Jerusalem does not, of course, prove that he followed exactly the code of Pharisaic Judaism as practised in Israel's heartland. For one thing, it is an extremely delicate matter to know what precisely did constitute the type of piety postulated of so-called normative rabbinic Judaism. Our extant sources are much later than Paul's own day; and not until after the reconstitution of Judaism in AD 90, following the break-up of AD 70 at the close of the Jewish war and the destruction of the second Temple, did Pharisaic Judaism become organised with its teaching set down. Moreover, as we have noted, the cross-fertilisation between Judaism and Hellenism even in Palestine was already much in progress by the time of Paul's early life, and we cannot suppose that he became a student of Gamaliel (according to the Acts record) or pursued the Pharisaic ideal (as he himself claims) in isolation from the swirling currents of many Oriental and hellenistic religious ideas all around him. Finally, recent studies, notably those by E. P. Sanders, have claimed that, although there are several items of religious vocabulary and expression which are common to Palestinian Judaism (as far as we can estimate it) and Paul, there is a decisive difference. That point of distinction which is traditionally linked to a different under-standing of 'grace' and 'works' as the basis of salvation is now more specifically to be seen in the total perception of the ground of God's approach to man. For Judaism the essence of the matter is 'covenantal nomism', i.e. salvation is offered to Israel out of God's grace, but Israel's obedience and 'works' are the condition of remaining in covenantal relationship with God. Paul stoutly affirms the primacy of grace but undercuts the Jewish exclusivist claim to be Yahweh's elect nation by opening the door of faith to believing Gentiles and applying the covenantal promises to all Christians, whether Jews or not (Gal. 3:15-29; Rom. 4:13-25). The heart of the covenant is, for Paul, Christ himself with whom the believer is associated by the intimate bond of 'participation' in his life and death. By this token which heralds a new age, Judaism's claim to be divine revelation is antiquated and Torah religion is set in direct antithesis to Christ, since now there is a new basis of religion altogether. If this estimate of the genius of Paul's Christianity is anywhere near correct, we can see in Paul both a common heritage with his Palestinian contemporaries in the ancestral faith and a striking novelty that emerged directly out of his union with Jesus Christ. Sanders has set the Jewish background on a firm foundation, even if parts of his overall thesis are to be questioned.

2. HELLENISTIC JUDAISM

The contention that Paul's religious views *after* his conversion are inexplicable unless we assume that *before* his conversion his exposure was to a type of religious piety different from rabbinic Judaism has often been made. C. G. Montefiore, E. R. Goodenough and S. Sandmel[12] have argued that the Judaism Paul knew in his early years was not rabbinic, but a poorer, gloomier and more fanatical species of Judaism associated with the Diaspora of the hellenistic world. The argument for this conclusion proceeds to show how later (AD 300–500) rabbinic religion was free from legalism and an introspective concern of 'salvation by works'. The notion of Torah as an oppressive burden does not chime with rabbinism's praise of 'the most adorable of God's gifts, the joy of the commandments' seen in Psalm 119. On both counts Paul's objection to legalism and his negative attitude to the law are held to be at variance with what emerges and to be more akin to a setting in hellenistic Judaism with its picture of God as transcendent, its pessimistic stance to life, and its interest in mysticism. The rabbinic joy in forgiveness that is available as men repent and return to God is singularly lacking in Paul, Montefiore concluded. The reason is to be sought in the statement that Paul had known a kind of Judaism other than Palestinian rabbinism; in fact it more resembled a syncretistic Judaeo-Hellenism which has left its mark on Paul with his interest in stoicism—terms such as 'conscience' (1 Cor. 8:7–13), 'nature' (1 Cor. 11:14), 'what is fitting' (Rom. 1:28) and 'self-sufficiency' (Phil. 4:11) are believed to prove the point — mediated to him through the book of Wisdom whose chapter 13 is held to run parallel to Paul's argument in support of natural theology in Romans 1.

The arguments adduced by Montefiore were handled by W. D. Davies[13] in an extensive critique. Davies laboured to show that it is impossible to keep Palestinian and hellenistic Judaism in separate spheres; he thus anticipated the fuller discussion of M. Hengel and others.

The acquaintance Paul shows with popular Jewish-hellenistic philosophy need not mean that he learned these matters in the Dispersion. 'At the feet of Gamaliel', as W. L. Knox pointed out,[14] an already mixed Jewish-hellenistic culture could be assimilated as part of the Jewish teachers' equipment in a cosmopolitan world. 'All this is the kind of thing which any intelligent young Jew would receive as the proper method for preaching to educated Jews of the Dispersion or the Gentile hearers who were to be found in almost every synagogue . . . .

There is no need to weave elaborate theories as to St. Paul's education in the Greek schools of Tarsus.' Moreover anxiety over the place of Torah and a certain distancing of God from human life was already part of rabbinic religion at its home base, and Paul finds no fault with the law in itself (Rom. 7:12). Human failure comes through the frailty of man's nature (Rom. 7:14; 8:3). The issue of Montefiore's major concern, however, is left untouched, as E. P. Sanders has pointed out:[15] what factor or set of factors will explain how Paul can pass over, in his critique of Judaism, the central matter of a rabbinic Judaism which is to do with repentance and forgiveness? Does this omission not point to the conclusion that Paul's background was set squarely in a type of Jewish religious practice which assumed a more sombre attitude to human need? If this conclusion is secure, it will put us on the track of seeking in Paul both a radical analysis of human nature as that of sinful creatures and an elaboration of the costly enterprise undertaken by God to rescue and restore his lost creation.

3. GNOSTICISM

The Graeco-Roman world in which Paul lived his adult life was full of religious ideas and practices. Above all we must rid ourselves of the common misconception that this was an age devoid of religion. Atheism — in the philosophical sense of a denial of the existence of the gods — was rare; the more characteristic feature is seen in the description given by Paul at Athens: 'I see that in every way you Athenians are very religious' (Acts 17:22). The impulse to religious observance was partly an intellectual quest for what is true and partly an aesthetic love of the noble and good, but as far as ordinary men and women were concerned, the prime concern was expressed in one word, salvation.

There was much to make the hellenistic world one of instability and fear. There were the political confusions that followed in the wake of Alexander the great's 'global' influence and its sudden decline. The wars and the disturbances of the balance of power brought an unsettlement to the lives of ordinary people across the Mediterranean world and the Syrian Levant. As was inevitable following the political upheavals and conflicts, social misery and economic ruin appeared on the scene; and these features contributed further to the sense of futility that fell across the spirit of hellenistic man. But there was a more serious dimension to the human condition in Paul's world.

A new view of the cosmos had been introduced by Greek scientists. The geocentric astronomy was formulated by Hipparchus (190–126 BC), who was the first man to construct a theory of the movements of sun and moon based on observation and to integrate this with the Babylonian eclipse-records to produce a notion of equinoxes. (He also goes down in history as the first man to have used trigonometry in a systematic way.) The geocentric cosmology taught that the earth floated freely in space, surrounded by seven or eight concentric spheres which rotated around it in perfect harmony. This view of the universe had a direct repercussion on the traditional Homeric theology that located the pantheon of gods and goddesses on Mount Olympus. At a single stroke they were rendered otiose as far as endeavouring to locate them in a mundane sphere, and they were driven to the outer regions of starry space. With the fateful exploiting of these astronomical and theological novelties by the astrologers religion entered a new phase. The realm of the gods or the forces thought to govern human life was fixed in the planets, and those gods became identified with the stars themselves.

The practical result was that religion entered on a phase of pessimism and despair. Once deny the existence of personal deities, who order mundane affairs in accordance with understandable motives of wisdom and justice, and no alternative seems left but that all things happen 'by chance'. The next step is to place the goddess Tyche (luck) on the throne vacated by Zeus, recalling Pliny, *Natural History* 2,5:22: 'We are so much at the mercy of chance that Chance is our god'. So it eventuated that everything in the world was placed under the control of astral powers which determined the lot of humanity. Men and women were made to feel that all things were ruled by an evil necessity and impersonal destiny which from birth determined 'the entire course of our lives, and which nothing can enable us to escape'.[16]

But escape was promised along certain paths. First, by seeking fellowship with a mighty god who was able to raise his devotees above the hopeless round of necessity and above the regions of the astral deities; second, by the cult of Serapis, Isis and the healer Asclepius — all deities who offered their worshippers victory over luck or fate and promised a new hope;

third, by renunciation, asceticism and magic — by all these routes the yearning of hellenistic man for 'salvation' and harmony with the eternal world was expressed and celebrated in praise, ritual, sacrament and experience.

One special way to overcome human meaninglessness and cosmic fear was the attainment of secret knowledge (*gnōsis*). By securing access to the esoteric formulas, thought of as passwords to ensure a smooth passage across inter-stellar space from earth to heaven, a person would enjoy both enlightenment and an entry to the ethereal realm where all is 'pure spirit'. In the classical systems of Gnosticism, dated in the late 2nd century AD there was an elaborate cosmological process to mark this transition; and it was based on a redeemer myth, i.e. the saga of a saviour figure who descends from the high God to enter our human existence. He experiences 'humiliation' at the hands of spirit-powers and thereafter rises to return to God, thereby opening a path for his adherents — the 'gnostics' — to follow in his train. It is still being actively debated whether this 'myth' existed prior to its use by Christian gnostic teachers in the period AD 150–200; the evidence from the Nag Hammadi library suggests that at least what may be called 'the gnostic religion' (Jonas' term[17]) was a pre-Christian phenomenon. This means that such important items in that religion as a dualistic view of the universe, a doctrine of man as a fallen and enslaved being, victimised by spirit-forces, and an interpretation of human experience based on man's homelessness in this world and his craving to attain unity with God who is spirit were all accepted articles of hellenistic religion in Paul's time.

To set Paul in this milieu is to say no more than that he lived in a real world, already facing deep cosmic and religious questions and acting out certain definite and highly popular solutions. The three basic needs of the hellenistic age have been outlined by P. Wendland:[18]

(a)   Men craved a freedom from the power or tyranny of evil spirits, and longed for a stake in immortality by a union with the divine. The answer to this elemental need came in the mystery cults which traded on man's frailty and finitude and offered an experience of rebirth through sacramental action. Reitzenstein expressed the hope in a crisp sentence: 'God who is spirit (*pneuma*), gives to the initiate pneumatic character by imparting immortality and knowledge (*gnōsis*).'[19]

(b)   As men and women groaned under the weight of astral

religion, which made them the sport and plunder of the star gods, they cried out for some mighty god or lord (*kyrios*) who would deliver them from pitiless fate and call them to a new allegiance. The cults of the various deities, part Greek, part Egyptian, part Chaldean, are all centered on the single idea of lordship. W. Bousset[20] saw in this the key to Paul's theology since it provided a setting — the contemporary desire to confess a cultic master and saviour — for Paul's declaration that even 'although there may be so-called gods in heaven or on earth — as indeed there are many "gods" and many "lords" (*kyrioi*) — yet for us there is . . . one Lord (*kyrios*), Jesus Christ' (1 Cor. 8:5–6).

(*c*) The soul of man, conscious of its divine origin, strove for redemption and release from its foreign and unrelated companion, the human body; and it sought either by ascetic discipline or bodily indulgence (a strange paradox!) to deny the material needs of a common humanity. By self-knowledge (*gnōsis*) the soul seeks release from earthly entanglements and an absorption with the divine that may be commenced in this life in anticipation of a fuller union when the body is cast off. R. Bultmann[21] finds in the gnostic view of human existence and destiny the background of much of Paul's anthropology and teaching on Christ as cosmic redeemer and man's enlightener and saviour. A reading of 1 Corinthians 2:8; Galatians 4:3, 9; Philippians 2:6–11; Colossians 2:8, 14–15, 18, 20–21 with these ideas in mind will demonstrate that much of Paul's language and idiom is dictated by a gnostic world view; but it is a different issue to decide whether he is employing such terms as his own or utilising the thought-forms of his opponents or his misguided converts to correct some false impressions.

What seems beyond doubt is the conclusion that Paul sought to express his missionary preaching in a language consonant with the cultural and religious setting of his day in order to be intelligible to the men and women he was addressing. The person and work of Christ as ruler of the cosmos, lord of men's lives and the fulfilment of their spiritual quest for meaning in life are the leading themes he handles. Much of his exposition is directly related to the pressing needs of the Graeco-Roman civilisation of which he was a part and in which he lived out his missionary career.

We may agree with G. H. C. Macgregor's verdict: 'Much of Paul's teaching on redemption is quite unintelligible except in the light of this universal longing for some scheme of cosmic salvation from these "principalities and powers" . . . which held the whole universe enthralled.'[22]

4. CONVERSION-CALL

But the phrase 'missionary career' in a preceding sentence stimulates the prior question, What was it that made Paul a Christian in the first place and gave him the desire to spend effort and energy as a missionary apostle? Was it a fresh orientation to what he had known as a Jewish proselytiser, assuming that his brand of Pharisaic religion engaged in active pursuit of the Gentile god-fearers with a view to their conversion to Judaism? Was it that as a hellenistic Jew he came to the conviction of the imminent close of history, believing that with Messiah's coming the course of history would soon run out and this apocalyptic vision impelled him to announce the arrival of the end-time? Did he already have a 'plan of redemption' in mind, supposedly learned from his knowledge of the Tarsus mystery religions or the hellenistic cults at Antioch where he first met hellenistic believers in Jesus whom they hailed as 'Lord'? All these proposals have been made,[23] but with scarcely any degree of cogency. Their fatal flaw is that they overlook what Paul, on his own admission, gave as the central motivating force in his life as a Christian and an apostle: *an encounter with the risen Lord and a summons to his service.*

One of the most provocative studies of Paul's conversion-call has been provided by K. Stendahl whose treatment deserves some attention.[24] Let the following paragraphs set down the gist of his argument. The ensuing response will give opportunity to offer an alternative treatment of the significance of Paul's experience before Damascus.

(*a*) He remarks on Paul's life as a faithful Jew both when he lived as a loyal adherent of his ancestral faith and later as a Christian. There is, Stendahl believes, no evidence of a struggle within his soul under Torah religion. We should appeal to his own unambiguous witness in Philippians 3:6 ('as to legal righteousness, I was blameless') as a ruling datum, and not be influenced by a false reading of Romans 7 which is often taken as evidence of a divided self.

Saul of Tarsus had no guilt feelings — on his own admission; nor was he obsessed with the quest of Luther, How can I obtain a gracious God? There was no 'introspective conscience' clamouring to be appeased and quieted. All such attempts to reconstruct Saul's discontent with Pharisaic religion owe more to a line of successive Christian saints and thinkers such as Augustine, the medieval monks and Luther.

(*b*) To that extent the term 'conversion' is a misnomer, since it implies dissatisfaction with one's present lot as a religious or non-religious person and/or a switch of religious affiliation. What came to Saul was a new vocation spelled out in terms of service to the Gentiles. But Saul did not jettison his Jewishness in exchange for a new religion. He remained a Jew throughout his life.

(*c*) Granted that Paul embarked on a new course of life following his encounter with the living Lord, it is still remarkable that he never once explains the beginnings of that new adventure in terms of the forgiveness of sins. Indeed, Stendahl comments, the language of forgiveness is restricted to one occurrence of the term in Romans 4:7, which is itself a quotation from Psalm 32:1. The reason for this de-emphasising of forgiveness is given as twofold. First, forgiveness of past sins is an inward-looking, anthropological idea, believed to be foreign to Paul who was indifferent to 'sins' (in the plural) both in his pre-Christian and Christian state. Normally he refers to 'sin' as a singular noun, thereby implying the notion of sin as a principle or personalised force. Secondly, Paul's more frequent term for human need is 'weakness', expressing both his own frailty as a man and an apostle and spotlighting the target at which Satan aimed his shafts either directly through Paul's bodily defects (2 Cor. 12:1–10) or circumstances (as in 1 Thess. 2:18). What Paul needed in these situations was divine strengthening and support — of which he has far more to say than of his needs as a sinner imploring the mercy and pardon of God.

The above statement, based on Stendahl's position and understanding of Paul's 'conversion', is open to criticism. We may set down the following responses.

(*a*) This estimate of the evidence relating to Paul's 'conversion' is certainly suggestive and some of Stendahl's points are well made. For example, there is no substantial reason to believe that Saul was caught in the throes of a spiritual struggle from which he sought release and which was resolved on the

Damascus road. The datum of Philippians 3:6 which certifies that Saul's Judaic life was one of self-satisfaction and confidence must stand and must not be absorbed into the drama of Romans 7 which, since W. G. Kümmel's monograph,[25] has been claimed as non-autobiographical in its relation to Saul the Jew. But Philippians 3:6 must also be read in context. There Paul is viewing his past life from the position of his new life in Christ. The turning point came in a renunciation of his former 'gains' of heredity, birth and religious zeal. But also his acceptance of God's way of dealing with men and women — devout Jews as well as pagans — made an end to all efforts at securing his own righteousness, whether on the basis of Torah or elsewhere, and cast him without qualification on the free favour of God. 'My own righteousness' is now seen to be an impossible claim, not so much because it eluded his grasp as a devout Pharisee but because it ministered to 'confidence in the flesh' (Phil. 3:4) which as a Christian he decisively renounced in his becoming a Christian (v. 3). This was the great discovery implied in the Damascus road experience. Attainment of nomistic righteousness which he claimed as a Pharisaic pietist is now seen to be invalid, not because he was self-deluded or had lowered the standard but precisely because it represented a mistaken goal for which he was then striving 'in the flesh'. The result was that he secured his objective but at the price of 'boasting' in the very achievement that can only be granted (viz. divine salvation) as God's gift and received in the pure gratitude of faith (Phil. 3:9; it is righteousness that depends on faith). And 'boasting', as R. Bultmann has shown, is the one human trait that stands in antithesis to trust and calls down divine judgment. See Romans 3:27; 1 Corinthians 1:29–31; 2 Corinthians 5:12; and later p. 60.

(b) A second criticism of Stendahl's reconstruction takes a look at what was the central issue in Paul's entry upon new life. For Stendahl the transition is a direct one from Saul's past to his new vocation as a commissioned apostle. But this is to overlook the middle term required both to show Paul his past life in its true light and to give him the driving force to embark on a new career. The intermediate term is Christ himself. What was at stake here was conversion to Christ, not to Christianity as an intellectual system or a new way of life and not to a freshly discovered task, arising from his commission. The central link, acting as a hinge to connect the old and the new for Paul, was *a revelation of Christ in his glory as the image of God.*

The data to show this are copious, not only in the Acts narratives with their use of language such as the radiant light (Acts 9:3; 22:6; 26:13), the heavenly voice (Acts 9:4; 22:7; 26:14) and Saul's falling to the ground (Acts 9:4; 22:7; 26:14) — all of which may be paralleled in Old Testament-Judaic theophany stories (Isa. 6:1–10; Ezek. 1:27–28; Enoch 14:8–16:4), but more importantly in Paul's own self-witness. The theologising of Paul's experience has already begun in 1 Corinthians 15:8 ('he appeared to me', suggesting a divine theophanic vision) and Galatians 1:15–17 in which prophetic (Jer. 1:4–7; Isa. 49:1–6) and apocalyptic (as in Paul's verb *apokalyptein* in v. 16) language and idioms are pressed into service. The fullest account is given in 2 Corinthians 4:4–6 where the 'glory of Christ' which became visible in his function as the divine image (*eikōn*) (Col. 1:15; Phil. 2:6; cf. Heb. 1:3; Wisdom 7:25) shone forth, reflecting and conveying nothing less than the glory of God himself. The allusions to the creation story (Gen. 1:3) are obvious; it is just as evident that Paul is comparing his experience to a new creation (2 Cor. 5:17) when on the darkness of his past life the recreating light of God shone 'in the face of Christ' who appeared in that moment of splendour, and he realised 'the new age' was already here.

The overpowering of Saul's hostility and his determination to root out the followers of Jesus is a marked feature of his story as he tells it in Philippians 3:4–10, 12. The last reference gives the key to all that Paul has related in terms of his decision to 'count everything as loss for the sake of Christ' (vv. 7–8). He writes: 'because Christ Jesus made me his own', where the verb is one that suggests seizure or arrest. Christ's firm hands were laid on him to reorient his life and set it in a new direction. Similar ideas of an almost forceable overtaking of Saul and turning him around are in 1 Corinthians 9:16 and 15:8 where 'abortion' (*ektrōma*) has been taken to imply the powerful intervention of Christ in his life. Allusions such as these could only have been made if Paul looked back to a dramatic encounter with the heavenly *kyrios* who as sovereign Lord of glory appeared out of the sky to apprehend him and redirect him to a fresh course of life.

Of course, conversion meant far more than an initial encounter of overwhelming and numinous effect. Paul came to see that the living Christ was the rationale behind the Christians' assertion that Jesus of Nazareth was the crucified Messiah — in itself a contradictory statement since 'Messiah' betokens divine favour and 'crucified' inevitably recalls the divine curse of Deuteronomy 21:23. But if the once crucified Jesus was living in the divine glory and radiated God's brilliance like the Jewish *shekinah*, as Stephen had confessed (Acts 7:56), then there must be substance in the shattering conviction that he was truly and validly God's anointed one. For Paul this inaugural vision and audition of the exalted Christ became henceforward transmitted into the awareness of his presence in the lives of his people (Gal. 2:20; Col. 1:27) who form his body (the question 'Why do you persecute me?' lays a groundwork for Paul's close association of Christ and the church in 1 Cor. 8:12; 12:12f.).

Moreover the reality of Christ's living among the Gentiles became the theme to describe and justify the Gentile mission for which Paul felt responsibility as the key eschatological apostle sent by God in the final time (Col. 1:24–29; cf. Eph. 3:1–13). Thus it may be argued that Paul's commission was certainly a part of his entrance into new life as a Christian but it cannot be the sum-total of it. Rather it is the immediate effect (Gal. 1:16: 'in order that I might preach him among the Gentiles') of an event whose cause must be traced elsewhere, namely in the epiphany of the glorious Lord who claimed Paul as his own and placed him in the sphere of being 'in Christ'. The christological dimension of Paul's conversion — strangely missing from Stendahl's exposition — turns out to be the indispensable factor in explaining it.

(c) J. Dupont[26] has shown that much of Saul's passion as a persecutor of the infant communities may be expressed in terms of his zeal for the Jewish law. At his conversion that zeal was redirected into an ardent love for Christ and his people based on the understanding that a new phase of God's dealings with the world had begun. Henceforth the gaining of nomistic righteousness would be an invalid exercise. Divine righteousness, i.e. a right relationship of acceptance with God was proffered as a gift to be received, not a task to be pursued with strenuous endeavour (Rom. 10:3–4; Gal. 2:16–21; Phil. 3:3–16). So Paul's conversion is best understood, from a theological standpoint, in terms of soteriology. Paul came to a dramatic new understanding of how God saves people and sustains them in covenant relationship with himself. Put sharply, it is not on the basis of the *old* covenant (that way leads to condemnation and death, 2 Cor. 3:6–11); nor is it on the basis of a *renewed* covenant as the Jewish

Christians chose to speak in their fragment incorporated in Romans 3:24f. (See p. 87.) Rather, Paul learned to express the faith as a *new* covenant (1 Cor. 11:25; 2 Cor. 3:6; Gal. 4:24–31). As E. Käsemann remarks,[27] 'Moses is for him the antitype, not, like Abraham, the prototype of Christ as the fulfiller of the promise . . . . For since Easter it has become clear that God's dealings are with all people and that Israel's election in days of yore points forward beyond Israel into that comprehensive history which began with Adam.' T. W. Manson puts the same thought more simply in his comment on Galatians 3:1–4:7 and Romans 4:

> In laying the supreme emphasis on this [promise to Abraham] Paul parts company with Judaism. For Judaism the great thing was the deliverance from Egypt together with the giving of the Law. In these passages, especially Galatians, Paul reverses the emphasis. Judaism would read the patriarchal narratives in the light of Sinai. Paul insists on looking at Sinai from the standpoint of the promise to Abraham.[28]

Paul's conversion entailed inevitably a measure of anti-Jewish polemic that marks off his old life as a Jew from his new identity. It is hardly adequate, therefore, to view his 'conversion' as in unbroken continuity with his previous life as a Pharisaic Jew and refer to the redirection in the form simply of his acceptance of a new calling to be 'apostle to the nations'. When Stendahl writes,[29] 'rather than being "converted", Paul was called to the specific task . . . of apostleship to the Gentiles', he has by-passed the question of how Paul's vocation differs from that of the Hebrew prophets such as Jeremiah (Jer. 1:5: 'I appointed you a prophet to the nations') and has failed to reckon with Paul's rationale for the revised place of Israel in the divine economy.

The new chapter that dawned in Paul's life as a Christian was opened by the conviction that the messianic age had brought Christ into history. The prophetic vision was that of a theocratic society; Paul's task was to announce the arrival of the messianic kingdom in Jesus, as the rabbi Leo Baeck has conceded.[30] Baeck declares with all candour that this is the novelty in Paul's preaching that separated him from Judaism and placed him in an antagonistic tension with his ancestral faith. Paul and his compatriots shared a common belief: when 'days of Messiah' come, the 'days of the Torah' will run to their close. The distinctiveness of Paul's position was that since Messiah had appeared, the validity of Torah had ceased and its function was discharged (Gal. 3:24–25). This accounts for the deep cleavage between Paul and the Jews and the virulence of their hostility to him. Yet he was shut up to that conclusion, expressed in Romans 10:4, once he had embraced the conviction that Messiah Jesus had inaugurated the era of eschatological salvation in those final days. From this new perspective he can go on to announce a society of messianic fellowship in which ethnic, racial and cultural distinctives are at an end (Gal. 3:28–29; Col. 3:11; 1 Cor. 12:13), since Abraham's promise is available to all Abraham's family, i.e. those who belong to Christ and are united to him by faith (Gal. 3:9). And Paul's conversion became a paradigm for others to follow.

(d) Paul's use of the term 'forgiveness' in the light of Stendahl's observations does not really fall to be considered here. It will be treated later. The final comment to be made, however, can take up an issue not handled by Stendahl; and this too seems to be pivotal to Paul's conversion as he worked out his later theology.

Above all else, Paul's understanding and explication of the Christian faith is in terms of personal relationships, of which 'forgiveness' may be suspected to be a prominent feature. To be sure, the verb 'to forgive' is only weakly attested in Paul, though the evidence is more plentiful if we go on to include the verb *charizomai* along with *aphiēmi* and *aphesis* (Col. 1:14; Eph. 1:7). W. Klassen[31] suggests that *charizomai* (to show favour) had appeal for Paul because it has root connections with *charis*, 'grace'. It has a softer ring than *aphiēmi* and stresses the personal since it occurs in conjunction with people rather than with sins. In any regard it is certainly a verb to be reckoned with in Paul's theology as we see from 2 Corinthians 2:7, 10; 12:13 and Colossians 2:13; 3:13 (cf. Eph. 4:32). Other verses (1 Cor. 2:12; Phil. 1:29) should be rendered 'show favour', 'do a favour', while Philemon 22 is different again. Paul stands out as the bestower of his generous forgiveness to the offender at Corinth (2 Cor. 2:10; 7:12) and counsels the Colossians: 'you must forgive as the Lord forgave you' (3:13 NEB). The link with the teaching in Colossians 1:14 seems firm; and it would be monstrous to suppose that Paul did not include himself in the coverage of the texts: '*we* have redemption, the forgiveness of sins', 'the Lord forgave *you*', in the light of Colossians 2:13, 'having forgiven us all our trespasses'.

'Trespasses' and 'sins' are clearly equivalent terms for Paul, but there is a frequently mentioned problem with the latter. He uses the singular 'sin' much more often than 'sins'. Paul's use of 'sins' (in the plural) in connection with Christ's death is found in 1 Corinthians 15:3. But this is usually dismissed as evidence on the ground that Paul is reciting a traditional formula. Against such a dismissal we should observe that (*i*) he does accept this formulation as his own and believes it to be a piece of generally accepted teaching (see 1 Cor. 15:11); and (*ii*) he returns to the plural 'sins' in 1 Corinthians 15:17: 'you are yet in your sins' if Christ is not raised.

True, it is left to a later statement in the Pauline corpus to reflect on Paul's conversion as a model of divine mercy and grace (1 Tim. 1:12–17), but it would not be overpressing the evidence to submit that Paul learned to forgive others and to be a messenger of reconciliation (2 Cor. 5:19–20) — his vocation par excellence — because he was made aware of God's grace and pardon to him in his first meeting with the living Lord.

That initial encounter, we have tried to show, left ineffaceable impressions on this man that were later to be worked into his mental system and whole life-style. *And out of it came directly his theology, fashioned and shaped as a reflective transcript of his own experience* as a person who had known at first hand the reconciling love and power of God in Jesus Christ.

CHAPTER 3

PAUL'S LEADING THEMES

The problem of trying to compress Paul's teaching into a single formula has daunted the best minds in Pauline studies. Let us pass under quick review some of the salient proposals.

I. JUSTIFICATION BY FAITH

Ever since the decade of the 1830s when F. C. Baur offered a reconstruction of apostolic history in terms of the conflict between Jewish and Gentile Christianity, it has been traditional — at least in Lutheran circles — to see Paul's response to this tension as all-determinative of his theology. Paul was concerned throughout his ministry with the Judaising faction within Jewish Christianity. This group insisted on Gentile believers becoming 'good' Jews as part of their acceptance of Israel's Messiah. The issue turned on the rite of circumcision, as we can see clearly from the debate in Acts 15 and Galatians 2. There is no consensus as to how these accounts are to be brought together. But they do agree at one point: from Paul's position male Gentile believers were not to be circumcised as a pre-condition of their admittance to the church. Paul's argument is emphatic (e.g. Gal. 5:2–12) because it seems clear that Gentile Christians in Galatia were being influenced by Jewish teachers who were seeking to persuade them to receive circumcision. The fullest picture of these infiltrators is given in Galatians 6:12–13 (where the details are admittedly obscure). They appear to have represented extreme nationalist sentiments and to have used the enforcement of circumcision as a way of ensuring ethnic unity at a time when Zealot pressures, especially in Judaea where they originated, were strong.

The historical circumstances of Paul's debate with Jewish Christians have given rise to the idea that his teaching was so contextually conditioned that it represented only an isolated phase of his thought. Both W. Wrede and A. Deissmann argued that the use of justification language was decided by Paul's

Jewish polemics. Wrede commented:[1]

> The Reformation has accustomed us to look upon this [the so-called doctrine of justification by faith] as the central point of Pauline doctrine: but it is not so . . . . It only appears where Paul is dealing with the strife against Judaism [citing Galatians, Romans and Philippians 3:6–9]. And this fact indicates the real significance of the doctrine. It is the *polemical doctrine* of Paul, is only made intelligible by the struggle of his life, his controversy with Judaism and Jewish Christianity, and is only intended for this [his italics].

Deissmann endorsed this verdict:[2]

> That the so-called doctrine of justification is so prominent in Paul's letters, which have come down to us, has less an inner, than an outer, cause. The hard fight against the Judaisers and the Law compelled the Apostle thereto. When, in the second century, the direct struggle with Judaism retired into the background, the necessity for strongly contrasting Justification by Faith with Justification by Works disappeared.

These negative assessments are not altogether fair. They skate too lightly over the full extent of the evidence and introduce extraneous lines of reasoning. For example, Wrede omits Paul's controversy with Jewish agitators at Corinth and he turns a blind eye to the ethical implications of justification (seen in 1 Cor. 6:11) by limiting the scope of justification to 'nothing else than Christ's historic act of redemption, namely, his death'. He fails to see the effect of Christ's death resulting in transformed lives. Deissmann, too, remarks on the fading of the teaching in later decades; he might have asked if there were other factors that accounted for the subsequent absence of justification language, such as the eclipse of Paul's teaching generally in the second-century church.

Wrede elsewhere correctly remarks that 'the framework of the whole Pauline teaching is formed by the Jewish idea of a contrast between two worlds (aeons), one of which is present and earthly, the other future and heavenly'.[3] This clue might have led him to give a more balanced evaluation of Paul's teaching, since it is the setting of his model of justification by faith.

That model is based on the Old Testament-Jewish understanding of 'righteousness'. As applied to man it connotes 'the status of being in the right'[4] when tested by the norm of God's righteous character. That happy condition lies at the heart of the covenantal relationship between Yahweh and his people, Israel. For the maintenance of covenant relations 'righteousness' on Israel's part is also required, with the prospect of attaining approval from God both in this life and at the final judgment.

Paul has set his face against this construction for two reasons. The Jewish claim that those who keep Torah and so gain 'righteousness' will be set right with God and given approved status before God is considered by Paul to be a vain hope; for this class of 'righteous' persons has no qualified member, because 'all have sinned and fall short of the glory of God' (Rom. 3:9ff., 23). There is no prospect of being put right with God as long as a person stays with nomistic religion (Gal. 5:3ff.). Instead the outlook on that basis is one of universal condemnation for both Jews and non-Jews, since all have become sinners (Rom. 2:17–3:20; Gal. 3:21–22). The way this has happened will concern our study shortly. It is sufficient here to express Paul's convictions that all stand under divine judgment (Rom. 1:18; 3:9, 19), and must remain so unless God takes action on their behalf.

The second reason why Paul opposed nomistic religion is that he believed a new era had dawned with the coming of Israel's Messiah. Moving from solution to plight — to use E. P. Sanders's recent procedural statement[5] — Paul knew he was living in days of eschatological renewal, and specifically in the matter of divine judgment. What Judaism anticipated as God's gracious intervention at the end-time — to vindicate and reward his people — Paul now declared as a present reality for all who were of faith (Rom 5:1) in the sure confidence that at the future tribunal the past verdict of acceptance and amnesty will be confirmed (Gal. 5:5; Phil. 1:11; 3:9). In this way the tension of the Christian life ('already justified. . . .not yet finally "saved"') is maintained as a part of Paul's proclamation.

Justification, as defined by Vincent Taylor as 'the gracious action of God in accepting men as righteous in consequence of faith resting upon His redemptive activity in Christ',[6] may serve as a starting point for a discussion of the meaning of the term. The definition, however, needs strengthening by a recognition that Paul constantly lays a basis for what he believed about God's 'redemptive activity' in Christ's obedience (Rom. 5:19) or sacrifice (Rom. 5:9) or righteousness (Rom. 5:18), and so more should be said in any summary statement about Paul's insist-

ence on 'imputation' — in spite of Taylor's disclaimer — as
providing a rationale for the divine enterprise in cancelling
human guilt and providing acceptance in his holy presence. The
paragraphs in Romans 3:24f. and 2 Corinthians 5:18–21 will
have to be examined in some detail. Also Paul's thought is as
much conditioned by promises of 'rectification of personal
relationships'[7] as by assurances of forensic acquittal. Indeed the
latter term is best avoided if it still conjures the notion of treating
sinners as though they were not sinners. Plainly in Paul's
theology there is no room for such exonerating considerations.
'Amnesty' is a term suggested by T. W. Manson,[8] and it recalls
that justification is above all a kingly act by which royal pardon
is freely bestowed on the undeserving. God's royal rule is
displayed in releasing offenders from guilt out of respect for his
son who stands as their sponsor. (M. Barth's interpretative
rendering of *hilastērion* is *Fürsprecher*, 'intercessor', 'mediator'.[9])
Jesus Christ by his undertaking engineers a new network of
divine-human relations — the element of novelty is seen by
Paul's statement that God's righteousness, i.e. saving power is
shown 'apart from law' (Rom. 3:21) — and the whole enterprise
springs from his free favour, his 'grace' (Rom. 3:24; 11:6). The
fresh start that is made by Christ's action ushers in a new order
that consists of 'a whole series of events which involve both
forensic and dynamic acts on the part of God'.[10] The refusal to
delimit justification to the initial act of acquittal and remission of
guilt, thought of in exclusively legal terms and played out in a
court-room drama, paves the way for a much richer understanding of the term. It certainly will include a forensic release from
sin's penalty, but justification will also entail the entire process
of the rectification of man's relationship to God who dynamical-
ly releases power to set this relationship in a new orbit. For Paul,
as we shall see, the new sphere of living is one of sonship within a
family context and no longer that of slavery under the taskma-
ster's stern eye.

Two direct consequences flow from these conclusions on the
modern debate over justification. First, E. Käsemann's important contributions have to be taken into our reckoning;[11] and
second, Paul's thinking on justification is such that he can
smoothly glide from that category of thought or model to
reconciliation, since both idioms are fundamentally dealing with
personal relationships. Moreover from this vantage point we can
see connections with those passages in the synoptic tradition

which stress the outgoing love of God for sinners in Jesus' ministry as he befriended outcasts and 'sinners', shared meals with 'publicans and prostitutes', and offered not only release from their past but new hope for the future in the kingdom of God already present in his person.

E. Käsemann has made two emphatic statements in his treatment of '"The Righteousness of God" in Paul'. (a) He has shown that basically God's righteousness is a gift that has the character of power. In fact the actual term is associated in the Old Testament with other expressions, such as 'love', 'peace', 'wrath', that are used in personified form and may connote divine power. That conclusion chimes in well with our earlier observation that what God does in rectifying sinners is characteristically a regal fiat, announcing a new day when past failures are put away, debts and liabilities cancelled, and guilt removed from those who otherwise must pay the price. The epiphany language of Romans 1:17; 3:21 is clear, and it is this coming-into-being of a new order that sets human relationships on a different footing from one of strict justice and merit. The divine power/energy now released and known in human experience is what the Pauline gospel is all about (Rom. 1:16; 1 Thess. 1:5).

(b) The second emphasis given to God's righteousness by Käsemann is one of its universality. He maintains that Paul stands directly in the tradition of the exilic prophet (Isa. 40–55) for whom divine ṣᵉdāqāh (righteousness) spills over into Yahweh's saving activity put forth on Israel's behalf and issuing in the promise of a new world. The apocalyptic dimension of Paul's mind is visible clearly in the way he celebrates God's power in reaching out to capture the entire world for the sovereignty of God. What seems a limited teaching in the Jewish Christian fragment of Romans 3:24f. is taken over editorially by Paul and enlarged to cover God's faithfulness not only to the covenant people of Israel but the whole creation. And that statement of a new creation brought into existence at God's command (2 Cor. 5:17) will play a significant part in Paul's developed teaching on reconciliation as he seeks to embrace the cosmic scope of Christ's salvific work (2 Cor. 5:18–21; Col. 1:15–20).

In summary, justification by faith, according to the more recent insight into the biblical usage of 'righteousness' and its cognate terms, *is a relational term.* Talk of forensic acquittal often suggesting a sterile setting free from immediate punishment is misplaced, and only serves to merit the criticism brought by Sanday and Headlam that Paul's teaching is little short of a legal 'fiction'. 'The Christian life is made to have its beginning in a fiction'[12] they conclude; but such criticism is deflected once we recall how this terminology is basically couched in the framework of inter-personal relationships, and carries for Paul a dynamic nuance of a new attitude of God to man as of man to God which in both instances leads to a chain of events. On God's part he takes steps to carry through the enterprise of human recovery and renewal, while on the human side the initial act of 'rightwising' — to use an old English term — begins a process of moral transformation associated with union with Christ that will ultimately reach its goal in the final homecoming of the people of God at the last day.

The way Paul can easily move from the idiom of justification to that of reconciliation is seen in the epistle to the Romans. At 3:21-31 the language is heavily indebted to the Greek root *dikai-* as in *dikaiosynē* (righteousness); the same is true up to 5:11 after which it is replaced by other ideas and recurs only at 5:16; 6:19; 8:33; 10:3; with 6:7 using the verb 'to be justified' in a special, non-technical sense. Moreover at 5:1-19 justification and reconciliation can be mingled as though they were interchangeable terms, at least in human experience. The relational dimension of justification could not be more clearly illustrated than by comparing:

We are now *justified* by his blood (5:9).

We were *reconciled* to God by the death of his son (5:10).

Both sentences say virtually the same thing: it is the assurance of being admitted to a restored relationship. But there is more to be said about this; see later p. 153.

2. SALVATION

Set against a background of political upheavals, economic stresses and intellectual ferment, the world of Paul's day was racked also by religious uncertainty. To meet this challenge contemporary cults of the Graeco-Roman period offered *sōtēria* or salvation. The term may be generally defined as an escape from the prison-house of bondage, from the pessimism of despair. The blind goddess of chance imposed a sense of life's meaninglessness; or else the more philosophical belief that the whole of life was determined by an inevitable link of cause and effect seemed to give a purpose to existence, but in the end it led to the same admission of hopelessness. Whichever way he turned, hellenistic man ran into a cynicism of 'failure of nerve', and called out for deliverance.

Edwyn Bevan reduces the variety of current philosophical and religious questings in Paul's day to the following items which are attested in 'hellenistic theology'.

> There was first the fundamental conviction that the world accessible to the senses, this material world was evil. . . . There was next the conviction that in the soul of man somehow or other an element from that divine world had got mixed up in the material sphere. And lastly there was the conviction that by some means or other the divine element could free itself and win its way back to the sphere whence it came.[13]

For Jews too the clamant need for salvation was no less real, even if the cry was couched in a different idiom. It was a need for sin to be forgiven with its guilt before a holy God removed. The one term that comprehensively covers both the Jewish and the non-Jewish areas of the human predicament is *peace*. 'Peace' can be understood on its Old Testament background as *šālôm*, an omnibus term extending over a wide range of meanings from soundness of body to the highest ideal of spiritual health and wholeness. 'Peace' spoke to the political turmoils of Paul's time as the much lauded promise of *otium* of the Augustan age failed to materialize and to yield lasting results of 'peace and order' under Gaius, Claudius and Nero. 'Peace' was the one great need of the restless spirit of the contemporary culture as it sought for an assurance of satisfying union with the divine and release from animal passion and instinctual forces. No word was more suited to express the answer to the widespread human condition across a wide cultural spectrum.

It is therefore not surprising that Paul's gospel is stated in terms of 'salvation' (Rom. 1:16) and 'peace' (Rom. 5:1). Indeed it is claimed that the whole of Paul's theology can be written in terms of these central and inclusive concepts, which 'cover the initial experience, the present status and the future consummation of those who are Christians'.[14] The lexical data supporting this programmatic statement are copious. Paul can employ the aorist (past) tense of the verb 'to be saved' to denote what has taken place in the hour of turning to God (Rom. 8:24; the perfect

tense, 'you have been saved', is found only at Eph. 2:5, 8 where
the emphasis on 'completed salvation' is needed to rebut a
gnosticising counterclaim and to assert by this creed-like
statement that no defect or inadequacy mars God's saving
purpose as it is viewed as an already accomplished fact). The
present tense, 'we are on the road to salvation', is also found (1
Cor. 1:18; 15:2), while the future hope of eschatological deliverance at the final day is mentioned as well (Rom. 5:9; 1 Cor. 5:5).

Salvation with its associated blessing of peace is characteristically depicted by Paul as a past event; and the Christian's hope
of being saved reposes on what God has done to achieve human
liberation from the thraldom of evil (Rom. 3:24; Col. 1:14). The
exodus motif with its passover ritual forms one aspect of this
teaching, and Christ is represented as the redeemer who secured
human freedom from the bondage of evil. Deissmann's well-
known attempt to understand Pauline redemption language
from the social context of his times and in terms of sacred
manumission, by which slaves in Graeco-Roman society were
set free by purchase, is conceded to have failed as a fully
satisfying background.[15] More likely is a common indebtedness
shared by other New Testament writers to the exodus tradition
that celebrated and proclaimed Israel's emancipation from
servitude to liberty, as in 1 Corinthians 5:7f.; Galatians 5:1. The
political dimension of this redemption — so commonly explored
in recent writing on 'liberation theology' — is largely passed
over (cf. 1 Cor. 7:17-24; Philemon);[16] the chief concern of Paul's
use of the term is metaphorical in order to enunciate and explain
what freedom from demonic forces means and how it is related to
Christ's victory on the cross (Col. 2:15, 20). 'Redemption' in
Paul's usage is an eschatological term to denote the action 'by
which God finally sets men free from bondage to evil powers and
to corruption'.[17]

For Paul the present experience is variously described as
being in a new realm (likened in Col. 1:13 to the counterpart to
Canaan, the land of promise), or standing on a new platform of
acceptance with God who bestows his peace (Rom. 5:1), or
enjoying a new relationship with God (Gal. 4:5-7; 1 Thess.
1:9-10). The immediate effect is safety and protection from
divine 'wrath' (1 Thess. 5:9; cf. Eph. 2:3) both in the present
(Rom. 1:18) and eschatologically at the day of judgment (Rom.
5:9). But the important rationale for this confidence is that the
new age of messianic salvation has already dawned (2 Cor.

6:2–3) bringing with it the 'new creation' (2 Cor. 5:17) or new order in which God and the world, formerly disunited and alienated by some mysterious cosmic rupture, are brought together and 'reconciled'. It is precisely at this point that Paul's salvation teaching is undergirded and supported by his presupposition of what God in Christ has already achieved, i.e. the reconciliation of the world. From that vantage point he is able to hold out the offer of salvation and peace in the empirical language of forgiveness and new life.

The critique that 'salvation' is exclusively experience-oriented and narrowly individualistic is valid up to a point. Pietistic religion talks of the salvation of the human soul (a phrase not found in Paul), and this practice only endorses the impression of Paul as a preacher of personal salvation. But just as Paul uses the title 'saviour' for Jesus only twice in his usually accepted corpus of writings and both references (Phil. 3:20; Eph. 5:23) are non-technical and are unrelated to what is normally implied in the word, so his salvation language is best seen as the language of experience that points back to a more fundamental work of Christ. The undoubted personal 'side' of Paul's preaching (for which there is evidence in, e.g., Acts 16:17 — 'a way of salvation'; 16:30-31: 'What must I do to be saved? Believe in the Lord Jesus, and you will be saved, you and your household') did evoke a believing response (Rom. 10:9-10) that led to salvation as an experience. Yet Paul never appealed to that experience as the ground of the Christian's confidence and hope. Instead he announced the arrival of the new age and cast his lot with the new beginning that had been made in world history. On the basis of a global reconciliation that embraces the cosmic powers, the forces of sin and death, and humankind as a sinful race in Christ's victory over evil, he moved to proclaim deliverance from all human ills that afflicted both his society and his readers.

To make our starting point in Christ's universal triumph (2 Cor. 2:14) as the great liberator is to begin where Paul's creative thinking took its origin. He depicted Christ as the victorious antagonist who raided enemy territory and delivered his prey (Col. 2:15), even when those hostile forces imagined that he was their victim (1 Cor. 2:8). In fact, he turned the tables and set the captives free (Eph. 4:8), so releasing men and women from their bondage to the tyranny of evil (Rom. 6:15-23; 7:14, 23; Gal. 4:3-8; Rom. 8:15; Col. 1:13f.).

It is important to fix correctly the sequence of Paul's soteriology. He began with observable facts of life, plain for all to see. The preaching of his message came as tangible good news, addressed to receptive hearers. They obeyed his word and accepted the invitation; and in the hour of conversion ('turning to God from idols' as 1 Thess. 1:9-10; Gal. 4:9; cf. Acts 15:19, describing the movement on its human side) they entered upon a new life marked by release from evil powers (implied in Gal. 4:8–9 which refers to 'no-gods' and 1 Cor. 10:20 which speaks of demons) and such polluting influences as those listed in 1 Corinthians 6:9-10.[18] Now they were in the realm of light and purity (1 Cor. 6:11; Col. 1:12-24; cf. Eph. 5:7-20), having received the gift of salvation and peace with God (Rom. 5:1).

Formerly captives, these men and women were released into freedom, with the tyrannical grip of dark forces broken. The question was bound to occur, How did this happen? Not that they would be questioning *that* it had happened; the issue is rather to do with *the process underlying the experience.* Paul's reply yields some surprising (to us, that is) 'behind-the-scenes' drama, which we may try to set out in sequential form.

(*a*) The 'rulers of this age' (1 Cor. 2:6, 8) conspired to destroy the glorious Christ. They rose against him in his 'weakness' (2 Cor. 13:4), but they were self-deceived as to the success of their endeavour.

(*b*) Christ turned the tables on them, and held them up to ridicule as he paraded them from the cross as *his* spoils of war (Col. 2:15).

(*c*) He was able to do this since he had already in that act of surrendering to the powers 'stripped off' (the verb in 2:15) the body of his flesh (his frail humanity, according to Col. 1:22) in what Paul calls his 'circumcision' (Col. 2:11). This is another name for his death. To be sure, Christians are said to be identified with that death; but it seems that Paul has Christ's own experience in mind as well.

(*d*) He put up the notice of his victory on the wood of the cross (Col. 2:14) and so announced that the reign of evil was at an end. He there began his reign from the cross. 'The paradox of the crucifixion is thus placed in the strongest light — triumph in helplessness and glory in shame. The convict's gibbet is the victor's car', is Lightfoot's picturesque comment.[19]

(*e*) So Paul can move on directly to enforce the appeal: 'Therefore let no one pass judgment on you' (Col. 2:16) . . . since 'with Christ you died to the elemental spirits of the universe' (2:20) which he so decisively overcame in his death with which you are linked by participatory faith (Col. 2:11-12).

The Colossians received the fruits of his reconciliation in deliverance from evil (1:21-22) because of their share in his victorious enterprise which is part of his larger work affecting the entire cosmos (Col. 1:15-20). Behind their personal experience of salvation and peace — to which they were summoned by Paul's proclamation (Col. 3:15) — lay the deeper, more comprehensive claim that involves the cosmic renewal and 'the reconciliation of all things' (1:20) effected by the 'blood of his cross'.

Salvation, therefore, suggests an omnibus term to embrace a wide range of human needs; but it presupposes and builds on the prior action of God who has reconciled the world to himself (2 Cor. 5:18-21). And with God's triumph in recalling the universe to himself in harmony it is not to be wondered at that Paul's theology will feature prominently the title of Jesus Christ which heralds the new aeon under its cosmic head, *Lord* (*kyrios*). Found approximately 184 times in Paul's writings, 'Lord' is essentially a title of liturgical origin, denoting a confessional statement in worship (1 Cor. 12:3), or at baptism (Rom. 10:9-10), or part of the acclamation that in worship reaches forward to actualize in the present the final consummation of the divine purpose (Phil. 2:11). *Kyrios* is equally a title of obedience and acknowledgment that expresses the believer's place under Christ's authority. It spells out 'the authority to whom men are accountable for their every decision',[20] and as such is a fitting response made to mark the initial passage from the old life to the new and its continuing pattern of 'being saved'. Transfer to the new domain of lordship (Col. 2:6) means leaving the old allegiances to idols, deities and earthly authority figures that offered no sure confidence in life and death, and an entry to a new realm of authority where Christ's victory has given him entitlement to control the lives of his people. They henceforth live in a new world which as a microcosm of God's final order proclaims and anticipates the time of his universal *de facto* reconciliation.

3.   COMMUNION WITH CHRIST

An earlier reference to Deissmann recalled his finding fault with justification by faith as the key to Paul's theology. In its place he proposed 'communion with Christ'. This emphasis which is well supported by the many Pauline texts adduced by Deissmann, notably 1 Corinthians 1:9; 6:17; 10:16, reminds us that 'to Paul Christ is not a great "historic" figure, but a reality and power of the present, an "energy" whose life-giving power [citing Phil. 3:21; Col. 1:29; Eph. 1:19] is daily made perfect in him'.[21] So in an oft-quoted sentence, for Deissmann, Paul 'is not so much the great *Christologos* as the great *Christophorus*,.not so much the great thinker in Christology as the great bearer of Christ'. Perhaps we are not compelled to choose between these descriptive titles, and it is certainly plain that for Paul Christ became and remained the centre and soul of his life (Phil. 1:21; cf. Col. 3:11). The autobiographical transcript of Philippians 3:7-12 is eloquent in its witness to Christ's personal presence in Paul's life, a thought he expresses more mystically in the limpid sentence, again self-reflective, 'Christ lives in me' (Gal. 2:20). So it remains a provable assertion that 'communion' (*koinōnia*) is a key Pauline term, describing 'the most intimate fellowship imaginable of the Christian with the living spiritual Christ'.[22]

With greater rigour and deeper penetration that takes us beyond the truism that Christ was all-important in Paul's life and theologising, Albert Schweitzer has referred to 'justification' as no more than a 'subsidiary crater' within the main rim of the what he regards as the main centre of Pauline teaching.[23] The latter he identifies as the mystical doctrine of redemption through 'being-in-Christ'.

The great merit of Schweitzer's approach to Pauline teaching is that it takes Paul's Jewish background seriously — at least in the matter of the division of history into two ages. 'The Most High has made not one Age but two' (4 Ezra 7:50). The New Testament writers use this framework of 'the present age' and 'the age to come' but reinterpret the time-line by announcing that the messianic era has already dawned with the coming of Israel's Messiah and the supervening of the new age while the present world order will run its course until the messianic age/the age to come is realised in its fullness. Schweitzer maintained in his book on Jesus that his mission could be understood only within the format of the Jewish belief of two ages but that, since Jesus' hopes of an immediate end of the world did not materialise, Paul was driven to reinterpret Jewish eschatological hopes in terms of hellenistic mysticism. And the essence of mysticism in Paul's vocabulary is 'being-in-Christ'.

With this reinterpretation Schweitzer could account for two features in Paul's thought. On the one side was his rationale of the time period before Christ's resurrection and his parousia or appearance in glory. Clearly this interval was not envisaged in Jesus' lifetime; he marched on Jerusalem 'solely in order to die there'[24] and so to expect that the end of the age would come. In the event, as Paul knew, it was not to happen, and so Paul was compelled to adjust his time-scale to accommodate an intermediate 'reign of the Messiah'. He did so by explaining the post-Easter period as the time when the communion of the elect with the heavenly Lord is actual. As Schweitzer put it:

> Paul's conception is, that believers in mysterious fashion share the dying and rising again of Christ, and in this way are swept away out of their ordinary mode of existence, and form a special category of humanity.

The modus operandi by which this being 'swept away' is effected is baptism. By this sacramental passage Schweitzer is able to answer the pressing question, 'How is it conceivable that the Elect, walking upon earth as natural men, should have fellowship with the Christ who is already in a supernatural state of existence?' Christians attain the 'solidarity of the Elect with Christ' by coming to share in a most realistic fashion in the same bodily existence. Christ and his people are thought of as 'physically interdependent in the same corporeity'. Dying and rising with Christ are descriptive acts that betoken a simple reality.

There is an important strand of the apostle's teaching that strongly emphasises the intimate union of the risen Lord and his people. Schweitzer has put his finger on a vital aspect in Paul's teaching when he writes: 'The concept of being-in-Christ dominates Paul's thought in a way that he not only sees in it the source of everything connected with redemption, but describes all the experience, feeling, thought and will of the baptised as taking place in Christ.'

His false step from this admirable statement is to insist that the formula 'in Christ' (where so much activity is located, as Schweitzer's recital of texts proves) is 'no mere formula for Paul', but a statement of literal, concrete fact, as though Christ were a substance or a fluid in which the believer is placed. It is one thing to assert, as a needed protest against the concept of justification by faith which easily becomes simply a forensic formula and suggests no more than a sterile, objective acquittal, that being-in-Christ is needed to add a dimension of warm, personal devotion to Christ in Paul's religion. But it is far different to insist that verses such as Galatians 2:20 speak of an undifferenti- ated mystical union whereby the believer is absorbed into Christ or that in the Pauline phrase 'in Christ' the preposition has a local force and indicates 'Christ' as a sphere in which the elect live.

The term 'being-in-Christ' has a built-in ambiguity. The result is that interpreters are hard pressed to say exactly how it is to be understood. There is one 'side' of the term that has overtones of a corporate nature, suggesting almost an equiva- lence of membership in the church as Christ's person and body. Analogies from Paul's Jewish past have been offered, such as 'in Abraham' or 'in the land of Torah'. Sometimes the term takes on a diffused meaning, implying perhaps no more than Christ as 'a sphere of influence' or a centre of consciousness. C. F. D. Moule has proposed that the phrase is to be taken locally but with metaphorical significance related to the exalted Christ who is the 'corporate representative' of his people.[25] This last notion seems the best current option. To this conclusion whose theme may be illustrated from 1 Corinthians 6:17: 'he who is united to the Lord becomes one spirit with him', and 12:13: 'by one spirit we were all baptised into one body', may be added one further considera- tion on the matter of Paul's so-called mysticism.

Théo Preiss has reminded us that 'life in Christ' does not mean a 'sphere of vitalism', as Deissmann thought, as if 'Christ' were an ethereal substance.[26] Paul's new life is no diffuse mysticism. 'On the one hand this mystical life flows directly from the remission of sins, from justification of which after all it is only another expression. On the other hand, it culminates in [a life that] does not fear to use the most common and secular business terms.' Social ethics for Paul directly stems from being-in-Christ as the background of his letter to Philemon shows, and this leads Preiss to comment on the christocentric nature of Paul's relationship with Christ and others. 'It seeks only to express in daily life the unheard-of fact that in Jesus Christ all are one: in him there is no more slave nor free (Gal. 3:28)'.[27]

So we infer that 'being-in-Christ' is a cipher for a network of relationships both divine (with the heavenly Lord as 'a man in Christ' [2 Cor. 12:2]) and human (as when Euodia and Syntyche are to agree 'in the Lord' or Onesimus is to be welcomed 'in the

Lord' [Phil. 4:2; Philem. 16]) that stem from Paul's orientation as a justified sinner and a redeemed man. The background of the idioms is different but essentially 'justification', 'salvation', and 'being-in-Christ' are all relational terms and take on meaning only in the context of personal relationships.

4. CONCLUSION

We have surveyed the chief attempts to set Paul's teaching under the rubric of its 'leading theme' or 'centre'. None has proved satisfactory since we really need a larger frame to encompass the apostle's diverse modes of expression.

It is for this reason that Paul's thought can best be captured in the omnibus term 'reconciliation'. We are seeking for an organising principle that will do some justice to at least three aspects of Paul's theology and religious experience.

The first is the cosmic predicament that in some mysterious way entailed the disorder of nature, the opposition of demonic 'principalities and powers', and man's need as an alienated and disconsolate 'sinner', bereft in the universe and estranged from the holy God.

Secondly, the saving action of God in Jesus Christ is directed to a process of restoration that will one day, Paul and his followers anticipated, lead to a reclaimed universe, at one with its creator. The sign and pledge of that cosmic renewal have already been given in what was taking place in the apostolic community — deliverance from demonic forces, the forgiveness of sins and life in the fellowship of the Spirit under the lordship of the exalted Christ. One token in particular was evidence of the new age that, it was believed, had dawned with the post-Easter triumph of Christ and his new life in the Spirit. Barriers of separation were being broken down, not only between God and the sinful race of humankind, but just as impressively between the inverately distanced groups in ancient society: Jew/ Gentile; slave/free; male/female. Life in the society of the new creation, the church, was a marker of what God was accomplishing in the world at large, and this revolution in the microcosm of the church was treated as a foretaste and promise of God's plan to embrace the whole cosmos in his new order.

Thirdly, Paul's own experience which dated from his encounter with the living Lord became a transcript from which he read off a major part of his theology, viz. the reconciliation and pacification of the world. This encounter, to which he constantly returns in his writings, left an indelible impression on him as a pastor-theologian that set the pattern for his proclamation of the kerygma and his expectation of what that preaching would achieve. He wrote therefore to men and women who, he assumed, shared his experience of God's initiative in grace, divine pardon and entry upon new life in Christ. His ministry was that of reconciliation — his own self-description (2 Cor. 5:18) — even if his terminology changed from time to time. He both rejoiced in the new status of friendship and amity that was his following his conversion, and went on to express the role of the church as a reconciling agent in God's design. The prospect of the church's mission is couched in terms embracing the entire world, of which the coming to existence of a new community in the church was a pledge. It only needed the letter to the Ephesians to elaborate and develop the teaching in order to produce a well-rounded philosophy of history in which cosmic reconciliation is the achieved goal.

So Paul's theology, essentially relational and concerned with the well-being of persons, took its starting point in what God had done and was still doing in the lives of his people. From this irreducible datum Paul extrapolated his teaching about soteriology (the work of Christ), ecclesiology (the role of the church in the world) and eschatology (the divine purpose in history).

CHAPTER FOUR

THE HUMAN PREDICAMENT

INTRODUCTION

The chapter title is intended to focus on Paul's background against which he erected his teaching on reconciliation. In one sense the setting reflects simply his observation that his world was less than the best. The indictment he used as a frontispiece to his announcement in Roman 3:21 that a new epoch has begun with the *manifesting* of divine righteousness (i.e. saving activity) began in a similar literary way at 1:18: 'For the wrath of God is *revealed* from heaven against all ungodliness and wickedness of men', even if the verbs are different.

Paul's world on its Jewish and pagan side is held up to the mirror in this lengthy section (1:18–3:20) and brought to see its deep need. In typical Jewish fashion, Paul traced the immoral ways of the Graeco-Roman society around him — and he wrote this section while living at Corinth — to the human propensity for idol-making (Rom. 1:23) in spite of what God has shown in his creation (1:19f.). G. S. Hendry rightly points out that Paul cannot here be conceding in the stoic tradition that there is a 'real' knowledge of God among the pagans, antecedent to and independent of his revelation in Christ. Elsewhere he forcefully denies just that (1 Thess. 4:5; 1 Cor. 1:21; 15:34; cf. 2 Thess. 1:8).

> What he is concerned to assert is that a knowledge of certain invisible attributes of God by inference from his works in creation has been given by God to men, but that men have rejected the inference and so forfeited this knowledge. The knowledge of God in creation remains an objective possibility, as it were, but the subjective condition for receiving it has been lost. And the consequence is that when man, alienated from God, yet haunted by the lost knowledge of God, attempts to recover it by himself, he reaches only distortions and perversions (Rom. 1:21–25).[1]

This statement is important since it shows how Paul is already testing human life by the revelation in Christ, and is arguing

48

back to human plight from the awareness he has as a Christian of all that God has done to rectify the situation. Such a line of reasoning is even clearer in Romans 2:12–3:8, where the Jewish world with its religiosity and outward devoutness is placed under scrutiny. The summarising verdict is clear: 'all men, *both Jews and Greeks*, are under the power of sin' (3:9) — a sentence with a middle phrase that recalls the announcement earlier made concerning the power of God to salvation already at work in the world with the good news that is addressed to men of faith, 'to the Jew first and also to the Greek' (1:16).

Paul faced the realities of the human situation based on the empirical knowledge that since the gospel was directed to all men and women, they needed to hear that message. And the sad tale of Gentile immoral ways (a commonplace in Jewish moral philosophy found, for instance, in the Wisdom of Solomon) and irresponsibility (Rom. 1:29–32) is matched by the equally observable realities of Jewish failure and lack of accountability as God's people (a verdict in which the rabbis concurred). These twin conclusions only served to reinforce Paul's conviction that 'the whole world [is] held accountable to God' (3:19) and remains under his judgment and righteous sentence. From this state there is no escape along the path of 'the law', for as we shall see 'the law' itself is a death-dealing instrument, and nomistic religion only compounds and intensifies the problem.

Paul's teaching on the human condition falls in two areas: cosmic rebellion and human need. In his view the first preceded the second in time, but it was from man's existing need in bondage to alien powers that Paul seemed to have argued back to the primal cause. The datum was what he knew of life outside of Christ; the inference he drew was that men and women were held in the grip of demonic forces — Satan, sin, the flesh, the law, death — because behind the current scene was the alienation of the world and the fall 'into' nomistic religion that looked back to a catastrophe 'in the beginning'. So we must examine first what Paul regarded as a cosmic disruption.

I.   COSMIC DISORDER

Paul insisted that the world is good since it was made by the good God, the creator. There is no pagan polytheism in Paul's cosmology. The scripture sentence, 'The earth is the Lord's' (Ps. 24:1) is quoted to prove the point that all God's creation is

wholesome against those who brought a super-sensitive conscience to their Christianity and advocated avoidance of fellowship
meals in certain circumstances (1 Cor. 10:26). Later the same
assertion that God's world and his gifts of food and drink are all
good would be made against a devaluing of these things in the
name of gnosticising asceticism (1 Tim. 4:3–5).

<h2>GOD AND MAN</h2>

God is the sole creator (1 Cor. 8:5), though he acted through the
agency of the preincarnate Christ (1 Cor. 8:6; Col. 1:15–17) who
was given, as the firstborn son, sovereign rights over the entire
creation, including its human inhabitants who were made by
God and for God. The phrase that is crucial here is that man is
seen in the new Adam, 'the image and glory of God' (1 Cor.
11:7), since it is this privilege of reflecting the divine splendour,
seen first in Adam according to Paul's Bible (Gen. 1:26–27; Ps.
8) that has been lost in man's fall — a lapse whose description is
seen in the wording of Romans 1:19ff.[2] and which is reported of
all Adam's subsequent family in Romans 3:23: 'All have sinned
and fall short of the glory of God.' It cannot be accidental that
what Paul regarded as Adam's chief loss — divine 'glory' (*doxa*)
— is exactly the quality that is restored to the new person in
Christ both in that person's present state (2 Cor. 3:18) and more
especially in his future prospect as 'eschatological man ...
[destined] to possess a spiritual body'.[3] The middle term
between that which man-as-Adam lost and man-in-Christ
regained is the image of God in Christ.

For Paul the divine image is seen in Jesus Christ (2 Cor. 4:4;
Col. 1:15; Phil. 2:6) — a set of references that borrow from
traditional teaching, but their use by Paul only emphasises their
suitability to convey the thought of what appeared to him in a
blaze of light before the city gates of Damascus. Jesus Christ
embodied the divine 'image' as the final Adam and brought the
divine form into focus with a human face. His saving work is to
reproduce that 'image' in his people who are both being
transformed by an ongoing process of renewal (Col. 3:10; 2 Cor.
3:18) and will at length be conformed to the pattern set by the
'image of God' in Christ (Rom. 8:29; Phil. 3:21). As J. Jervell
puts it in his exhaustive study, the heavenly Christ is the
prototype (*Vorbild*), setting a unique mould in which all repro-
duction (*Abbild*) in the lives of Christians is made.[4]

The christological model provides Paul with his hope for the future as far as man-in-Christ is concerned. The eschatological man, in Scroggs's phrase, is destined to share in the image of God in the last Adam. But this line of Jewish reasoning concerning Adam's high dignity above the angels and tragic loss of an estate which, the rabbis believed, would be restored to him in the age to come, gave Paul a framework to construct a rationale for the current plight. The world is astray from God's design because two forces entered the situation to spoil and deface the scene: these are 'sin' and 'death' (Rom. 5:12).

ADAM'S FALL

We should notice that Paul does not *explain* how this happened, except to shift the cause back to the personification (or personalising) of evil in 'the devil'; yet throughout he is bold to retain man's responsibility for what went wrong. The one place where he describes the stage-setting of man's fall is 2 Corinthians 11:3 (cf. 1 Tim. 2:13–15, which allows less room for human culpability since Eve's deception led to her transgression and she influenced her husband who otherwise would have stood firm; so too Sirach 25:24: 'From a woman did sin originate, and because of her we all must die', and *Life of Adam and Eve* 3, 'And Eve said to Adam: . . . it was only through my fault . . .'). Paul is content to state the fact evident to every faithful Jew without apportioning blame. He simply reports: 'sin came into the world through one man' (Rom. 5:12); 'as in Adam all die' (1 Cor. 15:22). And because of this one sin, 'the one man's trespass' (Rom. 5:17), death reigned and we all 'bear the image of the man of dust' (1 Cor. 15:49). Paul could well have expressed himself in the words of the apocalyptist: 'O Adam, what have you done? For though it was you who sinned, the fall is not yours alone, but ours also who are your descendants' (4 Ezra 7:118). But in fact Paul never apostrophises in this way.

SATAN/THE DEVIL

His interest is practical and pragmatic. He shows no knowledge of or concern for the Jewish legend told in the books of *Enoch* and *Jubilees* of the fall of the angels and Satan's dismissal from the heavenly courts. Both these documents offer an imaginative commentary on Genesis 6:1–4 and trace the origin of Satan's kingdom of demons to this source (1 Enoch 15:8–10; 16:1; 19:1; 69:4–6; Jub. 4:15–22).

(a) The chief instance where Paul could possibly have Satan's initial downfall in mind comes in a pre-Pauline passage: Philippians 2:6–11. There, some scholars hold, the contrast is made between Satan who tried to grasp at equality with God and was abased, and the obedient Christ who chose rather to receive his title to lordship by an act of submission and subsequent enthronement by God. The Enoch literature, referred to by E. Stauffer,[5] who champions this background of a conscious contrast between the two personages, describes the devil as a glorious angelic leader (*Slavonic Enoch* 39:4–5). In a decisive hour he refused to obey God and spoke out defiantly in words reminiscent of Isaiah 14:12f., which current Jewish tradition took as imaging the aspiration and fall of Satan. The penalty that followed was his expulsion from heaven — allusions to this are elsewhere in the New Testament (Luke 10:18; 2 Pet. 2:4ff.; Jude 6; Rev. 9:1; 12:9) and in 2 Clement 20:4.

On this view Paul is deliberately contrasting the picture of Satan and his *superbia* or pride with his depiction of Christ and his *humilitas*. The link term is the desire to rival God. The Enoch documents and the *Life of Adam and Eve* chapters 10–17 put this satanic ambition in a dramatic way. Satan had his heavenly nature as an angel of light and was honoured as the chiefest of God's creatures, but he strove after equality with God. The test came when he refused to worship Adam. Instead he proceeded to seduce Eve and in his proud disobedience he was robbed of his glory (a part of the story Paul was familiar with according to 2 Cor. 11:14) and disgraced. His role in this legendary story as 'tempter' persists in Paul's demonology where Satan is consistently spoken of as acting to place a roadblock in the path of the Gentile mission (1 Thess. 2:18), to upset the standing of Paul's converts (1 Thess. 3:5; 2 Cor. 2:11) and to assault Paul's own person (2 Cor. 12:7). Ephesians 6:11–12 is exceptional, not primarily because it uses the title 'the devil' where Paul normally has 'Satan' or 'Belial' (2 Cor. 6:15; a title shared in *Jubilees* and the *Testaments of the Twelve Patriarchs* with 'Mastema' for the personification of Israel's great enemy), but because it locates the sphere of the conflict 'in the heavenlies', thought of as the residence of evil intelligences (cf. Eph. 2:2). In other New Testament references believers face demonic powers on earth or from 'under the earth' (Phil. 2:10).

(*b*) A second possibility of Paul's side-glance at Satan's fall is raised when we look at Romans 8:19–23. The 'creation' (*ktisis*) which is the subject of Paul's paragraph means more than simply humankind. It is described as being 'made subject to futility, not of its own will, but through him who subjected it in hope', and is at present afflicted by 'the bondage of decay' awaiting its deliverance — as do Christians. Paul had earlier in this letter traced the human condition to man's responsible and deliberate refusal to acknowledge God, and men are confirmed by God in their fateful moral choices (Rom. 1:21). Here some extra-terrestrial power is at work enslaving the world and corrupting its fair beauty by subjecting it to 'decay' as well as imposing a curse on humanity (Gen. 3:17ff.). The result is that creation like the Christian (v. 23) 'groans and travails' (v. 22) as it waits for its final redemption and liberation — terms which indicate its present state as victimised by angelic powers and its future hope to be released from their malign grip.

The corrupting 'powers' are evidently treated by Paul as demonic, parallel to the 'elemental spirits of the universe' in Galatians 4:3, 9; Colossians 2:8, 20. These spirit-powers are most likely the astrological deities that the ancients thought of as controlling the universe and making man the plaything of fate, as we have seen. The exegetical question raised at Romans 8:19ff. is whether Paul has Satan's fall in view and whether it was this primal disobedience and rebellion that dragged down the whole creation. That it was so Karl Heim argues.[6] He suggests that the 'vanity', 'corruption', and 'death' of our passage are all attributable to the 'Satanic rebellion against the omnipotence of God'. Such a defiance has been in force in the whole creation even before the rise of man and 'the whole creation is under a curse derived from the Satanic power, which has brought the living world of creation under the bondage of corruption'. The charge that this interpretation postulates 'an un-Pauline dualism'[7] is perhaps not necessary, once we see how the passage refers to the temporary nature of the bondage and the creation's final hope that is the creator's design for its ultimate state.

In other places Paul describes how all cosmic agencies — 'thrones, dominions, principalities, authorities' (Col. 1:16; cf. 2:10; 1 Cor. 15:24) — have been brought into existence by the eternal Christ and find their rationale only in him. Clearly the statement, even if Colossians 1:15–20 has its origin in a pre-Pauline composition, is polemical and directed against a gnosticising world-view that regarded these 'angels' as mediators to be venerated (Col. 2:18). Paul denied them this role by his assertion that the entire 'fullness' (*plērōma*) of deity resides in the human Jesus (Col. 1:19; 2:9), who is the sole intermediary between God and the world. These 'elemental spirits of the universe' (Col. 2:8, 20) represent therefore the church's enemies and must be resisted. But they have already been overcome in Christ's triumph (Col. 2:15) and their hostility neutralised. So there is no need to fear them nor accord them a place in any theosophical or religious system. They are foredoomed in Christ's victory and will at length be 'destroyed' (1 Cor. 15:24).

Paul makes one further observation that complicates the picture. In Colossians 1:20 these cosmic agencies evidently belong to part of the object of Christ's reconciliation undertaken at the cross. 'Reconciliation' presupposes an original hostility since 'no one reconciles or triumphs over what is not opposed to him'.[8] So Paul's declarations in 1:20 and 2:15 can only mean that the powers were created to be subservient to the cosmic Christ (a thought implied maybe in the phrase 'for him', *eis auton*, in v. 16) but they have broken away from their primal station and 'deserted their appointed rank'. Their 'status' between creation and the time of Christ's triumph over them is one of rebellion, and the effect of his work is to neutralise or at least pacify their enmity against the day of their elimination.

All this drama suggests that their being wrenched from an original station or rank and their continuing malevolence reflect Paul's knowledge of the Jewish legend of Satan's primordial rebellion and his expulsion from the divine presence with his minions.

ANGELS

Paul's angelology includes 'good' angels (2 Thess. 1:7; possibly the same angels are mentioned in 1 Thess. 3:13 as 'saints', i.e. holy ones as in Dan. 4:23, 'watchers' — a name for angels in *Jubilees*), but his main emphasis falls on evil angels that try to separate Christians from God's love (Rom. 8:38). Other demonic powers are Satan's messiah, the 'lawless one' (2 Thess. 2:9) whose parousia in a show of triumph will not succeed since he will be blasted by a messianic parousia of Jesus (2 Thess. 2:8), and 'spirit forces' which comprise a kingdom of Satan.

Jewish apocalyptic ranging from Daniel to 4 Ezra and Baruch provided Paul with a framework of dualism. It is a set theme of these writings that there are two kingdoms that face each other in deadly opposition. Israel is caught in the middle and is the bone of contention between good and evil powers that claim her allegiance. J. Weiss[9] quotes the vivid imagery of *Testament of Dan* 6:1 to show how Israel is in the cockpit of a struggle: so 'beware of Satan and his spirits . . . the enemy is eager to destroy all that call upon the Lord'. Deliverance is promised along certain well-defined paths: Israel's repentance, full obedience, perfect sabbath observance are among the deciding factors that tip the scales and yield victory as they introduce the time of messianic salvation. On the other side Israel's failures and disloyalties impede the coming of the day of deliverance. So the warfare continues.

Paul could take over this frame of reference but he has made several important qualifications. Satan indeed is head of a kingdom, 'the domain of darkness' (Col. 1:13) from which believers are rescued (Gal. 1:4) but the possibility of their being sent back by excommunication is ever present (1 Cor. 5:5; cf. 1 Tim. 1:20). The Pauline pastor warns clearly that this is no idle threat: 'some have already strayed after Satan' (1 Tim. 5:15). There in the 'world order' that is soon to pass away Satan continues to rule (Eph. 2:2) and his influence poses a real danger against which Christians are warned (2 Cor. 2:11).

But Paul's dualism of evil and good powers in continuing contention is more apparent than real. 'The god of this age' (2 Cor. 4:4) may work his will to blind the minds of unbelievers but the light of the Pauline gospel that borrows its illumination from the 'glory of Christ' (4:4) or 'the glory of God in the person of Christ' (4:6) shines in the darkness and penetrates the veil cast over those who are 'perishing', whether Gentiles (1 Cor. 1:18) or Jews (2 Cor. 3:15). The emergence from darkness to light is a theme constantly recurring as a dramatic way of describing conversion in Paul's communities (e.g. 2 Cor. 6:14; Phil. 2:15; 1 Thess. 5:5; Eph. 5:8–14; Col. 1:12–13). The last reference is emphatic that just as there is a kingdom of evil from which believers are rescued, so there is 'the kingdom of the son whom God loves' which has opened its gates to receive them. To that extent Satan's realm is being despoiled and robbed of its prey – a rationale for Paul's antagonistic *Christus victor* christology that he will elaborate in Colossians 2:8–15. And that divine realm will last when Satan's empire is no more. Indeed already the process of its decay has begun (1 Cor. 2:6, 'the rulers of this age . . . are doomed to pass away') and when the messianic era merges into the final kingdom (1 Cor. 15:25–28) the enemies will be completely put down and their power destroyed. T. W. Manson neatly phrases it: 'Satanic power is limited in extent; he is the god of this world — and this world only.'[10]

A second reason why Paul is protected from the charge of dualism is that he seems to have used the role of Satan as a background idea — he has no speculative interest in demonology — against which to deal realistically with pastoral problems such as temptation and moral laxity (see 1 Cor. 10:6–13). And his employment of personalised language to describe Satan and 'the powers' serves to give a dimension to the cosmic work of *Christus creator* in refutation of incipient Gnosticism. Above all, satanic forces are like a foil against which Paul proclaimed the victory of Christ, already achieved in principle and in the end destined to lead to the actual overthrow and destruction of the church's enemies. So Paul's satanology is never pessimistic as though the struggle were unequal and the result in doubt. In Christ's triumph at the cross (Col. 2:15), the resurrection (Eph. 1:20–21) and his return to the Father (Eph. 4:10; cf. 1 Tim. 3:16), the age to come has already supervened on the stage of world history with the promise that as 'the form of this world' passes away (1 Cor. 7:31) the powers of the new age will grow stronger under the rule of Christ which has already begun (1 Cor. 15:25) in anticipation of the day of God's universal sovereignty (1 Cor. 15:23; Eph. 1:10). The church's lot is cast in the coincidence of these two ages (1 Cor. 10:11) and it is Paul's confidence about the flow of history that gives him the assurance: 'The Lord is faithful . . . he will guard you from the evil one' (2 Thess. 3:3, RSV marg.). Perhaps Romans 16:20 has this same optimism in view: 'The God of peace will soon crush Satan under your feet.'

2. THE HUMAN CONDITION

Paul's understanding of the supra-terrestrial forces, concentrated in Satan and hostile angels, is really (we have proposed) a piece of demonology used to explain the human condition as he knew it empirically. Just as Paul's gospel works from solution to plight — 'the view that all men are under the lordship of sin as a reflex of his soteriology', as E. P. Sanders maintains[11] — so it may be argued that his analysis of human needs leads him to erect a network of demonic evil.

Logically we began with the idea of a cosmic disturbance involving Satan's take-over of the world with divine 'consent' — he is still God's devil, as Luther remarked — and the baneful influence of the 'powers of darkness' from which believers are redeemed. These forces are on the road to ruin (1 Cor. 2:6), even if their opposition is still felt. Phenomenologically their present control of the world scene and contemporary society in Paul's day led him to formulate his paradox of 'already set free . . . not yet finally victorious' which he used to good effect against the Corinthian enthusiasts who believed that the life on which they embarked in their 'baptismal resurrection' was life in a realised kingdom (1 Cor. 4:8) and so they denied a future resurrection (1 Cor. 15:12). Paul's response was to insist on the incompleteness of present salvation in hope of its final phase after the parousia. In the interim the church has to live in an arena where contending parties still engage one another, even if the final issue is not still in the balance. The decisive engagement has been fought and won by Christ (Col. 2:15) and Christians have 'died out from under the elements' (Col. 2:20; Rom. 7:1–4).[12]

The continuing consequence of evil's assault is seen in several ways.

SIN

Sin is often personified in Paul's writing and pictured as an alien force lurking to pounce on a victim (Rom. 7:7–11; cf. Gen. 4:7 for the personification of sin as a demon waiting to spring forth like the Assyrian and Babylonian demon called 'rabîṣu', whose name is given to a whole army of demons. The word is cognate with *rōbēṣ* 'to lurk' (*rābēṣ*) in the Hebrew of Gen. 4:7).[13] F. J. Leenhardt and C. K. Barrett have pointed out the parallels (in Romans 7) with the account of Adam's fate (Gen. 3) though it is more likely that Paul is 'telling his own story in the light of Genesis'.[14] Paul's wording at Romans 7:8–11 reads like a transcript of the traumatic awakening which was his when at the Jewish puberty ritual, 'bar mitzvah', the boy was faced with a commandment of Torah (such as the tenth prohibition, 'You shall not desire') and 'sin' sprang to life, awakened in him the desire to achieve independence from God, and he 'died'. It is the sad tale of Genesis 3 expressed in personal terms and revised in the light of Paul's own Jewish experience with the 'holy commandment'. The commandment was turned into a death-dealing agency by being perverted from its good quality as a gift into a means of condemnation as it became an occasion of self-confidence. The deadliness of nomistic religion could be hardly more vividly shown, though Paul gives a more measured statement of the matter in 2 Corinthians 3 and Galatians 3.

The point to observe is Paul's picture of sin as an external force that came to him from outside and lay in wait to attack. The suggestion of sin as inherent in the human make-up is not Pauline, since he expressly distinguishes between 'I' and 'the sin which dwells in me' (Rom. 7:17). Nonetheless all are infected by a universal disease that has attacked them, and all human beings in Paul's view have given a permanent lodging to the invading demon and succumbed to its approach.

The result is that everyone is under 'sin's control' (Rom. 6:16–20) — without exclusion (Rom. 3:9–23; Gal. 3:22). Jewish devotion to Torah, often regarded by the rabbis as a prophylactic and preventative against evil, only exposes a person to sin's inroad as Paul himself found. The law which *eo ipso* is praised as 'holy', 'just' and 'good' could not countervail because of humankind's solidarity with Adam whose 'flesh' all share. All have gone the way of Adam (Rom. 5:12–19; 1 Cor. 15:21f.; cf. 2 Baruch 54:15–19; 4 Ezra 3:7, 21f.; 7:116ff.) because Paul views humanity as one entity: what we share with Adam is 'flesh', which is an easy prey to sin's approach. This notion of solidarity with Adam explains Paul's repeated emphasis on human frailty and finitude ('men of dust' is how he describes Adam's family, 1 Cor. 15:47–49) and the universal involvement in which all stand because they have never been free to shake off sin's stranglehold first applied to the Adam in Paul's scripture. The end result is expressed in a series of lapidary statements to do with society and individuals. They are 'under sin' (Rom. 3:9; Gal. 3:22); they are 'sin's slaves' (Rom. 6:16, 20; cf. Gal. 2:17), 'sold under sin' (Rom. 7:14), in service to sin (Rom. 6:6), living inexorably 'according to sin's law' (Rom. 7:23, 25; 8:3) and controlled by sin which moves a person's limbs as 'instruments of evil' (Rom. 6:13). The upshot is that sin is a universal master, a demonic despot carrying off humanity as a prisoner-of-war (7:23) and asserting proprietary rights over God's creatures. The term 'sinners by nature' is not precisely Pauline, though Ephesians 2:3 comes near to it; but it expresses the practical consequence.

It is misleading, however, if it obscures the emphasis Paul makes on man as a willing victim, attacked and overcome by an alien power and now in bitter bondage — all of which is his unnatural (if sadly all-pervasive) condition. And man is both responsible and culpable — a twin reality that occasions the just sentence of divine 'wrath', which is God's rightful opposition to evil and his resolute determination to eradicate it, however painful the process, from the human scene (Rom. 1:18; Col. 3:6; Eph. 2:3; 5:6). The end result will be the day of judgment and, apart from the divine favour, a sentence of perdition (1 Cor. 1:18; 2 Cor. 4:3; Phil. 3:19).

FLESH

The vulnerable area at which sin's attack is made is man's 'flesh'.[15] This term merits some scrutiny since its meaning is chameleon-like and alters according to context. And intrinsically, of all the Pauline anthropological terms, it is the most important for our understanding of man's alienated condition, even if the word for 'spirit' (*pneuma*, found 146 times in Paul) exceeds it in common usage. *Sarx* (flesh) occurs 91 times.

Occasionally and not frequently *sarx* stands for a person's physical existence as a living body. 'The life I now live *in the flesh*' (Gal. 2:20) is Paul's way of relating to his present life as a human being, sometimes (as in Phil. 1:22, 24) set in contrast with life beyond death. The RSV translation, 'our bodies had no rest' (2 Cor. 7:5), is legitimate and according to the meaning in context, even if Paul's Greek has 'our flesh' (*sarx*). The parallelism with 2 Corinthians 2:13 ('My mind — Greek *pneuma* — could not rest', relating to the same historical circumstance) shows the fluidity of Paul's terms.

The basic sense of *sarx* when used on a broader canvas seems to be man's earthly existence as a human being opposed to the divine. 'Flesh and blood' may mean simply 'members of the human race' (Gal. 1:16) but there is often an overtone of mere humanity both opposed to and different from God; and especially in regard to man's frailty (1 Cor. 1:29: 'no flesh might boast'; 1 Cor. 15:50: 'flesh and blood cannot inherit the kingdom of God'). The christological phrase 'according to the flesh' (Rom. 1:3) is used to indicate the concreteness of Jesus' earthly life, set in contrast to his post-Easter life in the spirit (v. 4: *kata pneuma*), while 'knowing Christ *kata sarka*' in 2 Corinthians 5:16 means treating him as an earthly Messiah.

So *sarx* has its counterpoint in *pneuma* (spirit), and Paul can contrast two ways of life by these formulas in Romans 8:4 (cf. 1 Cor. 3:1, 3). It is easy to see the transition now to the general Pauline use of *sarx* as the principle of sin that still remains to be resisted and neutralised by the Spirit's activity: so Galatians 5:16–26. 'The deeds of the *sarx*' are descriptive of the old life of believers, which theoretically they have abandoned but which are liable to reassert their attractiveness and become a viable choice once more. The appeal is to the *sarx* that responds to instinctual influences ('the desires of the flesh') and is 'weak' to resist since it has no inherent strength. On the contrary 'nothing good' dwells in the 'flesh' (Rom. 7:18). So sin finds it easy prey, and the result is 'with my *sarx* I serve the law of sin' (Rom. 7:25).

Yet *sarx*, which has links in Paul's thought with the rabbinic 'evil tendency' (*yēṣer hā-raʿ*) that entices men into sin, could be likened to a personal entity that boasts of its confident claim. Its proclivity to selfishness and pride is evident in Paul's statements in 1 Corinthians 1: 29-31 and Philippians 3:3–4. The appropriate stance of mortal man, faced with the creator God and holy judge, is one of 'trust'; but the opposite attitude is often found, an assertive self-confidence that Paul expresses by the verb 'to boast' (*kauchasthai*). Bultmann's lexical study shows clearly the importance of this verb in Paul who uses it frequently.[16] Specifically 'to boast' and 'to trust' are synonymous terms, deriving from some Old Testament examples (e.g. Ps. 49:9; 97:7; Isa. 42:17).

'Boasting in the law' is the hallmark of self-confident religion, quite different from Abraham's example since he had no claim before God (Rom. 4:1f.) whereas nomistic Jews register this protestation (Rom. 2:17, 23). From Paul's perspective as a Christian all boasting is excluded (Rom. 3:27) since it drives a wedge between the believer and Christ who is the sole object of trust (Phil. 3:3f.). To live by any religious confidence other than faith is exactly 'to boast in the flesh' — a contradictory phrase since all 'boasting' must be of what God has done in Christ. This is the 'only one legitimate' ground of confidence, Bultmann rightly concludes as he appeals to Romans 5:11, 2 Corinthians 10:17 and Galatians 6:14.

The 'flesh' then is anything that is placed in rivalry to Christ; to trust in the flesh is to place confidence outside of Christ, as Calvin noted. *Sarx* thus personalised is like a demonic force that seeks to intrude into the place of Christ and coax man's allegiance away from him.

THE LAW

The negative assessments of 'the law' in Paul may be seen in this light. To be sure, his many-faceted designations of the Jewish law, extending from adulation (Rom. 7:12) to downright condemnation as a lethal weapon (2 Cor. 3:6), are difficult to put together into a coherent pattern. The ruling idea is found, however, in the use to which the law is put. Paul has no hesitation in ascribing its origin to God, though its transmission to Moses via angels (Gal. 3:19) qualifies this proposition and suggests that Torah's inferiority to the direct promise to Abraham is shown by the manner of its delivery. 'Angels' in this context — and the deference to angelic intermediaries at Sinai is not a sign of dignity as the rabbis contended — act as 'go-between' and remain as guardians during the period of world history while Torah is in force. The law-giving angels of Judaism are one more proof to Paul of the 'demonic' way in which religion can interpose between man and God, since he says exactly the same about pagan gods in Galatians 4:9. He calls them 'weak and beggarly elemental spirits' which are seeking to re-establish control over the Galatians by their return to a pre-Christian system, whether Jewish or heathen.

The regime of Torah was a necessary interlude 'until faith should be revealed . . . until Christ came' (Gal. 3:23–24). Law gave a definition and focus to wrongdoing (Rom. 4:15) and so prepared the way for the gospel. It was a *paidagōgos*, 'an ambulant baby-sitter, a slave who took children to school . . . a custodian' (Stendahl),[17] who leads men to Christ. So far Stendahl's argument that Torah was the Jewish tutor-mentor who conducted Paul and his compatriots to the realised messianic hope in Jesus holds good. But elsewhere Paul attaches a negative significance to Torah's role when he confesses that Torah acted as an incentive or stimulus to sin and created an awareness of human need that it could not handle (Rom. 7:7–11). It supplied a commentary on human weakness by revealing to 'man-under-law' that such a relationship to God predicated on that basis would lead only to 'death' whether through frustration or, as in Paul's case — since he professed to be a blameless Jew (Phil. 3:6) — pride and self-sufficiency. The *hybris* which is the inevitable consequence of legal religion, however devoutly pursued and practised, is the law's inevitable goal. It became a 'dispensation of condemnation' (2 Cor. 3:9).

One way in which Paul was led to the conclusion that the law is man's enemy comes in his argument displayed in Galatians 3:10–13. There the law pronounces a curse on all who fail to live by it (Deut. 27:26); this verdict is set in opposition to the blessing that attends the person who lives in faith. The antithesis is clear: 'The law does not rest on faith' (v. 12). And so the law acts as a condemning judge who pronounces sentence on 'the man-of-faith.' It does the opposite of justifying him; it condemns him.

It has been suggested[18] that Paul was led to this understanding of the 'curse of the law' by what he knew had happened in one historical case: Christ had been put to death. Was it the law that did it? Apparently this was so if we read Galatians 3:11 with its citation of Habakkuk 2:4 [LXX reading] as 'the righteous one shall live by my faith'. When taken to refer primarily in Paul's mind to Christ as the obedient one, it implies that Christ did not live by adopting the law as his way of life but chose to live in faith as God's righteous servant. The result was that the law (here personified) rose up and killed him, but in so doing it brought its own regime to an end because Christ incurred the curse not on his own account but on ours. As the true 'seed of Abraham' (3:16) he received the promise in being raised after death to become the father of a new race, the family that looks back to Abraham, as Abraham in his day looked forward to the messianic era (3:6–9). Paul's conclusion stands. The law is now — whatever its original purpose — our enemy since it was Christ's. He conquered it — and so may his people who live not 'by law' but 'by faith'.

So Torah's continuance as a way of life is now antiquated for Paul. Abraham's 'seed' (Gal. 3:16) has come, and with Christ the promise is ratified introducing thereby a new order, 'apart from law' (Rom. 3:21) in which the demonic hold of nomistic religion has been broken. The 'legal demands' of Torah are met in the obedient, righteous Christ and cancelled on his cross (Col. 2:14), if that is the meaning of 'law', which is disputed: see later p. 184. The historical evidence of the way Torah's writ no longer runs is found in the emergence of a new community as Abraham's family where Jew/non-Jew distinctions are torn away (Gal. 3:28f.) and the barrier of Torah and its prescriptions which acted (as in the *Letter of Aristeas*) as a hedge to divide Jews and non-Jews has been as effectively demolished as surely as the balustrade between the court of (Jewish) women and the court of the Gentiles was obliterated at the fall of Jerusalem in AD 70 (Eph. 2:14-18). See the later discussion (pp. 185f.).

DEATH

The ultimate result of man's sin is death, not unexpectedly called a 'king' (Rom. 5:17) and the 'final enemy' (1 Cor. 15:26) because its effect is to oppose and deny all that God intended for his children. 'Death', wrote Denney, 'is the sacrament of sin,'[19] the outward and visible sign of an inward and spiritual dis-grace!

Paul's scripture in the Old Testament offered at least one clue to the reality of death in human experience. There was an intimate, cause-and-effect connection between sin and death (Gen. 3). But death is unnatural to man and is regarded as unmitigated evil (Deut. 30:15, 19), bitter (1 Sam. 15:32) and horrendous (Ps. 55:4f.). Death is treated as the antithesis of God who is life, and it is no part of God's original design for the creation. It comes on the scene as an alien intruder no less than does sin. Just how death originated is not spelled out — except in the context of man's primal rebellion that evoked the divine penalty of the 'death sentence' of separation (Gen. 2:17; 3:22f.). 'The soul that sins shall die' (Ezek. 18:4) is as much an observation of life as a piece of theological teaching, and Paul's sentence echoes the thought in Romans 6:23.

Sin and death are intimately linked (Rom. 5:12) by being traced back to the Adam story; thereafter death is as universal a phenomenon as sin. 'All sin' therefore 'all die' is Paul's conclusion; and both assertions are based on humanity's oneness with Adam (1 Cor. 15:21–22). Nor is the pain of death denied, for on the basis of man's state as a sinner he is faced with the prospect of death as a penalty for his sin (1 Cor. 15:56; Rom. 5:17, 21). Sin's regime leads inevitably to 'death'.

With the coming of Christ and his 'obedience unto death' (Phil. 2:8) a new face has been put on the question of life and death. That one death 'in the body of his flesh' (Col. 1:21) has dealt the monster a mortal blow. Death suffered its decisive defeat in Christ's yielding to its power and emerging victorious in the resurrection. So 'death no longer has dominion over him' (Rom. 6:9) and over his people who have shared his death in

their baptismal experience (Rom. 6:4; Col. 2:12). His triumph
has become theirs as they 'die to sin' (Rom. 6:11; 8:11), put to
death the old nature shared with the old Adam (Col. 3:5–9), and
receive the life of the last Adam to raise them to new life (Col.
3:3).

Death as a fact of empirical experience continues even in the
church of the risen one — a reality that evidently created
problems at Thessalonica (1 Thess. 4:13ff.), Corinth (1 Cor.
11:30;. 15:29f.) and Philippi (Phil. 3:10f.); but its power to hurt
and destroy has been drawn and its judgment-character as a
penalty for sin transformed (1 Cor. 15:54ff.). As one of the
enemies of the church it holds the same ambivalent place as sin
and the 'powers': it has been conquered in principle in the cross
and resurrection of Jesus yet its eventual elimination awaits the
day of his final triumph (1 Cor. 15:26). The virtual equivalence
of 'sin', 'flesh', 'death' — all Satan's instruments to wage a
warfare against the church — is accepted rabbinic teaching and
Paul's close approximation of these terms, turning them into a
hierarchy of evil under Satan's control, is one more illustration of
his indebtedness to his Jewish background.

The continuing reality of death's power is seen by Paul in the
following ways.

(i) Alienation from God is the most obvious and fateful
consequence. He picks up the Old Testament idea of death =
separation (cf. Isa. 59:2) and applies it to those whose life
(paradoxically) is no better than death. His disciple can echo
faithfully his ideas concerning the self-indulgent widow: she 'is
dead even while she lives' (1 Tim. 5:6). Sin manifests its deadly
effect in cutting off the individual and society from God: 'dead
through trespasses and sins' (Eph. 2:1; Col. 2:13) is a verdict on
the previous life of Christians now 'made alive' (Eph. 2:5). The
sad state of the pagan world is summed up in Ephesians 4:17–22
under the rubric 'alienated from the life of God' and so isolated
from his favour.

The objective side of being cut off from God (a fate with
irreversible consequences, apart from his grace, 1 Cor. 1:18) is
matched by the state of men and women as 'hostile in mind'
toward God as well as being 'estranged' (Col. 1:21). 'Enmity'
marks the condition of the man-outside-of-Christ (Rom. 5:10).
This condition of hostility, moreover, is such that man cannot
remedy or rectify from his side, for he is 'helpless' in his ungodly
estate (Rom. 5:6). He is both powerless to improve himself and

so make his life presentable to elicit the divine regard, and unable to escape the divine sentence of 'wrath' (Rom. 5:9) that rests on him as a sinner (5:8). The attitude of enmity is thus a mutual one: man-as-sinner is both suspicious of God and shows hostility to him, and he is condemned by God whose eyes must turn away from moral evil. He is both a rebel who has taken arms against his rightful master, and a blameworthy culprit who deserves a righteous sentence of judgment. He stands in dire need of both reconciliation and justification, but these are usually taken to be two aspects of the same condition, depending on one's point of view. They are 'different metaphors describing the same fact',[20] viz. that man is an alienated sinner *coram Deo*, before the face of God (but see later p. 153).

(*ii*) Paul deals realistically with the human state of sinnership by relating it to the conflicts and turmoil of his own society. If it is true that he theologises by using 'sin' (in the singular) of man's chief ailment and enemy, it is equally to be respected that he can categorise human failings and excesses in a most graphic, down-to-earth manner. He can spell out what 'sins' are included in 'sin'.

Ethical lists of vices appear in several places (Gal. 5:19-21; Col. 3:5, 8; Rom. 1:29-31; 1 Cor. 5:10-11; 2 Cor. 12:10; cf. 1 Cor. 6:9-10; Eph. 4:31; 5:3-5; 1 Tim. 1:9-10; 2 Tim. 3:2-4) in a way that owes only formal similarities to Old Testament and contemporary models, whether in stoic moral philosophy or the teaching of the Qumran sect, though there is an indictment of Gentile sins in Jewish literature such as the Wisdom of Solomon 14:23-26. Deissmann's ingenious suggestion[21] that the list in 1 Corinthians 6:9–10 was based on the practice of children's moral instructions where counters, as separate discs, were labelled with the names of vices and shuffled in a game, is now less well regarded. The parallels in Jewish proselyte catechism which the church took over as it came to see itself as a 'holy community' make it more likely that this source of borrowing is correct. Certainly the correspondences in Paul's use of traditional teaching in these lists and the catalogues in the 'Two Ways' of *Didache* chapters 1-5 and *Barnabas* chapters 18–20 point in this direction.

The intent of these lists is to address real problems in contemporary society and to alert Christians to steer clear of such moral aberrations and defiling practices. Paul sees his world as in moral disarray because of its idolatry (Rom. 1:21-23) which, for a Jew, was the tap-root of all evil (cf. Col. 3:5). The lines of demarcation drawn between the church and the 'world' would promote this abhorrence. Paul's teaching on the community as a neo-levitical society called to holiness, purity and dedication to God would reinforce the insistence that the Gentiles are in deep darkness (Eph. 4:17ff.) and guilty of nameless anti-social, immoral and magical practices (Eph. 5:11-16) that prove how 'evil' are the days and how deservedly 'the wrath of God' is coming on such 'sons of disobedience' (Eph. 5:6).

(*iii*) Physical death is, as we have seen, the final consequence of human sinning. Used of Jesus' terminus on the cross (Phil. 2:8; Col. 1:22) it carries a plain meaning, though E. Lohmeyer[22] had made the phrase 'the death of the cross' into an allusion to Christ's descent into hell where he was willing to yield himself to the servitude of malign demonic powers. Before we dismiss this daring suggestion out of hand it will be well to inspect its arguments. Lohmeyer begins by offering a brilliant insight. Only a divine being can accept death as *obedience* (Phil. 2:8). For ordinary mortals it is a necessity for which they have no choice but to accept it. For one who was in the divine 'form' and became a 'servant', the submission to his destiny, whether it entailed an affirmation of God's will to suffer (so most commentators) or an acceptance of bondage to the cosmic powers which sought to victimise him (E. Käsemann),[23] marked him out as the true epiphany of God. So his obedience is more than human; it is a condescension that took him one step further in the sweep of his incarnation and humiliation.

Lohmeyer pointed out how, in Jewish theology, death is likened to a king or a kingdom. He argued that 'obedience *up to death*' (*mechri thanatou*) should be construed spatially, i.e. he entered this realm and permitted death to enslave him as a demon power which holds men captive. The incarnation (his becoming a mortal man) and the abasement of Christ to the death of the cross 'both have to do with an entrance into the control of the powers' in a way parallel to the drama of Hebrews 2:15; Revelation 1:18. Jesus identified himself to the full with the fate of humanity, but with one vital difference. He placed himself under the yoke of submission to the elemental spirits of his own free will. When he was exalted by God, he broke the power of their iron control and brought their regime to an end. It is natural then that the proclamation of 'Jesus Christ is Lord'

(2:11) will include the confession of demonic forces 'under the earth' (v. 10), i.e. in that region where he carried his triumph and despoiled them (Ignatius, *Trall.* 9:1).

Whatever the merits of this theory regarding Jesus' 'obedience to death', it illuminates one aspect of Paul's teaching: death carries with it a forensic quality and marks the ultimate sentence on man as mortal sinner. It inheres in his humanity because that humanity is so easily and so pervasively the vehicle of sin. Sin likened to an intruding demon has attacked mortal 'flesh', and the hallmark of sin's victory is death's universal reign and kingdom-like embrace of all who belong to 'Adam'. Death also is given a personified character like a power that would oppose God and come as an interloper between him and man (Rom. 8:38; cf. 2 Tim. 1:10). 'In Adam' they die, not because they are fashioned after 'the man of dust' but because they participate in Adam's 'flesh', the target for sin's assault and possession. 'In Adam' men are subject to death's victimising control.

(*iv*) The finality of death in Paul is assumed. The 'state of the departed' is a theme exclusively — with perhaps the solitary exception of 2 Thessalonians 1:9 — devoted to the Christian dead. We must postpone how Paul views the 'reconciliation of all things' in Colossians 1:20 until we have examined his teaching on reconciliation in general. It will be sufficient here to call attention to 'death' as putting the fatal capstone on man's state as a sinner, and noting Paul's serious note on the eschatological consequences of wrongdoing that extend beyond this life to the next (Rom. 2:8–11).

PART II

THE PAULINE RESPONSES

CHAPTER FIVE

PAUL AND TRADITION

This section will consider in some detail the way Paul addressed the needs of his day. Bearing in mind the suggestion that his thinking moves from what God has done to the malaise itself, we shall hope to put this idea to the practical test of the evidence.

In setting 'reconciliation' at the centre of our discussion in regard to Paul's answer to the human predicament, we acknowledge that this procedure may seem to be arbitrary and one-sided. Later we hope to show that the term 'reconciliation' is sufficiently comprehensive to embrace several facets of Paul's theology, and has the added merit of being able to explain them as it provides a general frame into which they can fit. Above all, we plan to demonstrate that 'reconciliation' is adequate to account for Paul's own insistence that his theology is concerned with personal relationships; it relates to the cosmic disorder; and it offers a groundplan for resolving the problem of Israel — all leading themes in his pastoral writing. 'Reconciliation', moreover, reflects his own experiences as a 'man in Christ' who came to see life in a new way from the encounter he had with the living Lord on the way to Damascus. His 'conversion' marked the turning point and redirection of life best described by 'reconciliation'. The term, we shall hope to show in conclusion, meets most of the criteria for a New Testament theology.

But before these matters can be considered in the light of the evidence from Paul, we must look at a counterproposal that would ruin our plan and discourage any further enquiry along the lines we have chosen. Ernst Käsemann's essay[1] was intended to set Paul's teaching on reconciliation within the context of the New Testament as a whole and to offer some critique of regarding it as in any way central or determinative. We must therefore examine this matter.

RECONCILIATION: E. KÄSEMANN'S CRITIQUE

Ernst Käsemann touches nothing but that he brings an independent and provocative attitude to even well-worn matters. He

71

possesses the uncanny knack of posing questions to familiar
themes and interrogating the evidence in such a way that old
solutions seem inadequate and new paths are opened up. What
he rightly remarked about Ernst Lohmeyer is just as true when
applied to himself:

> Lohmeyer's works mark a turning-point insofar as they lift us
> out of the old ruts, and therefore have forced 'the exegetical
> fraternity' and their usual readers to face new and suggestive
> questions.[2]

This inquisitive and restless probe is applied to what is
traditionally called 'the New Testament teaching on reconciliation' in a phrase where Käsemann's *Versöhnungslehre* may just as
properly be rendered 'atonement teaching', as Fitzmyer has
noted.[3]

1.   Käsemann concedes that 'reconciliation' is one element in
the New Testament lexicon used to denote and describe God's
work and Christ's achievement *vis-à-vis* the world of men out of
harmony with the divine purpose. His first question is to ask
whether there is 'essential unity' in the various statements about
reconciliation. Can these elements be brought together to form a
synthetic whole, thus making it possible to speak of '*the* doctrine
of reconciliation in the New Testament'? That point is well
taken, since it is fatally easy, in this area as elsewhere, to rush
prematurely to a conclusion that there is an underlying unity
and commonality in the New Testament on one aspect of the
redeemer's work at the expense of ignoring the contextual
settings of the data, the theological *Tendenz* or bias of the
multiple authors, and the attested pluralistic evidence produced
by the New Testament documents. The temptation to 'over-
simplification' against which Käsemann would warn us is ever
present and must be recognised.

2.   His second observation is just as painfully obvious to those
who would find in 'reconciliation' an attempt to pinpoint a
'leading theme' embracing the major concerns of the canonical
documents. We shall return to this question shortly. For the
moment it is enough to note that, strictly speaking, the teaching
on reconciliation is concentrated in passages which employ the
verbs *katallassein* (to reconcile) and *hilaskesthai* (to expiate), along
with their derivatives and cognates. These two word complexes,
when we examine them in the concordance, yield a surprisingly

exiguous body of evidence. Aside from Matthew 5:24, the motif of reconciliation is limited to the Pauline writings. 1 Corinthians 7:11 may be discounted since, in Käsemann's view, it carries there only 'a secular sense'. The main significance of the term in the attested Pauline letters is found only in Romans 5:10f. and 2 Corinthians 5:18ff. where its 'theological emphasis' is dominant. Romans 11:15 is treated as unimportant since Käsemann regards 'the reconciliation of the world' as equivalent to eschatological consummation and, in any case, it is formulaic and represents simply Paul's borrowing of a 'fixed tradition'. That leaves only Colossians 1:20, 22 and Ephesians 2:16 which are then dismissed as 'deutero-Pauline' in origin and mere catch-words set in hymnic fragments. The result of this appraisal of the evidence is that what is obviously limited material is further reduced in size and scope; and we are left with Romans 5:10-11 — which is later accorded a subservient place of simply sharpening and underscoring the teaching of the 'justification of the ungodly' by introducing the notion of the hostility by which the human condition of estrangement from God is compounded and intensified — and 2 Corinthians 5:18-21. The latter section incorporates a pre-Pauline hymnic fragment, used by the apostle to serve as an appeal to the Corinthians on the basis of a statement of his authority as a preacher. It does not represent a statement of the Pauline kerygma, except incidentally.

Käsemann's conclusion is reached. It is a twofold one, based on his reading of the lexical evidence. There is 'no such thing as a doctrine of reconciliation which is regulative for the whole New Testament' — a conclusion it is hard to resist once we are bound to recognise the infrequent occurrence of the key-terms based on the *katallass-* word-root in large sections of the canonical documents. Secondly, 'it is a remarkable fact that the motif appears only in the general realm of Paulinism, though without having any significant meaning for Pauline theology as a whole' — a much more debatable statement, in the light of our subsequent discussion.

Nor is the evidence very much different if we examine *hilaskesthai*, the verb meaning 'to propitiate', 'to expiate', 'to atone'. Admittedly 'expiation' occurs in Paul only at Romans 3:25, though it features in Hebrews 2:17, 8:12, 9:5 as well as 1 John 2:2, 4:10. Käsemann is willing to include the ransom sayings of Mark 10:45 and 1 Timothy 2:6. He considers these references germane on the ground that reconciliation and expiation move in the world of the cult and there sacrificial terminology is evidently at home. This consideration tilts his interpretation of the Colossians-Ephesians evidence since he maintains that the hymnic fragments, while originating in a liturgical context, do not speak to a cultic situation. 'Cultic associations' are found only in Romans 5, which builds on the justification teaching of Romans 3:25. The effect of justification is the accession of 'peace', which is treated cosmologically as heralding the dawn of a new age in which God's righteousness is publicly proclaimed and his lordship vindicated.

3.   Thirdly, Käsemann is now ready to offer his individualistic interpretation of how the teaching on reconciliation developed. He grants that 'the variety is constitutive of the whole'; and this teaching cannot be reduced to a simple formula. In the New Testament a whole host of different conceptions are used to characterise the essence of the eschatological salvation. He catalogues several of these, and cautions against isolating any one of these themes or giving one pride of place over the others.

Nonetheless this caution does not inhibit him from moving on to offer what he regards as establishing the legitimacy and setting the limits of all varieties and even interpretations of New Testament teaching. So he concludes: 'for Paul the doctrine of justification is the heart of the Christian message'. Standing as it does in the final section of his essay, this conclusion has really been implicit from the beginning, though it is never openly stated as such. For Käsemann his criticism of motif-research rests on this prior understanding of the primacy and normativeness of *justificatio impiorum*, 'the justification of the godless'.

By this criterion he is able to explain why Paul did not take up and exploit reconciliation as his major interest. The hellenistic hymns of triumph and doxology — embodied in Colossians 1:15-20, Ephesians 2:14-18 — celebrate Christ as cosmic victor and regard reconciliation as an accomplished fact. They smack of 'fanaticism' and a realised eschatology that strikes at the heart of the man's status as *simul justus et peccator*, 'at once a righteous person and a sinner'. They proclaim as present reality that which awaits the parousia when final justification will be announced.

Equally it is justification that prevents reconciliation from slipping from its christological moorings and becoming attached to a species of ecclesiology in Ephesians where the 'early catholic' celebration of 'one holy church' (*una sancta ecclesia*) paves the way for a churchly triumphalism and makes the church both the realm and the means of reconciliation. Thus God's new order is domesticated and the nerve-ending of the kerygma is dulled.

Finally, the eschatological dimension of justification exposes and corrects the false step that was taken when in Jewish-Christian teaching reconciliation and expiation were tied in with cultic, forensic and sacrificial ideas borrowed from the Old Testament and Judaic tradition. Paul had skilfully taken over and edited existing Jewish-Christian fragments in both Romans 3:24-25 and 2 Corinthians 5:18-21; he has thereby reduced the force of the cultic element, and he is concerned simply to use these traditional materials to enforce the divine sovereignty and initiative in the Christ-event and to set his understanding in relation to apostolic preaching. Paul's characteristic emphasis is not 'satisfaction' — as Romans 5:9 might suggest — but liberation and release from an alien tyranny, and it explains how freedom is gained by a change of lordship proclaimed over all creation.

'Justification' functions throughout as a 'deciding criterion', a *norma normans*, as Käsemann concedes in his final paragraph. He has kept this part of his 'hidden agenda' until the end, but in retrospect it has become clear that this designation of a ruling theme at least in Paul has informed and controlled his pre-understanding, his selection of the material, his exegesis, his assignment of suitable life-settings and his conclusions throughout. So he remarks:

> The statements about reconciliation in the NT are protected from extravagance by primitive Christian eschatology and by the Pauline doctrine of justification.[+]

A SCRUTINY OF KÄSEMANN'S POSITION

1. A criticism of Käsemann's thesis must begin by taking issue with his statement of justification as the legitimating principle of Paul's theology as a whole and of reconciliation in particular.

Of lesser importance in the current debate on 'divine righteousness' in Paul and elsewhere is W. Wrede's attempt to regard justification not as 'the central point of Pauline doctrine' but as a secondary 'polemical doctrine' (*Kampfeslehre*) directed against the Jews, or Adolf Deissmann's similar proposal to attribute

Paul's long discussion of it to the 'hard fight' he had to wage with the Judaizers. Albert Schweitzer in a famous phrase, as we saw earlier, referred to justification as a 'subsidiary crater' (*ein Nebenkrater*) within the main rim (*im Hauptkrater*) of Pauline teaching which he in turn identified as the mystical doctrine of redemption by 'being-in-Christ'. It is conceded by most scholars that Schweitzer's chief point is well taken; and it is difficult to see the basis for Paul's ethical appeals as confined simply within the orbit of righteousness by faith, though Jeremias has faulted Wrede for not having perceived the ethical implications of justification as in 1 Corinthians 6:11.[5]

Schweitzer's counter-proposals do make it clear how the believer by 'participation in Christ' — to use E. P. Sanders's recently coined expression[6] — gains from Christ's work objectively wrought (*extra nos*), and his arguments based on the lack of evidence that would make righteousness by faith *the* central theme in Paul are important. Indeed, Sanders remarks, they have never been effectively countered, and Bornkamm has conceded that other important matters are not derivable from the Pauline teaching on justification.

But even if it were admitted that justification is 'at the heart of the Christian message', it still remains to be shown why 'reconciliation' may not be an appropriate expression of that teaching — unless we are persuaded on other grounds that Paul was hostile to 'reconciliation' *per se* because it had been misused in the enthusiastic hymnody of Greek Christianity. To accord 'reconciliation' a rightful place might conceivably deflect the criticism that justification lacks the basis for an ethical call, since it is obvious from 2 Corinthians 5:18-21 that Paul can use reconciliation teaching *both* to state the kerygma *and* to issue the appeal, 'Be reconciled to God' (cf. 6:1).

Moreover, we should want to take issue with Käsemann's remark that reconciliation serves a function merely to 'sharpen and point up the doctrine of justification'. It seems that he is at pains to maintain at all costs the centrality and pervasiveness of justification in the structure of the epistle to the Romans. In fact, recent studies in that letter point to an opposite conclusion, namely that the language of justification which predominates in 1:17-5:11 thereafter gives way to terms that describe the consequences of being set right with God.[7] After 6:7 the terminology of justification fades away and reappears only momentarily in 8:33 and 10:4, 10. In this last verse 'to be

justified' is equivalent to 'salvation'. The upshot is that Käsemann's statement about the relation of justification to reconciliation may be turned on its head, and it is just as plausible to
argue, with Fitzmyer, that 'justification finds a more adequate
expression in reconciliation; indeed, "reconciliation" becomes
the better way of expressing that process'.[8]

2.   The analysis Käsemann makes of the texts and the
inferences he draws therefrom are also open to question. For
reasons we have already considered he proposes to demote the
discussions in Romans 5:10f. and 11:15 to a level inferior to 2
Corinthians 5:18ff. on the ground that only there (in 2 Cor.) does
the word *katallagē* (reconciliation) have theological emphasis. To
make equally short work of the hymnic passages in Colossians
1:20, 22 and Ephesians 2:16 on the score that they are (*a*)
'deutero-Pauline' in origin, and (*b*) to be classified as 'catch-
words' in quoted materials is once more to tailor-make the
evidence according to one's presuppositions. This argument
forgets that, while Colossians 1:20 is part of the christological-
soteriological hymn that may be pre-Pauline, 1:22 belongs to the
pastoral and paraenetic context of the letter and is not part of the
'hymnic fragment', as Käsemann calls it. Moreover, the scope of
Ephesians 2:16 which involves the reconciliation of Jews and
Gentiles looks as though it represents some comment, whether
Pauline or not, on the same ethnic and eschatological situation
as that envisaged in Romans 11:15; and 'the reconciliation of the
world' (*katallagē kosmou*) has echoes which are reminiscent of 2
Corinthians 5:19:

God was in Christ reconciling the world (*kosmon katallassōn ēn*)
to himself.

To be sure, Käsemann has correctly noted that Paul often
takes up traditional material and reinterprets it according to his
own theological bent. Evidence for this is clear from the form
analyses of Philippians 2:6-11 and Colossians 1:15-20. In 2
Corinthians 5:18-21 the same procedure may be suspected. But
insofar as Paul finds relevance at all in the quoted material —
however much he may choose to adapt it by additions and
corrections — it seems evident that he has approved of it as
consonant with his general theological position. Otherwise why
did he bother to refer to it in the first place? Fitzmyer's question
is pertinent:

Once we ascertain that there is pre-Pauline material in Paul's

writings, does that mean that it is not really part of his
thinking or that it cannot be considered a part of his
theology?[9]

The matter is more delicate in the case of the Colossians-
Ephesians passages where a Pauline editor may have used
existing material and have stamped it with a different *Tendenz* or
theological purpose. The citation of Pauline tradition may have
been made to lend authority to the redactor's own position. But
this argument cannot be used in 2 Corinthians 5 since it is
universally agreed that Paul himself has done the editing of a
pre-Pauline statement, and for him to have employed quoted
material that was alien to his mind raises the problem of why he
should want to do so in the first instance.

3.   We come now to the issue of whether Käsemann has
cogently arranged the teaching on reconciliation into a meaningful pattern. Let us state his argument. For him the origin of the
teaching lies in the gnostic idea of the reconciliation of the world
and of 'the All' (i.e. the totality of the cosmic order) seen as part
of an eschatological myth. Virgil's Fourth Eclogue is appealed to
as evidence of this expectation of a utopian order soon to appear.
The illustration is hardly satisfactory, however, since the poet
has cast into the idiom of a fairy tale the 'last age' (*ultima aetas*)
which turns out to be his way of heralding the birth of a new age
with Augustus' coming to power. The language is mythopoetic,
certainly; but the harsh realities are political, social and
economic. To interpret this as a uniting of the heavenly with the
earthly as a token of 'cosmic peace' seems extravagant, when all
that is intended is a flowery, if appealing and lyrical, description
of *pax Romana*, similar to Horace's tributes in his poem *Carmen
saeculare*.

More apposite is the appeal to the gnostic hope of the union of
all things in the divine. It is this sentiment, it is suggested, that
lies at the heart of early Christian hymns, such as Colossians 1
and Ephesians 2. This view taken by Käsemann is supported by
H. Schlier and G. Schille (see later pp. 168, 179). The myth of
cosmic unification is taken over by Paul in 2 Corinthians 5 and
by his school in the later epistles, and christianised by being
related to the proclamation of Christ as *cosmocrator* (world-ruler)
and reconciler of the world by his cross. This 'reconciliation'
involves the transference of power, with the result that cosmic
peace is restored by the acclamation of a new lord. Only at that

point does Christian thinking develop to include the anthropological dimension. The statements of cosmic reconciliation precede those relating to the message for forgiveness and new life for individuals, as in Colossians 1:21-22; and the same pattern emerges in 2 Corinthians 5 where there is, says Käsemann 'a transition from a cosmological to an anthropological message of reconciliation'.

This proposal is very difficult to sustain. It gives precedence to an idea that appears only in the later Pauline letters or deutero-Pauline writings by reading it back into pre-Pauline Christianity as a formative influence. It makes 'speculation' the mother of Christian theology, and introduces only later the appeal to Christian experience in forgiveness and new life whereas recent studies have shown how early Christianity began primarily as a religious movement and engaged in 'theosophical speculation' (if that is the correct term) under pressure from later contact with the hellenistic world. It looks to an early appearance of the myth of 'one new man' (Eph. 2:15) which more reasonably only emerged once the Jewish-Christian/ Gentile issue of the Pauline period had been resolved, namely after AD 70 when the exigencies of history nailed down the lid on the coffin of Jewish Christianity as a valid rival to the predominantly Gentile-oriented church.

Dissatisfaction with Käsemann's interpretative programme, however stimulating and novel it may be, raises the question of whether a more plausible line of development may be traced. To this we now turn.

RECONCILIATION: ITS TERMINOLOGY

In proposing a single term or theme with its variations we are cognizant of an objection that is readily to hand. Aside from the criticism that it is inadequate to use one single expression to comprehend satisfactorily all the teachings of the New Testament in its multiplex expression, there is the statistical fact that both noun (reconciliation) and verb (to reconcile) are only sparsely represented in the New Testament literature. This last-named objection is true — if we are content merely to consult the lexicon under the root [kat]allass-. Conceivably the verbal root hilask- may be included, but even that addition does not greatly add to the fund of materials present under the categories of reconciliation/expiation. Moreover, apart from

Matthew 5:24, the term 'reconciliation' is found only in the Pauline corpus; and only in 1 John and Hebrews does *hilaskes-thai/hilasmos* occur in addition to the few references to *hilastērion* in Romans 3:25 and Hebrews 9:5 (cf. Luke 18:13).

Nevertheless this field of enquiry is surely one which should not be dominated by the law of the concordance. In fact as far as Paul's soteriology is concerned, we are in touch with a key-term when we examine these two Greek roots, and 'expiation' plays a not inconsiderable part in the leading themes of the epistle to the Hebrews. Moreover, as far as Paul's contribution is involved, it may be stated that soteriology is one of his major epistolary subjects and the canvas is much broader than would at first be suggested by examining just this solitary term in its few occurrences. Ideas of man's enmity and God's provision of peace; man's bondage to the cosmos and his 'flesh' (*sarx*) and the divine offer of release and emancipation; man's estrangement in a disordered world and all that has been accomplished to secure his pardon and a welcome back to God's family — as well as the universe's restoration to harmony — all these motifs could well be subsumed under the overarching rubric of 'reconciliation'. The term, therefore, is much more compendious than appears at first glance, especially if the investigator consults only one or two entries in the New Testament concordance.

This contention, of course, should not be equated with the insistence that all the references to reconciliation are to be understood in the same way. They are manifestly not so regarded. Matthew 5:24 and 1 Corinthians 7:11 have particular application to concrete situations in the early church, and may best be seen as the practical outworking and application of a general lifestyle by which Christians live. *That* conclusion would be important enough, once the matter of inter-personal relations in the community at worship and the Christian family unit were seen as coming under the rubric of the new life in Christ. To dismiss these examples as 'secular' as Käsemann does is to overlook the practical application of teaching that originated in the statements of God's activity in securing reconciliation for mankind (2 Cor. 5:18-21).[10]

THE TRAJECTORY OF RECONCILIATION

Once we concede at least the possibility that in the Pauline tradition the concept of reconciliation played a substantial role, given Paul's understanding of the human predicament as one of cosmic disorder and human bondage resulting from enmity to God and leading to the fear of death and alienation in society, it becomes possible to construct a trajectory to plot the course of development. That trajectory embraces the phases of early Christianity denoted by (1) Paul's predecessors in both Jewish and hellenistic Christianity; (2) Paul's own contribution in redacting and utilising these traditions; and (3) Paul's disciples. If there is substance in this arrangement of the material, it will strengthen the case for regarding 'reconciliation' as a *leitmotif* (ruling idea) since it will then be shown that the idea was current and was developed across a broad chronological and cultural spectrum of primitive and later Christianity.

In the area of *pre-Pauline materials* there are three texts that claim our interest: Romans 3:24-26; 2 Corinthians 5:18-21; Colossians 1:15-20, where in all instances it is probable that Paul has taken and edited Jewish or hellenistic Christian confessional, possibly liturgical, material. We shall deal with the first short text here, and leave the two other passages to be considered in separate chapters apiece.

Romans 3:24-26

24'They are justified by his grace as a gift, through the redemption which is in Christ Jesus, 25whom God put forward as an expiation by his blood, to be received by faith. This was to show God's righteousness, because in his divine forbearance he had passed over former sins; 26it was to prove at the present time that he himself is righteous and that he justifies him who has faith in Jesus (RSV).

R. Bultmann argued that this pericope was traditional by calling attention to the number of non-Pauline expressions (such as *hilastērion*, expiation) and he suggested that 'freely by his grace' and 'through faith' were Paul's own supplements added to enrich the text.[11] A. M. Hunter and Käsemann went on to propose, on the grounds of style (in v. 24 'being justified' is a present participle which is unattached to what has gone before and is unexpected; and it is not a smooth transition), literary form (the sentences are top heavy with genitives and prepositions betraying a hymnlike liturgical tradition) and exegetical difficulties ('passing over' trespasses, and divine forbearance are concepts reckoned to be at odds with Rom. 1:18), that two layers of the text can be separated.[12]

On this analysis 3:24-25 contain a non-Pauline fragment derived from Jewish Christianity; to this text Paul has added a corrective in verse 26 as he cites and comments on the tradition. There is thus a tension between the two sections, one of which is quoted by Paul though he does not wholly agree with it. The point at issue is whether the traditional exegesis of the two verses will stand up to examination. According to the accepted view, verse 25*b* concerns past sins which God has overlooked; verse 26 speaks of the present when God has dealt with those sins. But how can Paul describe the past attitude of God as one of indulgence or indifference when he believed God's wrath lay on humankind (Rom. 1:18, 32; 3:9, 19)? The simplest solution would be to allow that in verses 24-25 we have a pre-Pauline statement which Paul has taken over, subsequently to amend. His corrective addition is seen in verse 26. In effect, what originated as a Jewish Christian formula of covenantal relationship and renewal, required because of human sin, is changed by the Pauline emphasis added to the next line. 'Righteousness' in verse 25 which is equated with a divine attribute, his covenantal faithfulness, becomes God's saving action openly displayed. The Pauline note of *en tō nun kairō* — 'at this time in the present' — heralds the arrival of a new, universal age (cf. the phrase in Rom. 8:18; 11:5; 2 Cor. 8:14). Justification is not the putting an end to former transgressions, but the vindication of God's character as one who 'justifies the ungodly' (Rom. 4:5). Above all, God's righteous action is directed not to the covenant people but to individuals who are founded on faith in Jesus. Paul's universalism gleams in verse 26. Two opposing tendencies are thus brought together by uniting verses 25*b*, 26*a*, while Paul rounds off the sentence by adding his characteristic emphasis of 'to be received *by faith*' (in v. 25).

General acceptance of Käsemann's proposals, which involve the principle of tradition (here a specimen of Jewish Christian confession) and redaction (by Paul who adds interpretative comment in v. 26), has meant that the soteriology of Christ's expiatory sacrifice in 3:25 is firmly grounded in traditional teaching passed on to Paul (cf. 1 Cor. 15:1ff.) and it is not his own eccentricity. But in the apostle's hands some deficiencies and limitations are corrected as the scope of Christ's saving work is enlarged, given a more pointed, present relevance, and fastened to his insistence on personal faith directed to the justifying God who ushers in a new age of cosmic renewal.

ADDITIONAL NOTE: ROMANS 3:24-26 IN RECENT STUDY

This short excursus takes up some of the leading issues in the debate over the origin of Romans 3:24-26.

Two studies (by C. H. Talbert and N. H. Young) have challenged the position above.[13] Talbert argues that the pre-Pauline fragment is not verses 24-25 (26a) but is confined to verses 25-26. His arguments are:

> (a) the initial relative pronoun 'whom' in v. 25 is a sign of a piece of quoted material; (b) the lines in the two verses (25-26) can be arranged to form a symmetrical unit; (c) and there is a logical connection in thought between v. 23 (end): 'all . . . have come short of the glory of God' and v. 27.

None of these lines of reasoning seems to be compelling, and there are definite counter-arguments. (a) Granted that the presence of a relative pronoun is a tell-tale sign of a quotation, all the examples in the New Testament have the nominative ('who', as in Col. 1:15; Phil. 2:6; 1 Tim. 3:16). An accusative is 'evidence that 3:25 could not have been the beginning of the quotation' (J. Reumann).[14] (b) Talbert's symmetrical arrangement is secured at too high a cost. It requires taking the phrase *en tē anochē tou theou*, 'through the instrumentality of his forbearance', in an unnatural way, i.e. to effect a parallelism with 'by his blood'. And it overlooks the change of meaning given in the two verses (25-26). (c) It is no argument to produce a logical sequence to Paul's thought, since on the assumption that verses 24-26a are being quoted, verse 26b functions as a Pauline comment, and his discussions continue naturally at verse 27.

Talbert's case for concluding that the quoted fragment extends only from verse 25 to verse 26 might have been strengthened by reference to E. Lohse.[15] The latter wanted to exclude verse 24 from the pre-Pauline material on the ground that 'redemption' (*apolytrōsis*) is related to 'in Christ Jesus' — a set of Pauline terms, though it must be granted that *apolytrōsis* occurs only in Romans 8:23; 1 Corinthians 1:30 (a formulaic reference) and in the liturgical text Colossians 1:14 (= Eph. 1:7; cf. Eph. 1:14; 4:30).

'In Christ Jesus' has a Pauline ring, but it need not be an instance of his technical use of the formula. J. Reumann suggests it means 'through the Messiah Jesus' (*en* being taken as instrumental). The main objection to verse 24 being excluded from the traditional formula is that then verse 25 opens with a relative without an antecedent.

A further small indication that verse 24 contains some pre-Pauline material is that 'freely' (*dōrean*) occurs three times elsewhere in Paul but never with the precise sense of 'as a gift'. The liturgical assonance of *dikaioumenoi dōrean* ('being set right' — a present participle of the verb Paul does not normally use — 'as a gift') suggests a pre-Pauline origin which Paul has enriched with his favourite note, 'by his grace'.

N. H. Young's objections are more thoroughgoing since he wishes to deny the presence of any quoted or pre-Pauline allusion in the verses. His attempt to deny the lexical peculiarities of these verses (24-26a) hardly succeeds. To remark that *hilastērion* and *paresis* are rare in any context is no response. Words that are found elsewhere in Paul (*endeixis* [twice]) carry a different sense in other references (e.g. Phil. 1:28). In this context, *endeixis* means 'demonstration' (so Kümmel).[16] The noun *anochē* (26a meaning 'forbearance') is found only once again (at Rom. 2:4). The verb 'put forward' (*prostithēmi*) is rare in the New Testament (three times; one reference in Rom. 1:13 has a different sense, meaning 'intended'). Paul's noun for 'sin' is normally in the singular; here it is plural, 'sins' (3:25). 'Blood' (*haima*) is found elsewhere in Romans (5:9) and Colossians (1:20 where however 'cross' is added) but the word in the eucharistic texts of 1 Corinthians 10:16; 11:25, 27 is derived from a pre-Pauline tradition. Paul prefers the term 'cross', as Bultmann remarked.

The greatest vocabulary difficulty comes with 'righteousness' since the word must be interpreted on its background. 'God's righteousness' is shown (in v. 25) in that he passes over, or better 'remits' (so Kümmel), previous sins as part of his forbearing attitude. This allusion clearly reflects a comment on the divine attribute or characteristic. In verse 26 the righteousness of God is displayed in that he 'justifies him who has faith in Jesus' — a typical Pauline remark to be sure, making Talbert's setting in a non-Pauline world hardly credible; but this second reference to righteousness must be *either* a repetition of what has been already said (then, why is it there?) *or* an additional comment made to

enforce or alter the sense already given. The likelihood is that
with a fresh introductory time clause — 'at this time' — Paul is
setting up a contrast between 'then' and 'now'. Formerly God
overlooked sins; now he demonstrates his righteousness
(= salvific action) in accepting as righteous those who have faith
in Jesus. But the notion of divine indulgence (in spite of Acts
17:30)is not otherwise attested in Paul, and flies in the face of his
position in Romans chapters 1-3. If verse 26*b* is Paul's corrective
comment on a traditional formula, then we can make sense of
both statements and both hold true, given the differing circumstances of their origin.

Käsemann had argued that Paul already was preparing his
climactic conclusion in verse 26*b* by inserting 'as a gift by his
grace' (in v. 24) and 'by faith' (v. 25). The cogency of the second
item is more compelling for we can attest elsewhere Paul's use of
a faith-formula (Rom. 3:22, 30-31; Phil. 3:9 as well as Romans
3:27-28). Notice how *dia pisteōs* intrudes between *hilastērion* and
'by his blood' which belong together, as Reumann and Wegenast point out.[17]

Two significant phrases, then, appear to be Paul's own
handiwork, added to supplement a traditional Jewish Christian
(or possibly hellenistic Christian, as Reumann proposes) tradition. These are Paul's characteristic terms, and pave the way for
what he will add as a fitting climax which also sets the traditional
theology in a new light. The verses read:

> Being set right as a gift by his grace through the redemption
> that is through Messiah Jesus; whom God appointed as an
> expiation in his blood [to be received by faith], to prove God's
> righteousness in view of the remitting of former sins in the
> forbearance of God. [This was to prove at this time that he is
> himself righteous and he sets right him who is founded on faith
> in Jesus.]

THE MEANING OF ROMANS 3:24-26

Several important facts emerge from our discussion. There is the
intrinsic value of this section which is 'no peripheral text; rather
it is a passage acknowledged as the centrepiece of Romans'.[18] If
the conclusion is granted that we can separate out a pre-Pauline
tradition from our text, interesting questions emerge.

(*a*) What is the origin of the 'first draft' of the passage? Hunter agrees with Bultmann that we have here a Jewish-Christian formula — a conclusion that leads to the note of surprise: 'Then Jesus' death would already have been conceived as an expiatory sacrifice in the earliest church!' Käsemann adds that 'righteousness' in this context reflects the Hebrew *hesed* (translated in LXX sometimes by *dikaiosynē*, 'righteousness' in v. 25) and means God's covenant-faithfulness, his '*Bundestreue*' (cf. Ex. 34:7).[19] But Lohse has raised some objections. The earlier verses are lacking in Semitic constructions and there is difficulty in retranslating the Greek into Hebrew.[20] The style is Septuagintal, i.e. written in biblical Greek. He suggests a place of origin in Antioch where there was already a theology of martyrdom (cf. 4 Macc. 17:21f.) and we know that Paul had earlier associated with this hellenistic-Judaic church (Acts 11:25-26; 13:1ff.).[21]

The covenant-renewal theme suggests links with the world of thought of the Dead Sea scrolls and this would give plausibility to the idea that the original formula emerged out of a tradition of liturgy connected with the Lord's Supper, just as Mark 14:24 is full of similar echoes ('covenant', 'blood') and is believed to pre-date the text of the supper in 1 Corinthians 11:23ff. which Paul received from his predecessors. 'Redemption' is probably too general a term to link it with a eucharistic vocabulary as Käsemann wants to do, but it does not pose a threat to this overall theory of the setting of the passage in a Lord's Supper service.

Most suggestively J. Reumann locates this teaching on Christ as 'expiation' in a Lord's Supper celebration in Jewish Christianity in the world of the dispersion that innovatively adapted the 'Day of Atonement' to Christian purposes. It used the ritual as a foil to set out the gospel message of the new covenant relationship in which 'Christ the mercy seat' replaced the old order.[22] R. H. Fuller has attempted to trace the emergence of the eucharistic words in Mark 14:22-24 to a Good Friday service held soon after the year of the crucifixion;[23] and it would be a further suggestion that Romans 3:24f. reflects and echoes the language of that occasion.

(*b*) At all events, the teaching of the passage is clear. Divine 'righteousness' (*dikaiosynē*) is seen in his patience with Israel (a theme that marks out the early preaching in Acts chapters 2-4) and his fidelity to the national covenant. There is a continuity linking the history of Israel with the people of the new covenant, as Wegenast remarks.[24] The underlying idea is God's 'forbear-

ance' which is almost a synonym for his 'righteousness'; both
terms characterise his 'attribute' as one who keeps faith with his
people (cf. 4 Ezra 8:36).

The background of the formula is the exodus. Old Israel was
delivered; now the new Israel has been redeemed by Jesus, and
this is known in the forgiveness of sins. The eucharistic setting
fits in with the phrase 'in his blood', and we recall the Sinai
pericope of Exodus 24 where the 'blood of the covenant' plays a
leading part in sealing the agreement between Yahweh and his
people. This formula then reflects a covenant-renewal and sets
the refurbished covenant, broken because of sin, on a firm basis
laid in Jesus' death.

That death is called *hilastērion*, RSV 'expiation'. Clearly this is a
cultic term, whether it refers explicitly and exclusively to the
'mercy seat' of Leviticus 16 or not.[25] This golden slab (Heb.
kappôreṯ) covered the ark of the covenant in the most holy place
which was part of the Tabernacle's furnishings. *Kappôreṯ* comes
from the verb *kippēr* 'to cover', in the sense of 'atone', 'wipe out'.
So *hilastērion* could very well refer to the 'place where sins are
wiped out', with the added thought that since it is God who
provides the *hilastērion* there is no idea of pagan appeasement or
placating of the deity. God's initiative is clear here, as in the Old
Testament sacrifices (Lev. 17:11: 'I have given it to you upon the
altar to make atonement for your soul', a text which uses *kippēr*
and in translation a verb cognate with *hilastērion*). The reference
to the 'blood' which is the means of atonement (in Lev. 17:11)
reappears in Paul's text as 'by his blood', i.e. his death as a
sacrifice (F. F. Bruce[26]).

Perhaps the phrase 'God put forward' indicates a direct
contrast between the old and the new. Under the old covenant
the *hilastērion* was hidden within the sanctuary, and seen by only
one person, the high priest on the Day of Atonement. Paul's
allusion to the sacrifice of Christ indicates that this was publicly
displayed and set forth in the death of Jesus on the cross.

In terms of how this soteriological confession was understood
in pre-Pauline times we may remark that Christ's sacrificial
death was traced to God's free favour (his grace). It exemplifies
his covenant oath to restrain his judgment until the Messiah
should come. Now the day of redemption (i.e. release from sin's
captivity) has arrived and Christ is the expiatory sacrifice, the
new 'mercy seat' — the place where God shows forgiveness to his
people in accordance with the promise of Jeremiah 31:31-34 —

and sets them in a saving relationship with himself. They are 'justified', which seems to mean here no more than 'delivered', as Israel was released from the bondage of Babylonian exile (Deutero-Isaiah uses the verb consistently of God showing his 'righteousness' in bearing with Israel's folly and saving them).

(c) In Paul's hand the old formula takes on a new meaning. The decisive 'moment' (*kairos* in v. 26a) means for him the opening of a new epoch set in an apocalyptic framework. His way of viewing the time-line between the old and the new covenants is more in terms of disjunction than continuity. The old order is one of wrath and retribution; the new marks a break as it ushers in a novel dispensation of God's rectification (2 Cor. 3:6-11, especially v. 9: 'a dispensation of righteousness').

The climax comes in verse 26b: there is revealed God's righteousness, his vindication of lordship over all nations and his bringing into being of a new world where, irrespective of ethnic or religious qualifications, both Jews and Gentiles are set right with him. So Paul can conclude, in partial agreement with the formula and partial correction: it is true that God did show his righteous character (his '*Bundestreue*') in the Messiah of Israel but he also in this time of the new age reveals himself as the 'justifier of any one who has faith in Jesus', whether that one is Jew or pagan.

The emphasis 'by faith' was most likely added to verse 25 and we may also suspect that *hilastērion* has now taken on a deeper dimension for Paul. More than a term derived from the cultic terminology and restricted to the Day of Atonement setting, it stands for an expiatory offering that absorbed the wrath of God that Paul believed was released against all human ungodliness and unrighteousness (1:18; 2:5). Paul is likely, therefore, given the range of context in Romans 1:18-3:26, to have understood *hilastērion* as the place where God neutralised all human sin — not simply the cultic lapses of Leviticus — by accepting in Christ the penal consequences of evil, bearing those consequences in his exposure to the divine judgment and so freeing all, both Jews and Gentiles, from the guilt of alienation from God, which is the fateful result of human sinning.[27]

Paul's soteriology builds on and expresses the universality of Christ's atoning work, emphasises more clearly its representative and vicarious character (in a way absent from Lev. 16), and suspends the efficacy of the atonement more logically on the exercise of personal faith (against simple membership in a covenant community). Hence the climax centres on 'the individual who has faith in Jesus' (as in Phil. 3:9, against S. K. Williams).[28]

Two immediate consequences follow from this exegetical discussion. One is that Paul's thinking operates in the realm of personal categories. His accentuating of faith and his understanding of God's righteousness as relational — the beginning of a new age[29] is marked by God and the world being united by Christ's atoning deed more than by God's confirming the national covenant with Israel and liberating the people from physical slavery — are more obviously linked with all that has been done to restore men and women to God's favour in the dynamic-personal way that we earlier saw to be the meaning of the term.[30] Further illustration will come as we proceed to investigate the next section of Paul's salvation-teaching and understanding of Christ's death.

Secondly, the rationale of reconciliation is largely bypassed in Romans 3:24ff. For consideration of that theme we need to turn to a passage where Paul's writing addresses the questions, How did God set the world right? How did Christ assume the guilt of man the sinner? How do those who are deservedly guilty receive a share in God's righteousness in that 'sweet exchange' ('*im fröhlichen Wechsel*')[31] based on Jesus' death?[32]

CHAPTER SIX

RECONCILIATION AT CORINTH

THE HORIZON OF THE TEACHING

Before we are ready to look in some detail at 2 Corinthians 5:18-21, we should offer some observations regarding its background. The better and more modern term is the passage's 'horizon'. This word is in current use to denote something more than the background of an author's writing or the key to his thought. It is defined by E. D. Hirsch as 'that which was, consciously or unconsciously, in the author's intention'.[1] The term represents the datum to be investigated; or better it looks at the chosen passage under scrutiny as the datum and asks what inferences may be drawn by the modern interpreter as its meaning (or 'scope') within the context of the writer's known flow of thought.

There are many items in Paul's Corinthian correspondence that are, and must remain, obscure. In the familiar illustration used by several commentators (e.g. F. F. Bruce[2]) we are like those in the position of people listening into one end of a telephone conversation and 'trying, not very successfully, to reconstruct what is being said at the other end.' Bruce wisely concludes: 'There are many interpretative problems in the Corinthian correspondence the solutions to which can hardly be more than intelligent guesses.'

That assessment is true and just. It is, however, a verdict on the problems at Corinth as a whole and in regard to the more vexatious areas of Paul's pastoral responses as, for instance, in 1 Corinthians 11. In other parts of the correspondence the flow of the apostle's mind is more clearly logical and more easily comprehended. One such example is his writing at 2 Corinthians 2:14-7:4.

At the earlier text Paul has just concluded a narrative recital of events that, he explains, led him to move from a promising situation near Troas on the Asian coast and sail over to Macedonia. The narrative sequence is picked up again at 7:4 where he returns to his theme. In the interval he seems to digress and offer a resounding defence of his ministry and the gospel he preached. What led him to this extended 'diversion' (if that is the right word) in his letter?

A quick answer may be seen in his understanding of his mission. At Titus' return and meeting with Paul in Macedonia the news of the situation was uplifting to Paul's spirits (7:6), and it was time to celebrate the return of the Corinthian church (or at least the majority of its members) to the loyalty they once displayed to Paul. The disaffection in the main was over and it was an occasion for jubilant thankfulness to God that Paul's gospel and its advocacy in the apostolic ministry had overcome its detractors. The extravagant language of 2:14 is explained: God leads us in triumph, '[carrying] us along in the victorious progress of the Messianic triumph, which is sweeping through the world', as T. W. Manson paraphrases the verb.[3] Moreover, the progress of that triumph involves the success attending the life-giving message entrusted to Paul who, with his party, is like a fragrance of life to those who accept the gospel and yet a smell of doom and death to those who reject it. The latter are they who have fallen prey to an adulterated version of the apostolic preaching (2:17) and remain in a state of blindness like the unbelievers over whom Satan still has power (4:3-4).

The inference is that the message and the messenger are in some way inter-connected; to reject the message is to despise the ones who bring it and embody it in their lives (4:7). Conversely the Corinthians who have turned away from Paul, perhaps some who are still holding out and refusing to come over to his side, are rejecting not only his person but the very thing the apostle stood for and represented in his person, 'the word of God' with life-imparting power. The kerygma is a divine fragrance containing the 'knowledge of God' (2:14), but Paul can boldly claim 'we are the aroma of Christ' (2:15), since it is in our persons and ministry that 'God is making his appeal' to you (5:20).

The entire section (2:14-7:4) should be read as Paul's appeal. It is not so much a digression from what he had said about the 'tearful letter' pledging reconciliation if the Corinthian malcontents will deal radically with the offender (2:1-11) nor simply a rehearsal of past events up to the time of his leaving Troas and reaching Macedonia. It is an extension of the same spirit he has shown in calling them to repentance (2:2; 7:8-11) and obedience (2:9) and it is a fervent yet reasoned appeal to any who were still unyielding to the pressure of his earlier appeal and whose friendly attitude to himself he has reason to doubt. The plea is a renewed call to them to leave their hostile dispositions and suspicions of both his message and his ministry and accept his proffered reconciliation, already given to the ringleader (2:5-11; 7:12). (In my view, chapters 10-13 show only too clearly how well sensed were Paul's latent fears about such a continuing groundswell of opposition, and in 10:1ff. he, perhaps later in time than the writing of 2 Cor. 1-9, will answer vehemently the renewed troubles coming from the anti-Pauline group at Corinth and its alien influence which is abetted by some intruders, according to 11:4.)

THE APOSTLE'S APPEAL

The section in chapters 2-7 is arranged methodically in a set of contrasts.

(i) *Paul's teaching* is opposed to a different understanding of the Christian message which featured a promoting of Moses as a 'divine man' law-giver (3:1-18), a reliance on worldly success and lordly power to validate its preachers (4:1-15), and a type of eschatological thinking that saw the future already contained in the present and denied a future hope of resurrection (4:16-5:10; its slogan is 'we walk by sight', which Paul counters). Above all, this type of teaching raised hostility to Paul who was dismissed scornfully as 'out of his mind' (5:13). The only answer he could give in retort was to appeal to Christ's love for him (5:14-15) which has not only provided him with a motive power and a driving force for his ministry; it has most recently enabled him to forgive his enemies at Corinth (2:10) and now he extends to them and others who are still recalcitrant the same reconciliation. The appeal then embodied a piece of traditional 'church teaching' on God's reconciliation of the world through Christ (5:18-21), offered to enforce Paul's contention that his christological emphasis (5:16) meant the arrival of a new age in human history where 'the new has come' (5:17) but also to state that his attitudes to these Corinthian persons and problems were fashioned according to the new life that the new age had brought with it.

(ii) *Paul's person* belongs to that new aeon. He and his followers share a glory more illustrious than Moses (3:18) and what occurred in conversion (4:6) and his commission (4:5) has set the pattern for his ensuing life and ministry (4:7-12). It is essentially a career of human weakness and full reliance on God who will raise the dead at the end-time. The Spirit is our 'first instalment' (5:5) of the powers of the new age, but the end is not yet. Meanwhile Paul walks 'by faith' (5:7) and anticipates the resurrection in the future. The same tension between present possession and future hope is found in his mention of reconciliation.

God has reconciled the world in Christ; but the task of proclaiming the reconciliation goes on and, adds Paul, it must be applied to concrete human situations such as the one staring the Corinthians in the face. So he slips in the aside, 'Be reconciled to God' (5:20), as his earnest yet tender plea. So sure is he of the rightness of what he is doing in this move to secure full restoration that he can call upon God as his ally (6:1) and build on the fact that God is 'working together' (*synergountes*) with him as he is with God in this endeavour.[4] There are no hard feelings on his side (6:11); there should be no continuing resistance on theirs (6:12) as he works towards a complete reconciliation. His appeal — 'Mend your ways . . . live in peace' — is renewed in the closing verse (13:11), preparatory to the liturgical ending (13:14).

With this short attempt to 'set the stage' we can look more closely at the passage in question.

2 CORINTHIANS 5:18-21:
THE STRUCTURE OF THE VERSES

Our discussion will be helped if we set down Paul's writing in lines. Then we shall attempt to draw some conclusions as to the origin of the teaching.

> [18]All this is God's doing,
> 1a   who reconciled us to himself through Christ
> 1b   and gave us the service of reconciliation,[19] namely,
> 2a   God was reconciling the world to himself in Christ
>   [not reckoning their trespasses against them]
> 2b   and committing to us the message of reconciliation
> 3b   [20]We act then as ambassadors for Christ, as God
>   entreats through us [we beg on Christ's behalf, Be
>   reconciled to God]

3a   21The one who did not know sin   (A)
      on behalf of us   (B)
      sin   (C)
      he made   (D)
      that we   (A¹)
      should become   (D¹)
      the righteousness of God   (C¹)
      in him.   (B¹)

On three grounds this short exposition of Paul's teaching on reconciliation seems to have incorporated and adapted traditional material already in existence. First, in a context where the appeal is to pastoral problems at Corinth and is (presumably) addressed to believers in the church there, it is remarkable that Paul has used kerygmatic idioms more suited to a preaching of the gospel to unbelievers outside the church. The call 'Be reconciled to God' is the 'language of evangelism' (as I. H. Marshall calls it[5]), and is evidently explained by the secondary use Paul is making of the traditional preaching forms to enforce his concern for the Corinthians to be restored to good relations with himself as an apostolic leader (see 2 Cor. 6:11-13).

Second, the literary structure of the section suggests a carefully prepared piece of soteriological credo, that is, a specimen of confessional statement expressing in summary form what the first Christians believed about God's redemptive work in Christ. The two verses (18,19) stand together as dependent on each other, the latter verse enlarging and explaining what is contained in the former. Thus, line 1a (God reconciled us) is taken up and repeated with modification in line 2a (God or God-in-Christ reconciled the world). Similarly line 1b is parallel with line 2b and the terms 'service' and 'message' go together.

The structure in verses 20-21 is a little more complicated. Matching thoughts are repeated but in inverse sequence. The verbs in verse 20 ('act as ambassadors', 'entreat', 'beg') seem to be unnecessarily repetitous; this suggests a special reason for their use. At verse 21 it is fairly easy to see, even in the English translation, how the different lines are matched to form a series of contrasts.. The first part refers to the redeemer's work; the second half applies the benefits to the redeemed people.

Attempts have been made to trace a word-order chiasmus (suggesting a criss-cross arrangement) in the last verse, but its symmetry is less than perfect, as C. K. Barrett concedes.[6] The most he is willing to grant is that 'Paul is moved by the subject with which he is dealing to write in an exalted style that suggests the language of hymn or liturgy'.[7] All we know of Paul's literary habits indicates that when he uses hymnic or poetic speech he borrows compositions already formed and does not compose 'on the run'. Also his epistolary method is to add interpretative or explanatory or corrective comments to existing hymnic periods in such a way as to break strict symmetrical forms. Examples of this practice are seen in Philippians 2:6-11 and, as we shall observe, in Colossians 1:15-20.

This reminder brings us to the third reason for suspecting a pre-Pauline statement embedded in our text. Two lines look out of place, and we suggest that they were added by Paul's hand as he incorporated the formulation into his letter.

> verse 19*b*: not reckoning against them their trespasses
> verse 20*c*: we beg (you) on Christ's behalf, Be reconciled to God.

The interesting thing is that both these suggested additions are full of Pauline language. The verb 'to reckon' is used elsewhere in a similar context (Rom. 4:3f., 5f., 9, 11). The second verb 'to beg' is in 2 Corinthians 8:4; 10:2; Galatians 4:12. We suggest that these two lines are Paul's interpretative 'glosses' on a pre-formed tradition, and added to accomplish a double objective. On the one side (v. 19) Paul wanted to make it clear that the 'reconciliation of the world' was achieved by what God did in not holding trespasses against humankind — it is noteworthy that the line says 'against *them*', whereas elsewhere in the paragraph the language is first person plural (we, us) — and so he cleared them of guilt. It is the idiom of justification that Paul inserts, perhaps to safeguard the teaching against false understanding. Maybe 'reconciliation' was thought of as an automatic process or divine fiat, and Paul wished to anchor its rationale firmly in an act of God's power that dealt with human sin (exactly his teaching in Rom. 4:25; 5:15-18, 20). On the other side verse 20 opens with a somewhat harsh apostolic appeal as Paul appears in the role of 'ambassador' (*presbeutēs*). He does not use this title of himself elsewhere, except at Philemon 9 (where the reading is disputed), and the term reflects an authority only later accorded to Paul (as in Eph. 6:20). So we conclude that the appeal, 'acting as Christ's ambassador' is softened by the more moderate and tender call, 'we beg on Christ's behalf, Be reconciled to God', with half an eye on the Corinthian malcontents who were still resisting Paul's apostleship. This is evidently the sense of the appeal in 2 Corinthians 6:1.

As an extension of this third argument based on linguistic features we may go on to enquire if there are characteristically non-Pauline expressions in these verses. 'Righteousness of God' in verse 21 may be suspected since, while it is undeniable that Paul's salvation-teaching centred precisely on this phrase, as we have seen (Rom. 1:17; 3:21, 26; 10:3), it is there used of the power of God that introduced a new age of grace and forgiveness for the world. But in verse 21 in our text the thought of Christians 'becoming the righteousness of God in him [Christ]' is not paralleled elsewhere in Paul — the nearest he comes to it is 1 Corinthians 1:30, but with a significant difference, 'our righteousness' standing in some uneasy tension with the divine righteousness. In other words the anthropological application in 2 Corinthians 5:21 of the term sits awkwardly with the apostle's attested usage in other places.

The same doubt about another phrase in verse 21 may be registered. 'He made him to be sin for us' is a difficult sentence to explain precisely, because we do not know the background of the expression. Three possibilities are surveyed by L. Sabourin and S. Lyonnet[8]: (a) Christ was treated as a sinner in his own person; (b) Christ identified himself with sin in his incarnation (as in Rom. 8:3); (c) Christ became a sacrifice for sin. Their conclusion is that (c) is preferable, and cogent reasons are given for tracing this part-verse to the suffering servant motif of Second Isaiah, especially the teaching of Isaiah 53:10: 'When thou makest his soul an offering for sin' (Hebrew, RSV marg.). If this is so, it points in the direction of yet another instance of Paul's borrowing traditional teaching, for this verse falls under the rubric of an established modern consensus, namely: 'Paul never makes use of any of the Servant language, except where he is quoting tradition which he has received from pre-Pauline Christianity.'[9]

Our conclusion may be stated. In the course of a discussion with the Corinthian church Paul introduces a piece of accepted teaching on the theme of reconciliation. Arranged suggestively in lines, it has the appearance of a credal statement, with an introductory phrase ('All this comes from God'). At key-points in the quoted material Paul has inserted lines (verses 19b, 20c) partly to elaborate the meaning, partly to correct the sense of the pre-formed tradition. In so doing he has underscored those elements of the teaching on reconciliation that were in need of special emphasis.

So Paul, in quoting a current formulation, intended to make it his own. 'The pre-existing tradition is used to give a sharper profile to the apostle's own theology.' Yet, Käsemann continues, 'it is impossible to miss the fact that this tradition thereby takes on a new intention'.[10] What that 'new intention' may have been falls to be considered.

THE APOSTLE'S TEACHING

For Paul the 'reconciliation of the world' is interpreted in terms of justification as God does not impute trespasses to man's account and in this way he shows himself as one who 'justifies the ungodly' (Rom. 4:5). The call to live in God's justifying grace is one of perennial application. Christians are spoken of as 'already justified' by the past act of God's setting the world right with himself (Rom. 4:25; 5:1; 8:30, 33). To that extent the gift can be gratefully received and God's completed action in Christ celebrated as already fully and finally accomplished. There is, however, another side to Paul's thought. The present reality of living in God's favour of grace brings with it a sure confidence that at the future judgment the verdict of acceptance will be confirmed (Gal. 5:5; Phil. 1:11; 3:9). There is an open-ended aspect of justification that keeps the final day of acquittal in view (1 Cor. 4:5). The continual tension 'already justified . . . not yet finally saved' runs through Paul's correspondence and provides a basis for his paraenetic (i.e. hortatory) counsel to the churches.

The same tension is seen with 'reconciliation' which Paul re-interprets by inserting into a traditional formula both the negative element of God's not reckoning trespasses and the positive aspect of the need for Christians to be reconciled to God and so 'not to receive the grace of God in vain' (6:1). These two matters deserve extended comment, along with a feature that sets the teaching in this context on a firm Pauline base. That last-named item is treated first.

(a) Paul's earlier discussion had centred on a reminder that is singularly lacking in 5:18-21. The explicit mention of the cross and resurrection of Jesus is made in verses 14-15: 'one died for all . . . he died for all, that those who live might live no longer for themselves but for him who for their sake died and was raised'.

These words pick up and state clearly what were central assertions in Paul's public proclamation which in turn was based on teaching he had received (1 Cor. 15:3ff.). In his hands the statements, 'Christ died ... he was raised', became a summary of his message (e.g. Rom. 8:34; 2 Cor. 13:4). But it was not only the past event that interested Paul. He was concerned to underline the continued relevance of Jesus' death and resurrection to the Christian life. He died ... and we died in him; he was raised ... and God will raise us up (1 Cor. 6:14; cf. Rom. 6:1-11; 1 Thess. 5:10).

The effect of the cross and resurrection is to lead responsive believers to break with their old 'self'-life (Gal. 2:20) and to live henceforward under the dominion of Christ the Lord (Rom. 14:7-9). Paul has therefore safeguarded his use of the 'reconciliation' paragraph in 5:18-21 by prefacing it with a clear reminder that God's deed avails little unless it is 'applied' to those who are its beneficiaries. To maintain — as the credo evidently did in its stark simplicity and monumental grandeur — that 'God reconciled the world in Christ' is only part of the kerygma, albeit an indispensable foundation. There must be a corresponding personal dimension, otherwise the profound teaching remains *in abstracto* and detached from human experience. The objective kerygma requires a complementary call to faith; and Paul's 'faith' is a close identification with Christ in his death and rising that becomes part of the fabric of the Christian's life as he or she thereby 'dies' to self, and rises to 'walk', to 'serve', to 'live' in newness under Christ's lordship (Rom. 6:6; 7:6; Col. 2:6). And we shall show later how this 'personalised' application of traditional teaching is exactly what we see again when Paul comes to describe the nature of the Christian life (Rom. 5:6-11) and when he has occasion to press into service another example of hymnic celebration (Col. 1:15-23).

(*b*) If our submission is correct that the line 'not reckoning their trespasses against them' (5:19*b*) is from Paul's own hand, its value may now be assessed. As we have remarked, the 'non-reckoning' of human guilt is basic to his discussion in Romans chapters 4-5. The novel feature added here is a carefully worked-out explanation of the 'mechanics' of God's action in verse 21.

It involves several steps that we can tabulate even at the risk of appearing to give to Paul's words more logical coherence than they may originally have had. Obviously we do not have access to any early Christian 'doctrine of the Atonement' constructed as a piece of dogmatic theology. The best we can do is to summarise some ideas or convictions (see verse 14: 'we conclude', 'we have reached this conviction') that are salient in this brief report; and we acknowledge that later theology has used these verses to elaborate some intricate and detailed doctrines, a task that is not within our purview. With this caveat, the following scheme may be set down:

(i) *Identification.* 'God was in Christ reconciling the world to himself' (RSV) is capable of being taken in two or three ways. The phrase 'in Christ' may go with God to form a composite expression, thus 'God-in Christ' and the participle of the verb follows. Or else 'in Christ' is the means through which God reconciled the world (so Barrett).[11] J. H. Moulton prefers yet a third interpretation: 'God in Christ was reconciling' — giving the verb an imperfect tense — 'the world to himself'. Against the first view is the reminder that Paul's statement is to do with reconciliation, not incarnation, and the second translation seems better to continue the thought of verse 18 which attributes the initiative to God. Nonetheless it still remains true that Paul's Greek is less than precise; yet it is equally the case that the flow of his argument is to show how God himself is personally involved both in his acting through the agency of Christ (verse 18, *dia Christou*) and by coming himself in Christ (*en Christō*, verse 19) to our world. R. H. Strachan[12] speaks of a 'divine aggression' or invasion to underscore the personal presence of God who in Jesus Christ entered our temporal order and made himself one with the race he came to restore. At least we may take Paul's text to convey this: in Christ God became one of our human race and identified himself with it.

(ii) *Representation.* James D. G. Dunn[13] has rightly focused on 2 Corinthians 5:14-15 as 'one of the most explicit expressions of Paul's understanding of Jesus as representative man': 'one man died for all, therefore all humankind (*hoi pantes*) has died'. At face value this is taken to mean that Christ assumed the role of the last Adam and as man died because there was no other way for man — any man. 'His death is an acknowledgment that there is no way out for fallen men except through death — no answer to sinful flesh except its destruction in death.' Only through death, therefore and in consequence, does the New Man emerge in risen life. That hope of new life, however, is restricted to believers in a way not parallel with the earlier statement that 'Christ died, therefore all died'. The death is common to all humanity, Christ included; the resurrection (in verse 15) embraces only those who 'acknowledge the Risen One as Lord'.

The insistence on Christ as the representative man is correct, but we may hesitate to follow Dunn in taking the death of 'all' (in verse 14) to refer to 'all mankind'. The representation of Jesus is that of his people; it is they who are described as having died in the person of their representative; and as F. F. Bruce comments,[14] 'The "all" of this passage is synonymous with the second "many" of Rom. 5.15, 19.' Moreover, it cannot be a physical death as a terminus of life that is in view, since 'the all' continue to live (verse 15), albeit no longer to themselves but under a new head. The death is one to the old order of self-interest: 'He died for us that we might die to ourselves', observes Calvin, echoing Mark 8:34. The death of 'all' not only seals the grave on the old way of life, but liberates the persons who share Christ's death that they may share his resurrection newness, 'to become free for a new life with new goals and purposes'.[15] T. W. Manson crisply sums up:

> The death of Christ is something in which all his followers have a share; and equally they share in his risen life, which means that they can no longer live their old selfish life but must live for him who inaugurated the new life for them by dying and rising again.[16]

In the sentences 'one died *for* all', 'he died *for* all', the meaning of the preposition is obviously important. R. V. G. Tasker argues[17] (rightly, in our judgment) against the view that when Paul wrote 'Jesus *died for all*, the inference must be that all were liable to the death which was the penalty of sin'. But, Tasker concludes, 'It is not this truth that Paul is now stressing.' Tasker, however, takes the first part of the verse in precisely the way he has rejected for its second half. 'The apostle means that Christ's death was the death of all, in the sense that He died the death they should have died; the penalty of their sins was borne by Him; He died in their place.' Whether this notion of substitution is demanded in verse 21 will be considered later. It is doubtful, however, if it can be sustained as an interpretation of verses 14-15 where the phrase 'for all' (*hyper pantōn*) speaks more of the representative task of Christ who, acting on his people's behalf, died, i.e. so identified himself with their humanity and plight that his death to sin can be regarded as an act of obedience and surrender in which they have a share. The preposition in verse 20 (twice repeated, *hyper Christou*) describes the apostolic ministry in a similar way: it is representative of Christ, not only in that Paul acts for Christ as his servant but that God is personally present in Paul's ministry, 'as God were entreating through us'. Paul's preaching is given a word-of-God character by this close identification (cf. 1 Thess. 2:13), and proclamation is nothing less than the voice of God through Paul, as J. Murphy-O'Connor makes clear.[18] If this parallelism may be used, it would lead us to conclude that Christ's oneness with the race means his acting in their name and offering to God on their behalf an oblation of filial obedience and allegiance that God accepted and because of which he acted forgivingly to restore the race of sinners. At this point in the chapter Paul, it seems, says no more than 'he died for others' by acting representatively in their name, with the consequence that his act has the profound effect of changing personal attitudes and dispositions. They for whom he died no longer live for themselves but for him.

(*iii*)*Imputation*. The puzzling question, How is the sinful race restored to divine favour? is posed later, at verse 21. Its answer is given in terms of a transference or, to use Paul's word, 'imputation' (Rom. 4:4-8). The elements are presented in their bare simplicity. The sinless Christ took our condemnation, that for us there might be condemnation no more. On its positive side, the happy result of this 'transaction' is that as Christ in his sinlessness took responsibility for our wrongdoing, we are gifted with that entity ('the righteousness of God') that permits our acceptance with God. If this way of expressing the exchange is most suitable, then the appropriate term is substitution used to denote an interchange of guilt and righteousness, while imputation stresses how the two sides of the matter are related. A becomes B, so that B may become A.

The moment the process of transference is stated in these bald terms, we are struck by the fact that Paul elsewhere never so speaks and he in other places gives a more positive content to the matter. His attested teaching on the uniqueness of the redeemer in both his filial relation to God as 'son' and his pre-existence as being 'sent' — to which M. Hengel has drawn attention[19] — does not include a statement of his sinlessness. Indeed it has been argued by Karl Barth and others that Romans 8:3 — Christ 'came in the likeness of sinful flesh' — points in the other direction, namely that his complete humanity involved a taking of man's fallen nature. This is debatable, of course; and the debate, chronicled by Harry Johnson in his monograph,[20] continues. It is more significant to observe another part of Paul's discussion in Romans where the notion of 'interchange'[21] seems clear and so would offer a parallel. 'For as by one man's disobedience many were made/constituted sinners, so by one man's obedience many will be made/constituted righteous' (Rom. 5:19). The essence of that summarising statement is well stated by Cranfield: 'The many will be constituted righteous through Christ's obedience' — to God — 'in the sense that, since God has in Christ identified Himself with sinners and taken upon Himself the burden of their sin, they will receive as a free gift from Him that status of righteousness which Christ's perfect obedience alone has deserved.'[22]

With that explanation in mind we may observe the distinctive elements in 2 Corinthians 5:21: (i) Nothing is said there of Christ's freely willed obedience (classically stated in Phil. 2:6-8). Instead God 'made' him to be sin, perhaps in the sense of 'appointed' or 'designated' as in Mark 3:14; Acts 2:36. (ii) Adam's 'trespass' (paraptōma, Rom. 5:18) is not used as a foil to display more brightly the illustrious obedience of the Second Man. Interestingly it is precisely this term for human sin — 'trespasses' (paraptōmata) — that Paul has inserted in 5:19 using the language of imputation. (iii) 'Becoming the righteousness of God in him' poses its own problems, not least being the unexampled way this phrase 'righteouness of God' is used. Paul's normal usage (Rom 1:17; 3:21; 10:3 may be taken as characteristic, since they appear at pivotal points in the epistle) carries the sense of a disclosure of divine power leading to salvation and new life for the world. The thought of believers 'becoming' (genōmetha) part of that enterprise is strange for Paul, and is in no way parallel with Romans 5:19 where believers are 'constituted righteous', i.e. justified by Christ's vicarious obedience. In other words, the idioms of 2 Corinthians 5:21 are not justification terms and state simply a substitutionary change. The issue of how God has dealt with human sin is left open and no rationale, such as the Pauline justification teaching offers, is given to throw light on the pressing moral conundrum: how did Christ's identification with sin open the way for Christians to receive his righteousness? The verse then needs to be understood in the light of Paul's teaching elsewhere, and to that extent to be amplified and corrected by what we have in Romans. In specific terms, Christ's sharing our sin, whether as a sin-offering or a sacrifice or saviour figure modelled on Isaiah 53's *'ebed Yahweh*, is viewed by Paul as *his obedience* or *faithfulness to his mission as filial redeemer of the new humanity*. Those who stand as beneficiaries of his saving work are given acceptance with God because they are 'justified' or 'constituted righteous' in their status before God, *coram Deo*. This has come about by God's gracious decision not to reckon trespasses against them exactly as in Romans 5:18f., and to accept the filial obedience of the righteous one, the last Adam, on their behalf. To that extent 'they became God's righteousness in him', i.e. they are not divinised by God *but given the salvific status as men and women rightly related to God*. That conclusion, we submit, emerges from Paul's insertion of his distinctive comment in verse 19: 'not counting their trespasses against them'.

(*iv*)*Reconciliation*. And so we come to the quintessence of this stately credal paragraph. Paul is led to his theme by reflecting on the new order that came into being with Christ. The epitome of what he had discovered about the new age is summed up in 'the love of Christ' that impelled him to his service (2 Cor. 5:14). That love expressed itself supremely in the cross, a theme to which Paul returns in Romans 5:1-11 where he offers a concise statement of his understanding of reconciliation.

The 'cross of the Messiah' raised for Paul, as for Jewish hearers, an intractable problem. If he was simply an earthly Messiah, seen from a 'human point of view' (v. 16: *kata sarka*, a phrase with a negative connotation in Paul, suggesting horizons bounded by man's forlorn and arrogant wisdom), there is a fundamental contradiction in the statement that he was crucified. Whoever died in this manner fell under the deuteronomic rubric of a divine curse (Deut. 21:23); he was 'under a ban' (*ḥērem*) and an outcast from Israel's community. In another place Paul lets us see how the puzzle was solved. 'Christ became a curse *for us*,' he remarks (Gal. 3:13) to account for the strange fulfilment of the deuteronomic text. Here he denies the basis of the alleged objection. 'We do not now regard him from an earthly viewpoint,' since no nationalist or politicised categories will suffice, and 'Christ' (= Messiah) is a term Paul came to use less as a title of office meaningful only to Jews, and more as a personal appellation.

As a universal person, set free from all limiting restrictions, Christ ushered in the new era, at the 'turn of the ages' (v. 17). It was like a new order of creation, remarks Paul as he reflects on the Genesis creation story not for the first time in this letter (2 Cor. 4:6). The old world, with its enslavements and fears and ruled by its god (4:4), is on the way out; already it is replaced by the new age, promised in the glowing words of the exilic prophet (Isa. 51:9ff.;54:9f.; cf. Isa. 42:9; 43:18f. for the contrast between the old/new worlds) and already entering human experience as forgiveness and accompanied by baptismal joy. But we must be careful not to reduce the phrase to 'new creature', in a way similar to what the rabbis promised to pious Jewish converts.[23] Paul is not describing *in this context* the personal dimension of a new birth; rather he is announcing as a kerygmatic statement *the advent of the new creation 'in Christ'*, the dramatic recovery of the world, formerly alienated and dislocated, by God who has acted eschatologically in Christ, i.e. the world is placed now under his rule.

It is strange that C. K. Barrett should write in reference to verse 18: '*Up to this point* Paul has been describing the work of God *in nobis*, that is, the new creation that takes effect in and for a man who by faith comes to be in Christ'.[24] The flow of Paul's argument suggests the opposite. It is God's work 'outside of us', (*extra nos*), objectively viewed and independent of human application that Paul has recited, at least until he reaches the quoted formula of verse 18. Then, in our view, follows a piece of cosmic soteriology stated as a Christian 'confession of faith' — the language is both personal ('reconciled *us*') and universal ('the world'),except for verse 19*b* — and expressing in non-Pauline terminology the achievement and the demands of reconciliation. The note of authority runs through the statement, since those who are charged to undertake 'the ministry of reconciliation' are no less than 'ambassadors for Christ'. As was earlier observed, this singular title prompts the enquiry whether the next line, 'We beg you on Christ's behalf, Be reconciled to God', may be a Pauline aside, slipped in to temper the appeal. We proceed to test this assumption by remarking that in the quoted sentence the verb takes on an altered nuance since it is applied to pastoral problems at Corinth and so is lifted out of its earlier cosmic setting.

(*c*) The semantic field of the verb 'to reconcile' (*[kat] allassein*) has been investigated by several scholars.[25] At its simplest the verb denotes 'the action by which peace is made between personal enemies', as Moses brought together his estranged compatriots (Acts 7:26: the verb here is *synallassein*). It is the work of a mediator whose office is 'to make hostility cease, to lead to peace'. Applied to divine-human relations, the verb 'to reconcile' does not describe a change of feelings or disposition whether of man to God or of God to man but rather 'an objective change of the situation' in which God and man face each other, as Collange remarks.[26] Reconciliation 'denotes a change in the relations between God and man and more particularly a change in man himself' (T. W. Manson).[27] The verses of Paul's text say two important things: it is God who has acted to reconcile men and women to himself, and this reconciliation is effected through the mediation of Christ, with the thought left implicit that the phrase 'through Christ' (*dia Christou*, v. 18) includes his cross and resurrection. If, as is likely, verse 19 should read 'in Christ God was reconciling the world to himself', then the 'in Christ' (*en Christō*) formula is to be explained either as a stylistic variant of the more normal 'through Christ' (so Neugebauer, Lietzmann) or the sign of a more obvious non-Pauline usage (Collange; the usage would be even stranger if we adopted Collange's translation following Allo to the effect, 'God was in Christ, reconciling . . .').[28]

The periphrastic tense of the verb in verse 19: 'God was (*ēn*, imperfect of the verb 'to be') reconciling (*katallassōn*, participle)' has caused a problem. Does it imply that reconciliation is a process (Plummer) or an incomplete action (Windisch) or 'open-ended' in that while from God's side the reconciliation is total, there is the possibility that 'some men may not accept their being reconciled to God' (von Allmen)?[29] Collange believes that the shift in verb tenses is slight and is made on grounds of rhythm and style, with the imperfect tense disguising an aorist of past action. The last-named explanation may be too simple, and we are bound to observe that the ambiguity in 2 Corinthians 5:18-19 is not present in Romans 5:1-11 where reconciliation is an event in past time, once and for all.[30]

The difficulty for the interpreter comes when the verb is used passively, referring to the action of a person in giving up his hostility to another individual. Then, an offended person is appealed to that he may set aside his enmity or anger. Josephus (*Ant.* 7:184) uses the verb of David who was asked to be reconciled to his erring son Absalom and let his anger cease.

In 2 Maccabees, as Dupont says, there are several examples of situations where Israel has justly deserved God's wrath by apostasy and is suffering in consequence. Judgment has a salutary effect as the people pray for Yahweh to be reconciled to them and cease from his anger (2 Macc. 1:5). Martyrs whose suffering is both for their own sins (2 Macc. 7:18) and on behalf of the nation as a whole offer especially powerful prayers since their sufferings have a vicarious value. They bear the divine wrath, so (the prayer proceeds) in effect 'let the people be spared'. God is implored to be reconciled to the nation (2 Macc. 7:32ff.).

A sharp point may be put on the Pauline text if we ask whether this usage in Jewish literature offers any kind of parallel. There is, however, an obvious difference. The Maccabean martyrs urge God to be reconciled to them and offer both their lives and their sins to him as acts of vicarious piety and merit. This picture stands in direct antithesis to Paul's teaching whether that teaching was inherited or is his own formulation. Consistently the stress falls, in the apostolic preaching, on God as the originator of the act of reconciliation; he is always the subject and never the direct object of the verb. He is never said to be reconciled to us; on the contrary the passive 'be reconciled' is directed to men and women (or 'the church', since verse 20*c* is the solitary place where this imperative form of the verb is found and we shall argue that it has specific and specialised reference to Paul's Corinthian scene). To be sure, it may well be insisted that God's wrath (*orgē*, Rom. 1:18, 3:5) and judgment (*dikaiokrisia*, Rom. 2:5) are terms that presuppose God's being 'offended by the sins of men', and he has 'dealt with the sins which aroused his wrath', so removing the barrier on his side to the establishment of peace and friendly relations. This line of exposition goes on to conclude that 'in dying Christ exhausted the effects of divine wrath against sin'.[31] But it has to be said in all fairness that our passage hardly demonstrates this construction, since it says no more than that God in Christ has acted in such a way as to restore friendly relations between the world and himself. 'He has reconciled us to himself' means simply 'he has put us in right relations with himself'. As Dupont expresses it, 'God does not reconcile himself to the world, he reconciles the world to himself.'[32]

The participial phrase in verse 20*b*, 'God making his appeal through us' needs discussion from an exegetical standpoint. The basis of that appeal is, as we have seen, God's decisive act in the person of Christ by which the world is returned to God from its estrangement. 'Reconciliation' is a word that rests on prior disagreement and animosity; but, in this case, on whose side? Undoubtedly the cause is double-sided. On God's side there is that manifestation of his holy love called his 'righteousness' in the light of which the world stands both condemned and 'lost'; it is alienated and under the foreign domination of evil powers (see ch. 4). On the human side, there is all that is summed up in terms such as 'enmity', 'hostility', 'bondage', 'fear', 'despair' — language of the human condition, that is part of Paul's anthropology (see ch. 4) This barrier too must obviously crumble and fall if a genuine rapprochement is to take place.

The 'appeal' rests on the prior move God has made. Paul's ministry comes to his contemporaries with the news that God has taken the initiative and now offers peace. His hearers are bidden to receive it with a trustful welcome, not so much to lay aside their suspicion and enmity (though it is hard to deny that element) as to greet the good news with joyful acceptance. Or, as Paul would more carefully express it, with the obedience of faith (Rom. 1:5; 6:16; 16:26). The office of ambassador is one that 'stands upon [its] dignity',[33] since Paul's text sounds the note of authority in its call for such obedience (see Phil. 2:12, on which Bonnard comments, 'The obedient one must be obeyed' through the voice of his servant Paul).[34]

But we must notice two matters that demand caution in the above comment. We have had to introduce Paul's teaching on 'enmity' and 'peace' from other places to flesh out these sentences of our passage. And the 'appeal' is a general one, not directed to the Corinthians, *who do not come into the picture until verse 20c.* The result is that, while the call, 'Be reconciled to God', may be a legitimate extension of the apostolic kerygma, there is no proof of this. The call is issued with the Corinthian congregation and its pastoral problems in view, and should primarily be interpreted in that context. The awkward point of connection in verse 20 may be explained once we postulate a non-Pauline provenance of the part-verse: 'We are then acting as ambassadors for Christ, with the conviction (*hōs*: this is not translated in RSV) that God is *making his appeal* through us.' The italicised verb is *parakalountes* — a frequent term in Paul, especially in 2 Corinthians — but with the normal sense of God 'comforting' or 'strengthening' his people and not of directing an appeal to sinners. Paul's customary usage of the verb in this context is seen in 6:1: 'We appeal (*parakaloumen*) to you not to receive God's grace in vain.'

CONCLUSION

'Reconciliation' is a noble term in a pericope (5:18-21) on which Calvin rightly remarks: Here is a remarkable place, if there is such in the entire writing of Paul.[35] And regarding verse 21 P. E. Hughes writes, 'There is no sentence more profound in the whole of Scripture'.[36] Certain features of the apostolic message of Christ's work stand out. But much is tantalisingly obscure. We may affirm the divine initiative in reconciliation, both in its origin and total execution. Humankind plays only a passive role as those who are 'acted upon' by being 'reconciled' and then 'appealed to'. The cosmos is affected, presumably in the sense of being brought back to harmony with the creator and reinstated in right relations with him, 'becoming the righteousness of God' in Christ. The teaching and pre-Pauline provenance here are similar to those in Romans 3:24ff. where, as we saw, a Jewish-Christian tradition has been taken over and edited by Paul. E. Käsemann[37] offers three pointers to this conclusion: (*i*) Paul does not normally use 'sin' (*hamartia*, v. 21) in the sense of 'punishment for sin'; (*ii*) the close of verse 21 is less christological than 1 Corinthians 1:30; (*iii*) 'righteousness' is here used in a way different from Paul's attested usage. The Pauline clause in verse 19, however, we may submit, has recast the setting of what follows. It has introduced the framework of justification and so ensured, from Paul's perspective, that the 'double imputation' —our sin is borne by Christ/Christ's holy status is transferred to us — is understood in categories Paul's teaching regarded as central, namely (*a*) God has reconciled the cosmos made up of sinful men and women; (*b*) He has taken action to deal with their sins in Christ; (*c*) reconciliation is intimately related to personal and moral concerns to do with his apostolic responsibility at Corinth; and (*d*) 'righteousness' is both God setting men and women right with himself, and justifying himself: in so doing Paul's own gospel is 'justified', i.e. vindicated. Not least is the Pauline announcement in verse 17 which is not of a refurbished Judaism with the old order of Moses revamped but a new age with a new covenant (2 Cor. 3) and a new start made to world history.

The focal point of this enterprise is 'Christ became sin', again presumably on the cross, though that fact is not mentioned explicitly. It could be that the 'original version' of this soteriological credo simply announced the new age by divine fiat —

E. Güttgemanns[38] goes so far as to postulate a gnostic doctrine of creation's 'self-redemption', which Paul opposes in verse 18: 'all is God's doing' — and replaced the divine condemnation of the sinless Christ with a new status accorded to those who belong to him. But once verses 18-21 are introduced by verses 14-15, there can be no mistaking the dimension set by the self-giving of the historical Jesus, his death on the cross and his resurrection.

Paul's taking over this credo has clarified its meaning in ways we have already drawn attention to. In one other regard he has done something editorially that has put a fine point on the teaching *in the light of his customary method attested elsewhere*.

Paul has added, 'We beg you [Corinthians] on Christ's behalf [who did so much for us, *hyper hēmōn*], Be reconciled to God.' The apostle in tempering the strident apostolic voice to suit a more affectionate tone, repeated in 2 Corinthians 6:11-13, has recast the kerygmatic announcement to give it a personal dimension. He has taken language more germane to a call to unbelievers and has applied it to the strained relationships with the church by calling on them to accept his God-given authority implicit in his apostolic office (2 Cor. 10:8; 13:10-11) and to return to his side as children to a grieved father. How far this winsome appeal reflects the kerygma addressed to sinners is an open question. Given the scantiness of the evidence in Paul, we may never know whether he or others called on the hearers in synagogue or market-place to be reconciled to God. The inference is that they did not, any more than that their message was a pleading with or commanding men and women, 'Be justified before God.' The language is more declaratory than hortatory, as the data in Acts (13:39) and the capital epistles indicate.

But the link between kerygma and exhortation to Christians is important. In both cases, for Paul if not so clearly for his predecessors, the announcement of reconciliation is *expressible only in personal terms*, whether we recall Christ's obedience to God or the believer's response to all that reconciliation involves as a vital, loving relationship set up with persons always in view. And that we shall see is precisely what Romans 5:1-11 is all about. In a helpful summary Wiard Popkes writes in regard to our present passage's exegesis:

Paul wants to describe the new kind of life which he lives and which determines his outlook and behaviour. He approaches the matter from three angles: (i) new creation, (ii) reconciliation, and (iii) the righteousness of God. All of these concepts reflect God's character. He is the creator, the father and the judge. All of them reflect our situation. Without Christ we belong to the old, perishing creation; we are alienated from God; and we stand under the judgment of sin. All of the terms reflect the great change brought about by God in Christ. We stand in the new world; our personal relation to God has been restored, and we are free from judgment.[39]

To this final statement perhaps one more item needs to be added. Paul interjects the pastoral call of 'Be reconciled to God' to professing Christians as if to emphasise (a) the continual claim of the new life embarked on by the act of justification and grace (see 2 Cor. 6:1); and (b) the need for Paul's apostolic authority expressed in the proclamation he has quoted as commonly accepted material to be re-established at Corinth where it was under attack. Against those who prided themselves on 'the outward' and despised 'the inward' (2 Cor. 5:12) Paul's kerygma centred in the weakness of the crucified Christ (2 Cor. 13:4a) and the frailty of his messengers (4:7-12; 13:4b). But Paul appeals now to the greatness of his gospel that in some way embodies his own office as herald. So to be open to *his* apostolic person is part of the human response to the message.[40] To alienated 'children' (6:13: cf. 1 Cor. 4:15-21) at Corinth, the call is renewed, 'Be reconciled to God.'

CHAPTER SEVEN

CRISIS AT COLOSSAE

INTRODUCTION

While Paul was using Ephesus as a base of operations, according to Acts 19:10, 'the whole population of the province of Asia, both Jews and pagans, heard the word of the Lord' (NEB). The suggestion seems reasonable that during this lengthy period of time Paul sent out his representatives to carry the message to outlying cities and districts of the province. Epaphras, a native of Colossae in the Lycus valley some eighty miles or so from Ephesus, seems to have visited Paul, become a Christian and expressed a desire to return as Paul's emissary and evangelist. See Colossians 4:12-13 for these pieces of information.

Paul pays tribute to Epaphras as a 'faithful minister of Christ' (1:7) who had evangelised the Lycus valley region and had brought back a report of some success in his work (1:8). But some news at least was disquieting and further tribute is paid to Epaphras' prayerful concern for these infant communities (4:12).

The report Epaphras gave to Paul evidently included the threatening danger of some teaching that caused alarm. A recent attempt (by M. D. Hooker[1]) to deny the real existence of this alien teaching as a present threat to the apostolic mission at Colossae is hardly convincing. Her denial is based on the absence of any clear reference to the supposed error and the fact that Paul does not seem distressed in his response. Yet several verses he writes do have the appearance of being actual quotations of the teachers' slogans (clearly in 2:21; and very likely in 1:19; 2:18, 23 where rare terms and words found only here in Paul and only in the entire NT are used). A good illustration of the rivalry set up between Paul's kerygma (called 'according to Christ') and the position of the teachers whose influence is 'according to human tradition' is seen in the wording of 2:8. That verse uses the key phrase 'the *elemental spirits* of the universe' (*stoicheia* is the central term as italicised and is much disputed).

111

Given the rise of Christian groups in the Lycus valley in circumstances we have outlined it is not surprising that Paul felt no direct responsibility for these churches except through his emissary. He regarded the church at a distance (2:1-5) and made the apostolic traditions in 2:6 the basis of his appeal. He also drew on a pre-formed hymn which was evidently in vogue in Colossae (1:15-20), as we shall argue shortly. He chose to do this most likely to share some common ground with the church-members who were being threatened, and maybe to use a traditional hymn to the cosmic Christ, which he then adapted for his own immediate purposes. Furthermore, it is hard to discount the presence and influence of troublemakers who encroached on the church's life once we examine Colossians 2:8, 16, 18.

THE COLOSSIAN PROBLEM

The aberration Paul was quick to expose and warn against was one with serious consequences, as he viewed them. The end result of this 'heterodox' understanding of Christ was that it cut off its proponents from union with him (2:19) and so from the source of spiritual life and access to God.

The basis of its teaching was dualistic, thus setting God in opposition to the material world and denying his direct contact with or control over the cosmos. The inter-space between God and the world was peopled with emanations or aeons which, in gnostic cosmology, formed the 'fullness' (*plērōma*) and acted as a buffer-zone between the high God and the physical universe of matter regarded as evil. In the Christian version of this cosmology that was making a bid for acceptance at Colossae, Christ was given a place as one such aeon but God was far removed and Christ held only an inferior position. The 'angels' (2:18) or *stoicheia* as angelic spirits (2:8, 20) played the role of mediators and, it was alleged, they must be venerated as part of the Christian's approach to God. Only, it was suggested, in this way could 'fullness of life' — perhaps another propaganda slogan (2:10) — be reached, since there were practical taboos and restrictions to be respected as part of the cult and its way of life (2:20-23).

PAUL'S REPLY

The main affirmations of Paul's letter centre on the primacy of the cosmic Christ in creation and redemption, especially stated in the impressive two-panel statement of 1:15-20 and also in 2:3 9, 17; 3:1, 11. Against a proto-gnostic world-view Paul maintained the sovereign control of God in his world which left no room for a competing aeon to intrude between the high God and Christ or between Christ and the church. He bases this theology on the goodness of creation in answer to Manichean-like taboos of asceticism and self-depreciation of all that God has made.

The more serious peril is the possibility of a rival form of Christianity that is subtly flavoured with what Paul regarded as alien notions. We can watch the development of these ideas in the later church: (a) a devaluing of Jesus as a fully historical person living an empirical human life (denied by Paul in 1:22, 24; 2:11); (b) a version of cosmic salvation and recovery which did not place the atonement of Jesus' death at the forefront (denied in 1:20, 22); (c) a minimising of the need for forgiveness as sin was glossed over (denied in 1:14; 2:14), and above all, (d) a lingering fear of the demonic world where the hierarchy of malevolent spirit-forces was treated as real (denied in 1:16, 20; 2:14-15, 20).

CONCLUSION

In our reading of the Colossian letter we are witnessing, possibly for the first time with (it may be) the exception of the situation in the Corinthian assembly, an attempt to turn Paul's Christianity into a species of hellenistic philosophy and to regard a Christian congregation as just another gnosticising conventicle akin to the mystery cults and associations that flourished in the first two centuries of our era. The confrontation was a serious engagement of thought and practice at many points but none was more significant than in the area of an understanding of the cosmos. The prime questions raised in the debate were these: Is the world the battleground of warring forces, demonic and human, and full of uncertainty, or is it God's arena where his fatherly control and care spell confidence in life and death? Is life, on the one side, beset by cosmic fear of the unknown and hedged about with a regimen of taboos and prohibitions or, alternatively, is life based on fellowship with a personal God whose character is both known and loved and whose plan for his children is wholesome and kindly?

In a word, is this a world still at the mercy of uncontrolled forces of cosmic proportions, or is it 'reconciled' to a holy God who in Christ the son has entered its lifestream, purified it and made it a home for the people of God?

Questions such as these are offered as incentives to a study of Colossians 1:15-20.

COLOSSIANS 1:15-20

Strophe I

v. 15   (He) is the image of the invisible God,
          The firstborn over all creation;

v. 16   For in him all things were created, both in heaven
              and on earth
          [Visible and invisible,
          Whether thrones or dominions,
          Or principalities or authorities]
          All things were created through him and for him.

Strophe II

v. 17   He is before all things,
          And in him all things cohere;

v. 18a   And he is the head of the body [the church]:

Strophe III

v. 18b   (He) is the beginning,
              The firstborn from the dead
          [In order that he might be pre-eminent in all things]

v.19   For in him all the fullness was pleased to reside,

v.20   And through him to reconcile all things to himself,
          Whether things on earth or in heaven
          [So effecting peace by the blood of his cross]

THE FORM OF THE PASSAGE

Arranged in the way set out above, this section of Paul's letter is easily seen to be poetic and confessional. There is a virtual consensus among recent interpreters that 'the hymnic character of Col. 1:15-20 has long been recognised and generally acknowledged'[2] and that Paul has not only taken over and utilised a pre-formed hymn, but has edited what originally was composed as a tribute to the cosmic lordship of Christ and used it to give the hymn a new twist. These two propositions are not of equal cogency, and should perhaps be taken and inspected separately.

(i) *The hymnic character.* Attentive readers of Paul's chapters will observe that the address to the Colossian readers in 1:12-14 is couched in the language of a personal nature ('us', 'we have redemption, the forgiveness of sins'). Verses 15-20 are strangely impersonal, making no allusion to either writer or readers or the church as a local community. Then in verse 21, the personal element is resumed, 'And *you* . . . he has reconciled in his body of flesh by his death, in order to present *you* . . .' (v. 22). The intervening verses 15-20 give the appearance of being inserted into the flow of the apostolic message to the Colossian community.

Moreover the six verses have a literary and lexical stamp all their own. They are (a) credal or confessional, directing attention to the person and achievement of the redeemer; (b) liturgical with sonorous nouns and verbs, such as 'image of the invisible God', 'firstborn' (twice repeated), 'all the fullness', 'reside', 'be pre-eminent'; and (c) artistic, evidence for which trait is seen in the careful positioning of some key phrases such as 'firstborn', and the use made of the device of chiasmus (i.e. a criss-cross arrangement), as in verses 16c and 20:

A   All things ——————— B¹   And through him
B   Through him and ———— A¹   All things

If we add in the features of some rare words not used elsewhere by Paul or other Christian writers, and traces of alliteration, antithesis, and lines arranged as couplets, it seems reasonable to suppose that we are looking at a piece of early hymnody of a confessional and doxological type. This means the hymn was offered in praise to the regal Christ by the believing church at its worship. The overall conclusion, now pretty generally accepted, has given impetus since E. Norden's time — he was among the first to detect a pre-formed passage, in 1913[3] — to the endeavour to set out the verses in lines and stanzas. Of the several attempts to do that, E. Schweizer's versification given above seems the most satisfying.[4] But there are some debated aspects.

(ii) *The 'original' and Pauline versions.* In order to secure something of a model of exact symmetry and compactness, Schweizer had to leave out four phrases. They are bracketed in our translation, and contain elements that (a) cannot be fitted into an arrangement of three three-line strophes with rhythmical and metrical agreement, and (b) are thought to be Paul's own additions supplied to correct and modify the teaching of the original hymn. Thus, the reference to the cosmic powers added in verse 16 orients the hymn more pointedly in the direction of the false teachers at Colossae who were advocating that a superior place be given to these 'powers' (2:8, 18, 20). Paul's additional terms amplify the more general description of 'all things' to include specifically those powers as falling within the sphere of the creative work of Christ; so their independent existence and authority are 'debunked'. The same motive has inspired the assertion of Christ's cosmic pre-eminence (in v. 18), since he is now exalted to fill the entire universe which contains no part untouched by the total sweep of his reconciling work: 'he is head [or ruler] of all rule and authority' (2:10), Paul will maintain later in the letter.

Our interest focuses more keenly on the remaining suggested Pauline additions. First, by adding 'the church' (the simple genitive, *tēs ekklēsias*) in apposition to 'he is head of *the body*', Paul has effectively turned an original tribute to Christ (or the redeemer if the first draft of the composition had a non-Christian, gnostic origin, as Käsemann thought; but this is not likely) as the lord of the world into a statement praising him as head of the body, now identified as the church. So Christ's body is no longer confused with the physical world — an idea Paul combats or at least treats as less than adequate. It is equated in a characteristically Pauline way with the company of God's chosen ones, the believing community (so 1 Cor. 12:12-13; Rom. 12:5; Ephesians represents an extension of Paul's thought redirected to the cosmic idea). The notion that Christ as the risen one fills the universe with his power and so brings heaven and earth together in a physical way seems implicit in the earlier version. Paul's criticism of that hellenistic idea is seen in his corrective adjustment to verse 18, and he has done it in a way that adds a minimum of words (so as not to spoil the symmetry unduly; we can see his normal way of writing in Col. 1:24: 'his body, that is, the church', *tou sōmatos autou ho estin hē ekklēsia*, a much more expansive addition).

The second supplement added by the apostle brings us to the

heart of his teaching on reconciliation. At verse 20 the redeemer is the agent in a cosmic reconciliation that embraces 'all things'. Lest this deed should be thought of as an automatic fiat or a cosmic miracle which merely changed the state of the universe outside of man, Paul has added a word coined for the occasion (since it is rare to the point of uniqueness): *'making peace* by the blood shed on his cross'. The syntactical awkwardness of this addition serves only to emphasise its being inserted, and its content puts into clearer focus Paul's accepted teaching on the alienation of the cosmos (see ch. 4) and the centrality of the historical drama of Jesus' death on the cross.

If we needed confirmation that at Colossae these were precisely the twin elements of the alien doctrine that menaced the church, we should find it in Paul's insistence elsewhere in the letter that Christ has pacified the powers and neutralised their hostility (2:15) and that he did so by a real incarnation (1:22) and an atoning death (1:14; 2:13-14; 3:13). The fuller implications of these statements will be before us later.

In fine, there is much to be said for Schweizer's arrangement which includes a middle strophe (vv. 17-18a) that functions as a 'hinge' or 'bridge' to unite the pre-existing Christ and resurrected/exalted Lord and entails the principle of Paul's own redaction of an earlier, less adequate hymn to bring it into line with the problems at Colossae and offers his answer to them. For our purpose, which does not here include a defence of Schweizer's position against his questioning critics,[5] it will be enough to remark on the immediate relevance of the discussion. This centres on 'reconciliation'. One criticism of the above theory touches directly on our concern. N. Kehl asks,[6] How can a universe which is already united to Christ as its 'head' (assuming this to have been the original meaning of v. 18a) stand in need of a 'reconciliation'? The answer must lie in the different sense given to the verb 'reconcile' in that original version of the hymn which Paul has adapted and changed bringing it into conformity with his own purpose by the significant addition of 'making peace by the blood of his cross' (v. 20c) and so paving the way for an extended application of 'reconciliation' to his readers' situation in verses 21-22.

PAUL'S TEACHING

Assuming the existence of a pre-Pauline 'hymn' underlying our text, we can now offer a statement of what that earlier hymn taught, especially in the matter of reconciliation.

(*i*) The three stanzas of Colossians 1:15-20 cover a wide range of ideas. The scope of Christ's accomplishment embraces the orders of creation, their maintenance in being (v. 17: 'in him all thing cohere', since like the figure of wisdom in Prov. 8:30, Sirach 43:26; Wisdom of Solomon 1:7 he is thought of as a uniting principle which holds the universe together and in place. Plato and the stoic philosophers had a similar idea about the unity of the world) and their final destiny. The universal Christ is the head of the cosmos in a way some interpreters think of as parallel with hellenistic philosophy. An Orphic fragment speaks of Zeus as the 'head' of the universe, with his power running through the entire creation as his body. In stoic cosmology the world is pervaded by its soul, the logos, thus producing a perfect 'body' as it is unified by that 'reason' or indwelling principle. The cosmos and God, for the stoic, are virtually the same. Philo the Alexandrian Jewish thinker has similar teaching of the heavenly world over which the logos was set as head (*On Dreams* 1:128). That head gives directing force to the world as the human head controls and guides the body of a man (*On Special Laws* 3:184; *Questions on Ex.* 2:117).

The original draft of these verses went on to make even more audacious claims for the exalted Lord. Verse 19, however, is troublesome in its ambiguity: 'in him all the fullness of God was pleased to dwell' (RSV) is a straightforward rendering into English, but the meaning is unclear. Does the statement personalise the concept of 'the fullness of God' and make it the subject of the verb 'was pleased to dwell'? C. F. D. Moule[7] opts for this meaning with hesitation on the score that the personification may be too violent to be credible. It is possible also to offer a meaning according to the intended sense, namely 'God in his fullness' similar to the Pauline statement in Colossians 2:9: 'the whole fullness of deity dwells in Christ'; or else to infer that God is the 'hidden subject': so 'God was pleased that all fullness should dwell'. The first possibility may be defended; and indeed it is insisted on by E. Käsemann who uses its meaning to argue for a gnostic background of the two verses (17, 20) and to interpret 'reconciliation' in a specially nuanced way

Käsemann's position is that 'all the fullness' (*plērōma*) is a technical term, anticipating the part played by the word in second-century Gnosticism. Valentinian Gnosticism spoke of the pleroma as the totality or fullness of aeons or emanations that were put forth by the supreme God to fill the vast void of space between heaven and earth, though the term belongs more properly to the upper ethereal world near to God (Lohse[8]). In gnostic thinking under Valentinian influence (i.e. partly christianised) Jesus descended from the divine fullness as redeemer and executed a work of restoration by reassembling all things of pneumatic or ethereal origin to form the total pleroma; that last term explicitly excludes God who is not part of the pleroma. Käsemann seems to postulate a conflict within the pleroma which the advent of a new aeon or emanation (incarnate in the redeemer) resolved. This is how he understands reconciliation, 'Thereby the All is "reconciled", its conflicting elements are pacified . . . in that they have found their Lord' to whom they submit. This dependence on a gnostic world-view is interpreted by Käsemann in reference to cosmic peace, and he then proceeds to see a parallel with Virgil's Fourth Eclogue where the *pax Romana* is a historicised version of global harmony that mirrors the peace made in the heavenly realm. We have already doubted the legitimacy and relevance of this background (see p. 78).

There is one obvious point of distinction between the Christian version given in Paul's verse and the later gnostic speculation: *plērōma* in verse 19 (as in Col. 2:9) refers to God, not the interstellar region from which God is excluded. It may be that this distinction is exactly what the first Christians were insisting on in a way that showed how much they drew on their Old Teastament heritage. In the Old Testament God fills the entire universe (Jer. 23:24) with his glory (Ps. 72:19; cf. Isa. 6:3; Ezek. 43:5; 44:4). Not to be understood as pantheism or confusing God and his creation, this line of teaching at least left no room for competing agents to come between God and his world and was a firm rebuttal of dualism.

The essence of Gnosticism was a dualism that set the high God and the material world in antithetical relationship. Our passage by asserting that 'all the fullness' ('all' is really superfluous, since 'fullness' implies totality, and so 'all' may be a polemical thrust against a proto-gnostic world-view) chose to reside in Christ is opposing any such dichotomy between the creator and the creation. 'Reconciliation' takes on the meaning of harmony and peace within the cosmic order. Notions of supermundane disturbance in the astral regions were part and parcel of hellenistic religion, as we have described earlier (see pp. 21 f.);

the immediate and practical consequence for men and women in Graeco-Roman society was a sense of life's meaninglessness and lack of purpose since their fate rested in a cosmic strife over which they had no control and had little power to resolve. Nor did they have much hope to expect deliverance. To such people the christological tribute to the lordly Christ who embodied in himself the total pleroma of the creator would come as good news of hope and freedom. At a stroke this message spelled out the end of astral religion which traded on the disharmony and discord between heaven and earth as seen in the conflict in the ethereal sphere. The assurance of Christ's sole supremacy not only as the origin and sustainer of all cosmic elements but more particularly as the controller of those intractable forces would be heard as indeed 'the message of reconciliation'. The universe was no longer to be regarded as an alien, threatening sphere; its 'principalities and powers' were dethroned because of the supreme lordship of Christ the *cosmocrat* (see p. 78) who had taken his place as the agent of the divine restoration by which 'all things' were put into his hands. A new beginning in world history had been made (v. 18) with his elevation to supreme power as 'firstborn from the dead'; and by that act of enthronement all the refractory elements of the universe had been united under his headship and authority.

(*ii*) We may now proceed to see how in Paul's hands such a statement would need modification. He is partly motivated to address head-on the situation at Colossae where strange, theosophical theories were posing a threat to the apostolic message carried first by Epaphras. Paul was not the founder of these churches in the Lycus valley, and needed to handle the pastoral problems with tact and delicacy. If the basic pattern of a hymn underlying 1:15-20 was known and valued in the community, he can justifiably use it as his starting point. This may explain why he does not scrap the hymn entirely and reproduce a christological statement *de novo*; and this suggestion would answer P. T. O'Brien's criticism[9] that fastens on the way Paul seems to have dealt drastically with and changed the pre-formed hymn (whose existence O'Brien denies). Paul can utilise much of what is accepted teaching and liturgical confession at Colossae, but he needs to amplify (as in the additions we noted) to make the coverage of Christ's primordial creation even wider (v. 16), to lift the original cosmological tribute on to the plane of ecclesiology as the church's place under Christ's universal

authority (v. 18) is spelt out explicitly and to assert unequivocal-
ly the pre-eminence of Christ the risen Lord over his people (as
in Col. 2:10; 3:11) as well as over the created orders.

But it is verse 20 that demands our closest scrutiny. If we
assume that verse 19 was allowed to stand, since it could
admittedly be taken in several ways, it was otherwise with the
following lines of the hymn. Originally they stated a reconciliation which brought together in cosmic harmony the regions of
heaven and earth. Paul was presumably familiar with and able
to endorse such a statement. It is in the background of
Philippians 2:6-11. But it represented a species of hellenistic
doxology that was open to misunderstanding: (a) it moved in
exclusively cosmic and 'speculative' categories, and thought
more of a physical miracle by which alien elements were fused
together; (b) it attributed to the regnant Christ an authority that
was not rooted in redemption. Rather it was by fiat, announcing
the epiphany of a new age and a new ruler, that peace and
concord were restored; and (c) it could easily minister to an
ecclesiastical 'triumphalism' by which Christ promoted his
kingly power by his exaltation and enthronement as world-ruler,
a trend seen in 1 Timothy 3:16 and Ephesians. His death on the
cross is by-passed as saving message or else put into a place
where it is overshadowed by the glory of the exaltation which
involves both Christ and the church. 'A metaphysics of supernatural factors, structures, and orders'[10] has edged the kerygma
of the crucified Jesus out to the periphery of Christian proclamation and living and filled the centre with the picture of Christ
triumphant and the church all-glorious.

Paul, as theologian of the cross, addressed a set of corrective
measures to the scene at Colossae. By focusing on the phrase
'making peace by the blood of his cross', he has ensured that
several central emphases should not be lost.

First, he has shown that reconciliation is primarily concerned
with the *restoration of personal relationships*. Granted that Christ
restored the universe to its true state under God, Paul goes on to
insist that speculative interest is not adequate to match a moral
problem. 'The blood of the cross where he died' anchors Christ's
work in his sacrificial death for sinners. This is the Pauline
content now given to reconciliation: it is more soteriological than
cosmological in its scope. He has picked up a word ('to
reconcile', *apokatallassein*; his usage in 2 Cor. 5 is the simpler form
of the verb, *katallassein*) and changed its nuance so that its scope

embraces both the overcoming of the cosmic hostility through the lordship of Christ (explained in Col. 2:15) and the restoration of sinful men and women to God's favour and family (1:22). At 1:20 the verse *as it now stands* includes both ideas, as Dibelius-Greeven note.[11] The proof of this contention seems clear. Paul can glide smoothly to the discussion of verses 21-22 where both pronoun ('And you') and verb ('he has now reconciled by his death') stand in an unusual and emphatic position.

Quite evidently this way of writing is part of Paul's set purpose. Having shown how the scope of Christ's work reached every part of creation, he can apply this teaching to his readers who have not been mentioned since verses 12-14. But now the reconciliation touches human lives and produces the effect of a changed human character and conduct. Hence the purpose of reconciliation is spelled out: 'in order to present you holy and blameless and irreproachable before him' (v. 22*b*), a purpose which says nothing about mastering the hidden secrets of the universe or indulging in gnostic speculation regarding the pleroma. Later on in this letter Paul will offer a rationale of the way in which the evil powers were overcome and forced to surrender their claim on Christ and his people (Col. 2:14-15; see p. 41). At this point Paul's teaching remains within the orbit of the personal dimension of reconciliation by which its moral power is known in the restoration to God's favour of men and women who formerly were estranged and hostile in mind and open transgressors (v. 21). The sum of that experience is: the Lord has forgiven you (3:13; cf. 1:14) by his becoming fully human 'in the flesh-body' of a true man — a cumbrous expression added, it would seem, as an aside to underscore a real identity with humanity in a polemical manner — and by his death as a sacrifice (v. 22, repeating v. 20).

Second, the nature of reconciliation is seen in the vocabulary used in both verses 20*c* and 21-22. One of the aspects of the problem at Colossae had to do with the place accorded to 'the elemental spirits of the universe' (2:8, 20). The phrase renders *ta stoicheia tou kosmou*, and the exact meaning is not certain. The most likely background is that of cosmic forces that were thought to control and tyrannise over human lives. Admittedly the connotation of the phrase may originally have been neutral, denoting simply 'created orders' or the 'powers that control the universe' (so G. Delling[12]). It may be that, since they are not called 'evil' in 1:15-20, the original version of the hymn simply regarded them as part of the created order, made by and for Christ. Then their 'reconciliation' would mean no more than their finding their true place under his lordship.

Paul, however, has given to *stoicheia* a moral character since, in the Colossian teaching espoused and advocated by some group there (2:4, 8), these powers were becoming a rival to Christ and so were in dualistic tension with the Christ of Paul's basic monotheism. His naming the powers in 1:16 may be part of his response, which from Romans 8:38f. we know to be an almost altogether negative attitude to 'angels' (see p. 54).

Such a background illumines a difficult area in Paul's thought and eases the problem referred to by N. Kehl (see p. 117). Paul agreed that Christ was indeed creator of all, including these cosmic agents, but he has a lively sense of the danger such a cosmology could bring with it. When these powers break free from their station as 'created orders' and claim an independent status, demanding veneration and allegiance (as evidently Col. 2:18 implies) their role has been reversed. 'No longer do the Powers bind man and God together; they separate them'.[13] To that degree these created powers are in rebellion and need to be 'reconciled' by having their hostility drawn and neutralised.

So Paul expounds the need for their rebellion to be put down and for peace to be restored in a universe that — for him, if not for the Colossians who were open to the error present on the threshold of their church — was out of harmony with its creator. Moreover the creator-God in a moral world cannot deal with rebel spirits — or agencies that are being claimed as rivals to Christ, as Colossians 2:8 certainly shows — with a wave of the hand. In some way they have to be exposed, at least for the susceptible Colossians to see how specious are their claims, and their demand for human obedience denied.

That engagement between the *stoicheia* and Christ, Paul says, took place at the cross where the issue of God versus the powers was joined (Col. 2:14-15). Their accusation and condemnation of humankind was levelled at Christ who in his representative person met the demand and took it upon himself. He both submitted to and triumphed over the spirits; but it was no show of force or display of omnipotence that won the day. He died on the cross and shed his blood. Only then did his reign begin and only thus does it continue. Reconciliation whether of super-beings or of mortals was not easily secured nor was it accom-

plished as an other-worldly drama or automatic process.
E. Schweizer so contrasts two ways of looking at reconciliation:

> [It] does not work like, to use a Gnostic image, a magnet put
> up in heaven and drawing those who are brought into its
> magnetic field irresistibly after it. The effect of Christ's death
> is the effect of a deed of love bringing its fruit in a human life
> which is touched by it.[14]

CONCLUSION

The 'high' point, as Kehl calls it, of the passage is attained in its
statements regarding divine reconciliation. If we rightly discern
that there are two layers in the hymnic celebration offered to the
cosmic and enthroned Lord, the theme of reconciliation has
undergone in Paul's redaction a significant shift of meaning.
Both strata — pre-Pauline and Pauline — presuppose a
situation within the cosmos wherein the 'elements' need to be
dealt with so that 'peace' and 'harmony' may ensue. Nothing is
implied in the first draft of the hymn to indicate a rupture within
the cosmos: the scene is that created orders, brought into being
through the pre-temporal activity of Christ, are at length united
under his exaltation since he is the risen one. To that extent the
scope of the hymn parallels that of Ephesians 1:10, 22, where it is
God's design to set all things under Christ as their rightful head.

Paul viewed these powers through the prism of his pastoral
responsibility and saw how the cosmological theories at Colossae have a dangerous — because seductive — thrust. The
Colossians were threatened with a departure from the apostolic
tradition by their sympathy with this 'speculation' (see how Paul
so brands it in 2:8, 18). The threat is that his people may become
'detached from Christ' by ceasing to 'hold fast' to the rightful
Lord of the universe. These powers were therefore viewed as
positive evil and in rebellion against their creator since they have
set the pattern of a breaking away from him and have aspired to
independent, rival existence. This led Paul to an 'explanation' of
their malignancy, their opposition to the church, their conflict
with Christ and their defeat by him on the cross. Their
'reconciliation' involves their subjugation and submission to his
sovereign power, involving their having relaxed their grip on
men and women who have 'died with Christ out from under'
their power (2:20, as J. A. T. Robinson paraphrases the verb;
(see p. 57) and been 'delivered from the dominion of darkness'

where these malign forces held sway. The Colossians are now brought over into the realm of the son whom God loves (1:13). The hallmark of that emancipation, to which Paul appeals, is the forgiveness of sins (1:14). That is the ground of Paul's pastoral appeal: from the experienced reality to the more speculative conclusion. He argues from what he can confidently state of the converts at Colossae, namely they have been forgiven and are incorporated into Christ. The church as the company of the baptised shares in the new life (1:12). That common ground offers him a platform from which to answer the theorising of cosmic threats and promises, such as were evidently being actively discussed and promoted in the church according to 2:16-18. Once more the thesis given out earlier (p. 46) gains in strength: *Paul bases his theology on known experience of Christ and his saving power*. For him what counts is 'to know Christ' and live in the sphere of his salvific ministry. Whatever threatens that life — in this case, fear and superstition regarding the demonic and all the subliminal dread created by enquiry into and overzeal for the dark world of cosmic spirits — must be firmly put down by his unequivocal assertion of Christ, crucified and risen. The cross and resurrection of the historical Jesus brought pardon and renewal to these people; as a blessed corollary, Paul would contend, they may enjoy liberation from the spell of the demonic.

> Whoever is baptised into Christ is placed under the dominion of the beloved Son of God, who as Lord holds in his hands authority over the whole world as well as the salvation of those who belong to him — freed for the new life of obedience that confesses his rule.[15]

Perhaps one advantage of this approach to exegesis is that it enables us to move from the reconciliation verb in one verse (1:22) to the same verb in 1:20. We suggest that this is the correct sequence. First, Paul established the reconciliation between God and sinners as a datum of experience, already attested (1:12-14, 2:20). To explain its rationale he then invited his readers to consider the antagonistic drama of Christ versus the powers in 2:14-15 — an issue which Christ's resurrection and enthronement has shown to have been decisively and 'openly' settled in Christ's favour. The corollary is then drawn, to reinforce his earlier claim of the validity of Christian experience based on the apostolic gospel (and per contra not on man-devised traditions, 2:8, 22), regarding the total 'reconciliation' to those spiritual 'super-beings', namely that they have no more power to hurt the church because they were 'pacified' and neutralised in Christ who is their master.

Of the several ways 'reconciliation' in 1:20 may be understood — whether of God's glory filling the entire creation (so Kehl), or of angels, demons or sinful men restored to God (so Wambacq, Michl) and so denoting the scope of God's mercy to all, or conferring universal salvation upon everyone willy-nilly (so Michaelis), or else as confined to asserting simply the sole supremacy of Christ in every sphere of existence (so Mussner, Vögtle, Schweizer), or as stating comprehensively that heaven and earth are now at one (so Lohse, O'Brien), the line we have taken may be recommended as having at least one strength.[16] It deals with the plausibility that 'to reconcile' may have had one meaning in the pre-Pauline hymn and yet another in Paul's hands. But more particularly it is able to relate meaningfully the adjacent verses (20 and 21-22), and show how Paul's taking over a verb, otherwise not found until Ephesians 2:16, is pressed into paraenetic service in a way that elsewhere is typical of Paul's pastoralia. The 'subjugation' of demonic agents, following on their resounding defeat and open ignominy on Jesus' cross, is the scenario used to establish more firmly these infant believers in their knowledge of personal reconciliation to God by the same historical event of Jesus' death on the cross and to give them renewed assurance that as they have been forgiven by that death, so they may be set free from any kind of bondage that would rob them of their liberty as God's children. The dear son of God has undertaken a cosmic reconciliation that can never be reversed; it is their privilege as children of the same Father to rejoice in their reconciliation, actualised in forgiveness of sins. *Their reconciliation as sinners to God points back to Christ's cosmic reconciliation which in turn reinforces their faith against the sophists knocking on their church door.*

From Romans 3:24-26, 2 Corinthians 5:18-21 and Colossians 1:15-20, in their respective contexts and given the acceptance and modification of some earlier confessional matter by Paul, we can see the consistency of his main emphasis. He stresses that to be set free from sin's tyranny as we enter a new world,[17] put right with its God through all that God did in Christ's death on the cross at a point in time, is to enter upon a relationship with God marked by the joy of forgiveness and acceptance with God which no force, angelic, demonic or human can touch or destroy. It is to live in a new age of filial relationship with God.[18]

CHAPTER EIGHT

PAUL'S TEACHING IN ROMANS

INTRODUCTION:
THE PURPOSES OF THE LETTER TO THE ROMANS

The letter to the Romans has always been regarded as the centrepiece of Pauline theology. It is, said Luther, 'the chief book of the New Testament, and the purest Gospel'. It is, 'one of the classic documents of the Christian faith, the theological epistle *par excellence* in the New Testament'[1]; and it has been valued in every age as a quintessence of Paul's teaching. Even a shadowy figure in church history like Saint Patrick of Ireland prized it highly.

Yet the reason for Paul's writing this letter remains a matter of scholarly debate and extended enquiry. Obviously the letter has something to do with both Paul's missionary determination to visit Rome as a springboard for a further outreach to Spain (1:11-15; 15:22-29) and his offering practical counsel to the Christians at Rome on various domestic issues (chs. 14-15). The question remains whether these purposes can satisfactorily explain the form of the letter and its inclusion of such passages as chapters 9-11. There appears to be a set of deeper reasons why Paul would want, at the close of his Aegean mission (15:23), to send an epitome of his preaching, his 'theological self-confession' (as Kümmel calls it[2]), to the church in the Roman metropolis which he had never visited. We may surmise that he sensed intuitively the strategic importance of the church at the heart of the empire, and perhaps he wanted this community to be in no doubt that this statement of the gospel, announced programmatically in 1:16-17, was the message God had so signally honoured throughout the 'successful' Gentile mission in the eastern Mediterranean area. And the letter is a tacit if tactful call for them to embrace that message also.

If Paul's intention was to change the course of his missionary career and head in a westward direction as a matter of settled policy, we can well understand why he would want to 'sum up' in this formal way the salient features of his kerygma. But he had an earlier responsibility to discharge before accepting a missionary obligation in the west; he must go to Jerusalem with 'the collection for the saints' (15:25-27). Only when the relief money raised in the course of his mission to Macedonia and southern Greece has been safely delivered to the needy Jewish believers in the holy city would he be free to move out in the direction of Rome and Spain. To ensure a good hearing for his message among Jewish Christian groups at Rome — 'the weak' of Romans 14:1, 15:1 — he must show his personal concern for the mother church in Jerusalem. And he must define closely what his attitudes were to the Jewish law and the place of Israel within what he conceived to be God's unfolding purpose. Hence he includes a treatment of Israel as an integral part of his letter (2:17-29; chs. 9-11).

Paul remained, however, an apostle committed to the charter of Gentile freedom. That position is stated and enforced throughout the epistle, with sustained expositions of God's saving grace extended to all persons, whether Jewish or non-Jewish. God is God of all races, he affirms (3:29), and he returns to this central statement in 10:12-13. Therefore salvation can only be on the ground of his grace exhibited in Jesus Christ and his cross and available to all who will come and receive it 'by faith'. The law is set on its true basis (3:31) when it is seen as pointing to Christ who is its goal (10:4). Christ is the universal saviour, and his people whatever their racial origins should find a centre of unity as members of his one body in the one church (12:4-5). 'Welcome one another, therefore, as Christ has welcomed you' (15:7) is the force of his logic as well as his pastoral advice given at a distance.

Part of the problem within the church at Rome was evidently a suspicion created by Gentile arrogance, as this faction within the multiracial house congregations was over-emphasising its independence of the church's Jewish origins in the Old Testament and becoming forgetful of its indebtedness to historical Israel as God's dear people (11:28). Paul tackles this issue in 11:13ff., and by use of the figure of the olive tree endeavours to show how Israel's rejection of the gospel has given an opportunity for that message to be offered to the Gentiles: 'for if their rejection means the reconciliation of the world . . .'. By thus widening the scope of the ministry of salvation and permitting missionary efforts to be directed to non-Jews, this is a cause for celebration, since now it becomes clear that 'reconciliation' is a term as expansive and far-ranging in its scope as 'the world' (recalling

2 Cor. 5:19) and offered freely to all people.

The future of Israel, however, in this verse (11:15) is not one of permanent refusal and 'hardness of heart' (11:25). Paul goes on to refer to their 'acceptance', by which we should understand their being accepted by God after their being rejected by him. The two terms (*apobolē*/*proslēmpsis* are correlative) are Paul's proposed answer to the rhetorical question raised at 11:1: 'I ask, then, has God rejected his people? By no means!' Since this topic played a central part in Paul's missionary preaching and praxis and bears upon his understanding of reconciliation, it will require separate treatment, if only in abbreviated form.

PAUL AND ISRAEL

In his contemplation of 'the mystery' of Israel's strange refusal to receive his message (Rom. 11:25) Paul was caught in a genuine dilemma — or, more accurately, a 'trilemma'. Three forces pulled at him as he reflected on the fate and fortunes of his own people, the Jews.

(*i*) We have noted already his Jewish ancestry and heritage (Phil. 3:5; 2 Cor. 11:22) which he never disowned, even when he became a Christian believer and was spurned by his compatriots. His calling to be 'an apostle to the nations' (Rom. 1:5; 11:13) was never regarded as excluding him from a responsibility to 'win Jews' to their true saviour (1 Cor. 9:20). He announced this continuing missionary mandate at the 'prologue' of Romans (1:16: 'to the Jew first'; there is no reason to dismiss this, as Stendahl seems to do).

(*ii*) As a faithful member of the nation Paul mourned Jewish unbelief and hardening (Rom. 11:7, 23, 25). With a patriot's intensity he grieved over the obstinacy and opposition of Israel. His poignant language in Romans 9:2-3 is a moving tribute to his continuing solicitude for his people.

Yet he could not deny Israel's current resistance which is rationalised by the considerations Paul introduces in Romans chapters 9-11. These may be set down:

(*a*) God's promises touching his people have to be seen in an Old Testament context; there it is not all the descendants of the patriarchs who are given the promises but only the chosen ones (9:6-13). The reasoning runs parallel with that in Galatians 4:21-31 where Abraham's two children, sons of Hagar and Sarah, are promised different destinies.

(*b*) The divine choice of a 'true Israel' within the framework of the national covenant (reverting to distinctions already drawn in Rom. 2:27-29 on the question, who is the 'true Jew'?) is justified by reference to God's inscrutable will (9:14-18) and his role as 'supreme arbiter of mankind', as J. Munck[3] so describes God according to Romans 9:19-21.

(*c*) God's patience in not inflicting condign and immediate punishment on his rebellious people allows at least some, both Jews and Gentiles, to accept the gospel (9:22-24). Otherwise there would be no hope and his 'wrath' would be visited on rebels. This passage recalls 1 Thessalonians 2:14-16 which is Paul's strongest word of condemnation of Jewish unbelief: 'God's wrath has come upon them *eis telos*.' The last adverbial phrase can be taken in several ways. It may mean 'at last', 'for ever', 'completely', or with a final sense 'to the end', i.e. until the events at the end of the world. In the latter case, the judgment may be remedial and salutary by leading rebellious Israel to repentance. If 1 Thessalonians 2:16 is not to be dismissed as a later post-Pauline addition (and it is hard to accept this theory since Rom. 9:22 repeats the same idea), we should safeguard our interpretation against the charge of anti-semitism by the reminder of Paul's continuing love for his own people, and either interiorise the allusion to God's wrath 'coming upon them' by seeing Paul's 'real adversary as [the] devout Jew', the religious man of Philippians 3:4-9, who nevertheless lives in every person of whatever race and who stands condemned in spite of his religiosity (so Käsemann[4]), or relate Paul's condemnation to Jewish leaders or false Jews who betrayed the name (as in 2 Cor. 11:24; Rom. 2:28; cf. Rev. 2:9; 3:9; also in Ignatius, and the *Martyrdom of Polycarp*).

(*d*) God has done everything, especially in the sending of a Messiah to Israel, to lead his people to faith; but they have persisted in their hardened attitude and have resisted all overtures (10:1-21). Nonetheless there is a token response, alluded to in 9:6 and picked up negatively at 10:16. This thought will give Paul his springboard into chapter 11 where he comes to grips with the real issue: If the Jews have rejected the message of 'righteousness by faith' in Jesus and the Gentiles have gladly and savingly received it (9:30), what hope is there for Israel? Is this impasse the end of the story of salvation, of *Heilsgeschichte*? Does 'salvation history' virtually exclude the Jews?

(*iii*) Paul cannot and does not allow that possibility. He is

confident that his people has a hope and he anticipates their
salvation (11:1-2). He can even look ahead to 'all Israel' being
saved (11:26) when the deliverer comes, and he builds his case
on God's electing grace that never lets the chosen people go
(11:28-29). But it is precisely this governing idea of a 'chosen
people' that gives him the right to distinguish between the nation
on the one hand, and the 'now believing' and 'yet-to-believe'
remnant (11:23) on the other. The negative response he gave to
the question, Has God rejected his people? is justified by his
arguments that (*a*) the rejection of Israel by God is only partial
(vv. 1-10); (*b*) such blindness is only temporary (vv. 11-27); (*c*)
there is a deep purpose in the 'mystery' which no one can fully
explore but which points to the climax of the ages when God's
saving plan will be realised to the full (vv. 28-32). The fitting
note on which to close the disquisition is that of liturgical
doxology offered to God, perhaps in his trinitarian person (v. 36:
'from him and through him and to him are all things. To him be
glory for ever. Amen').

PRESUPPOSITIONS IN ROMANS 9-11

Paul's teaching in Romans 9-11 is expressed according to certain
presuppositions which he either accepts or for which he argues
with varying degrees of cogency.[5] At least to his mind the
following principles were assured.

(*a*) He never contemplates any way to please God or to be
accepted by him other than by his grace and through faith in
Christ (9:30, 31; 10:2-4). There is no suggestion of a 'double
covenant', one relating to Jews and a second for the Gentiles; nor
does he offer a two-track salvation, depending on one's racial
origin, ethnic status or religious affiliation. 'There is no distinction' (10:12) is posted as a warning sign to the acceptance of any
such idea that would undercut his teaching of 'by grace alone',
'by faith alone', *sola gratia, sola fide*.

(*b*) The term 'Jew' is ambiguous, since 'not all who are
descended from Israel belong to Israel' (9:6). The two sons of
Abraham represent two ways of understanding God's plan: the
one son prefigures slavery, the other sonship. There is hostility
between the two as fierce as the Spirit opposing the flesh (Gal.
5:17). For Paul the 'true Jew' stands over against the unreal and
bogus (Rom. 2:28, 29) just as 'true' circumcision (Phil. 3:3; Col.
2:11) is different from a mere cutting or minor surgical

operation, which he disdains as 'mutilation' (Phil. 3:2; cf. Gal. 5:12). The Jewish teachers who make these outward marks the essence of religion are woefully mistaken (by the criteria set out in 1 Cor. 7:19; Gal. 6:15), and it is worse when they advocate the imposing of circumcision on Gentile converts. This is tantamount to an alien gospel (2 Cor. 11:3f.) and they are doing the devil's work (2 Cor. 11:13-15).

(c) A fundamental postulate of Paul's 'salvation history' is that there is only one church, made up of believing Jews and Gentiles (1 Cor. 12:13; Gal. 3:28; Col. 3:11). Just as important is the assertion that both groups of believers are Abraham's family, whether they were originally ethnic Jews or not (Gal. 3:14, 29, texts which are elaborated in Rom. 4:1-25). In one place (1 Cor. 10:32) Paul can coin a phrase for a third group made up of 'believing Jews and Gentiles' when he distinguishes between two ethnic classes of 'Jews' and 'Hellenes' (= non-Jews) and 'the church of God'; elsewhere this new creation is called 'the Israel of God' (Gal. 6:16). Later the full rationale will be offered for the emergence of 'one new man' in place of two (Eph. 2:15). Paul had not yet reached that last phase and since the racial conflicts were for him a recent memory he was content simply to accept the co-existence of Jewish Christians along with Gentile believers, but with equality on both sides in an *entente* which he strove to make *cordiale*.

ISRAEL'S SALVATION AND THE GENTILES' RECONCILIATION

The last part of this summary takes another look at the initial problem. How does Israel-in-the-future fit in to God's plan of salvation? Paul's starting point is that Israel's Messiah (Rom. 9:5) came to bless all nations (Gal. 3:6-9, referring to Gen. 12:1-3). Israel has always had an outer shell and an inner core of the faithful, called the 'remnant' who lived by grace (Rom. 11:5). God, for Paul, was seen always to be working through this responsive remnant. The apostolic kerygma as Paul proclaimed it was directed to all who would believe; they were drawn from Israel's true members (Rom. 2:28-29) and equally included under Paul's ministry responding Gentiles. Paul himself belonged to the first group, but accepted responsibility for the second.

God's saving plan in the future will be to graft the 'Jews-as-

Israel' likened to cultivated olive branches (Rom. 11:24), broken off because of unbelief, into the parent stem — *if* they do not persist in their unbelief (11:23). Already the wild olive shoots have been inserted into the stem as a tribute to Paul's ministry (11:17 — a course of action, Paul recognises, that is 'contrary to nature', v. 24, since he is expressing something miraculous, not what was then horticulturally practicable; cf. Matt. 3:9).

By the same miracle that grafted in wild shoots God, it is said, can return the natural branches to the parent tree. But with the clear proviso that 'they do not persist in unbelief'. Paul is thus asserting two principles of ecclesiology simultaneously: (*a*) God's people is one and the same throughout the ages (Rom. 4:12; Gal. 3:6ff.) — a conclusion shared by most commentators; and the new Israel or the church is a continuation of the original Israel, where the common element is faith in God *either* in anticipation of *or* in realisation of his promise in Christ. And so Jewish Christians ought to be grateful now that they have Gentile partners in the same olive tree; and Gentile Christians ought to recognise their debt to Israel and not assume a false independence because 'true Israel' supports them (11:18); moreover Israel's future will enrich them in due time by accelerating the close of the age (11:5; this idea is expressed possibly in 2 Cor. 8:14: 'their abundance may supply your want'). (*b*) Paul's second statement holds out the hope of a 'homecoming of all the people of God' based on his illustration of the olive tree. When the natural branches (Israel *qua* people of God) and the wild olive shoots (Gentiles *qua* believers) are united, they will form one tree. Two events are needed to bring about this happy result. On the one side, 'the full number of the Gentiles' will be added — there is an obvious change of metaphor in 11:25, which implies that the totality of the Gentile world, perhaps representatively as in 11:30-32, has responded to bring about 'an eschatological universalism'.[6] On the other hand, there is the anticipation that God's acceptance of his people will be like a resurrection to life in the coming age. The promise of 'life from the dead' that follows on God's admittance of Israel to the community of faith has been interpreted in two quite opposite ways.[7] For one group of commentators it is a figurative expression implying that Israel's final conversion to God will lead to a spiritual renewal throughout the world. But as Cranfield is quick to point out, this view hardly agrees with verses 25f. according to which the total number of Gentiles has already been added *before* the turning of Israel to God and so further enrichment of the Gentiles numerically is ruled out. The alternative is to take 'life from the dead' literally and see in the phrase the resurrection that will usher in the consummation. Paul is then setting in tandem association the two eschatological 'events' that will be harbingers of the end-time and the final wind-up of the ages:

(i) Israel's fall into unbelief (11:12a), however temporary, has resulted in the 'riches for the Gentiles' and 'the reconciliation of the world' (11:15a);

(ii) Israel's recovery of faith (11:12b) will lead to its 'fullness' in the final resurrection of the dead and the eschaton (11:15b).

The advantages of this latter interpretation may now be assessed: (a) it sets the twin nouns 'rejection'/'acceptance' in obvious parallelism, with God as the implied author in both cases; (b) it allows 'reconciliation' to be taken in the sense already established in Romans 5:1-11, i.e. the breaking down of barriers of estrangement between God and sinful persons, which is the leading theme of Paul's ministry to the Gentiles (2 Cor. 5:18-21). Indeed, as will be claimed later (p. 153) 'reconciliation' is *the* term par excellence for the salvation of the Gentiles in Paul's formulation; (c) it permits a second parallelism between the 'full number (*plērōma*) of the Gentiles' (11:25) and the 'full inclusion' (*plērōma*) of Israel (11:12) to be drawn, and this paves the way for (d) Paul's triumphant conclusions in 11:26 and 32, which have the consummation of all things (*apokatastasis*) in view.

'And so (*houtōs*) all Israel will be saved.' There is a consensus that the text does not mean every individual Israelite, but at least 'Israel as a whole' (Sanday and Headlam[8]). Munck relates it to 'the remnant' (11:5) plus 'the rest' (11:7), at present hardened in unbelief but in God's good time to be aroused from unbelief and 'grafted in' (11:23).[9] The word 'all' suggests completeness embracing Jews of all ages. Further, the believing Gentiles should certainly find a place in this category since (i) they have been mentioned in verse 25, and (ii) they will surely feature in Paul's universalistic thought of verse 32. The phrase 'all Israel" looks to be an omnibus expression covering all types of believers: elect Israelites from the beginning; responsive Gentiles who hear the message from Paul's lips; and (when the Gentiles' full tally is complete) the 'Israel-of-the-future' who in faith will embrace the messianic salvation. Paul concludes, with an

Old Testament citation to buttress his eschatological hope, 'So in this way all Israel will be saved . . . God has consigned all men (Jews and Gentiles alike in Adam, 1:18-3:20; 5:12-14) to disobedience, that he may have mercy upon all' (Jews and Gentiles alike in the new Man, Jesus Christ).

Paul's soteriology and eschatology are linked by their common anchorage. They are both fideistic and christological through and through. His ground of salvation and confidence for the future are centred in the person of Jesus Christ, the reconciler of the Gentile world and the hope of Israel. And both offices are predicated on faith. From his initial announcement in Romans 1:16 of a gospel for the Jew and also the Greek he has laid out a groundplan of what God in Christ has done to meet human need for the Jew (in justification) and for the Gentile (in reconciliation). Both provisions are bound up with Christ's achievement in history and by his death on the cross where Gentile enmity was exposed, judged and forgiven and Jewish religion was tested, condemned and superseded. Yet there is new life for all in Christ crucified and living who meets both Jew and Gentile on the ground of faith. Both synagogue and church find their common meeting point in the new relationship with God made possible through his reconciling work in Christ that has a historical mooring in Christ's death (Rom. 5:6, 8, 10; cf. 2 Cor. 5:15, 19-21; Col. 1:20-22) and also a message of hope for the Israel-of-the-future whose reclaiming by God will usher in the eternal world and make the reconciliation of all things complete (Rom. 11:15).

We turn now to look more closely at that exposition of past reconciliation in Romans 5:1-11.

ROMANS 5:1-11 (omitting vv. 3-4)

1 Since then we have been justified through faith,
    let us enjoy the peace we have with God
        through our Lord Jesus Christ:
2 Through him moreover we have secured access [by faith]
    to this grace in which we abide,
And we exult in our hope of the [coming] divine glory.
5 [That] hope does not put us to shame,
    For God's love has been poured out in our hearts
        through the Holy Spirit who was given to us.

6   For when we were still powerless, at the appointed time,
       Christ died for ungodly people.

7   For it would be difficult [to find] someone
         to die for a righteous man;
      For a good man perhaps someone may even bring
         himself to die;

8   But God proves his love for us by the
      fact that while we were still sinners,
        Christ died for us.

9   Since then we have now been justified
      at the cost of his blood,
     We shall be saved with greater certainty
     from [God's] wrath through him.

10   For if when we were enemies we were reconciled to
     God
      through his son's death,
      now that we are reconciled, we shall with greater
      certainty
      be saved by his life.

11   Not only do we have this as our hope, but
      we also exult in God through our Lord Jesus Christ,
      through whom we have now already received recon-
      ciliation.

THE HORIZON OF THE PASSAGE

In using 'horizon' we press into service — as we earlier observed — the contemporary term for an author's intention, the purpose of his writing in so far as that purpose may be ascertained and understood today. It also means a term that relates to the context of his material, in this case the surrounding context of Paul's closely-knit discussion in the letter to the Romans.

Earlier debates centring on the way the epistle should be divided appealed to this short passage as being either a conclusion to all that had gone before or a 'bridge' to the opening of a new section (Matthew Black's word). One noteworthy feature is the lexical texture of Romans 5:1-11 which is heavily coloured by the vocabulary of earlier passages in the letter, thus:

'justified' (2:13; 3:4, 20, 24, 26, 28, 30; 4:2, 5): then twice in 5:1, 9, and recurring only in three places in Romans (6:7; 8:30 [twice], 33).

'this grace' (5:2), recalling 3:24.

'hope of the divine glory', recalling 3:23.

'exult' (5:2-3, 11), reverting to 2:17, 23 and not repeated later.

'by his blood' (5:9), a phrase virtually the same in 3:25.

'wrath (of God') in 5:9 picks up six references in chapters 1-4, but there are also later occurrences.

The verb 'to prove' (5:8) is found in 3:5 of the divine righteousness.

The conclusion of Cranfield seems supported: 'that there is a significant linguistic affinity between chapter 5 and chapters 1 to 4 is not to be denied'.[10] This conclusion would equally justify the view that at 5:1-11 Paul is consciously summing up the drift of his argument heretofore and drawing out some practical results. If the earlier section (1:18-4:25) has been devoted to the themes of universal need under God's judgment and the divine provision of justification by grace, then F. F. Bruce's title, 'The blessings which accompany justification: peace, joy, hope', may serve to encapsulate what these verses contain. C. K. Barrett brackets the description of the former section and what he evidently regards as a term to parallel it from verses 1-11: 'Justification and Salvation'. C. E. B. Cranfield follows suit with the caption, 'A life characterised by peace with God' for 5:1-21, though Barth's title is more comprehensive, 'The Gospel as Man's Reconciliation with God'.[11]

From one point of view then, 5:1-11 may be said to 'recapitulate and develop further the Pauline doctrine of justification'.[12] The new language introduced here for the first time — and admittedly for the last time except a single reference at 11:15 in our letter — is 'reconciliation'. Barrett regards justification and reconciliation as 'different metaphors describing the same fact', and his statement looks cogent when parallel verses are set side by side:

verse 9: 'justified' — 'by his blood' — 'we shall be saved'
verse 10: 'reconciled' — 'by the death of God's son' — 'we shall be saved'.

But appearances like these are deceiving, and certain assumptions need to be watched. For example, it is treated as axiomatic that 'blood' (v. 9) and 'death' (v. 10) are the same in theological 'weight' (*Sache*), whereas the former is a cultic-sacrificial term, used in Romans 3:25 in an Old Testament setting and matched with the verb 'to expiate' (*hilaskesthai*), whereas 'death' is theologically neutral as signifying the means (*dia thanatou*) of divine reconciliation in a manner akin to, if deeper than, the meaning of 2 Corinthians 5:18, 'through Christ'. 'Saved' may be taken in two different ways: in verse 9 the deliverance is from God's wrath, reverting to Romans 2:5-8; and in verse 10 the salvation may still be eschatological, i.e. forward-looking. But 'saved by his life' is a phrase that has puzzled the commentators who think that the verb may be equivalent to 'life in Christ' and so to be rendered, 'preserved', 'kept safe'. We are disposed, therefore, to refuse a too facile running together of Paul's verses and so to question whether justification and reconciliation are virtually the same ideas.

One way, recently discussed by Michael Wolter,[13] to relate the key terms in Paul's theological discussion starts from the observation that the infrastructure of the letter is fashioned with fixed points in view. These latter are found in the turning points of the letter, commencing with Romans 1:18: wrath is revealed on human ungodliness (*asebeia*, matching 5:6, *asebēs*) and unrighteousness (*adikia*; cf. 5:7, *dikaios*). The era of divine judgment extends to the time of God's saving action in Christ: then a new age opens with the revelation of God's righteousness in his son (3:21-26). We have already seen the distinctives of that passage where it is likely that Paul's final use of a Jewish Christian formula has (*a*) clarified divine righteousness as God's salvific power to reclaim the world; (*b*) emphasised the universality of God's grace to the Gentiles, and (*c*) set the contrast 'formerly . . . but now' on a more firm base by accentuating the previous age of Torah religion as one of condemnation, now succeeded by the age of Messiah. Through faith in Jesus (3:26) men and women enter into a new relationship with a God who both justifies himself and declares 'just' (*dikaios*) those who have no claim on his grace. Or, to express the contrast in yet another way as a prelude to Romans 5:1-11, what humankind has lost by its connection with the race's progenitor, namely the divine 'glory' (3:23; cf. 1:23) is now restored in the new humanity in Christ (5:2; cf. 8:17-18, 21, 30; 9:23).

Chapter 5 is another major landmark in the letter's configuration. But 5:1-11 does more than recapitulate and restate the argument in Paul's existing terms. It marks a decisive move forward in his thinking, raising it to a new plateau. Up to 4:25 he has utilised the schema or framework of Jewish apocalyptic with its time-frame of the two ages. 'This age' is one of God's wrath; in the coming age God's righteousness will be seen in justifying and redeeming his people and ushering in a new era. Paul, to be sure, does not disown and discard that world-view entirely, but reinterprets at 5:1 the language of justification to state God's power in salvation, his righteousness, in reference to the human condition more relationally and personally. The new idiom is 'reconciliation', first introduced here and then unfolded in subsequent chapters in terms of membership of the new family of God, the power of the Spirit, likeness to the image of Christ and the social implications of life-in-community in the world, the state and the fellowship of the church. In fact, the groundplan of this letter is now set by Paul's fresh nomenclature based on the new relationship with God described at 5:1-11. What has gone before has been preparatory — and indispensable as a basis — to Paul's later construction. But we should not fail to notice how the language of justification at this point gives way to a lexicon of terms referring to the new life in Christ on more personal levels. J. A. T. Robinson writes of the place of 5:1-11:

> Here are sketched the themes which will occupy the second half of the doctrinal section of the epistle and as though in an overture to Act II the tunes are played over. The new words are peace, glory, endurance, hope, love, the Spirit, salvation, reconciliation, life. They are all given their full orchestration and reach their crescendo in chapter 8. These verses, which raise the argument to a new level, are to chapter 8 what 1:16-17 were to chapter 3, where the key words were 'to Jew first and also to Greek, righteousness, faith'.[14]

This statement may be accepted with the further observation that 5:1-11 functions both as a summary of what has gone before (we have seen the lexical affinities) and a preview of all that will follow not only up to chapter 8 but in the rest of the letter. But 'reconciliation' is not one term in a laundry list of several items, as Robinson suggests; it is an overarching term that includes the list and describes a new relationship with God that may then be further described under the headings he proposes, and goes on to embrace the new Israel of chapters 9-11 and the social dimensions of chapters 12-15.

The link at 5:1 is the noun 'peace'. Like 'reconciliation' (*katallagē*, in v. 11), *eirēnē* is a relational term and is its synonym. Moreover, both words have their opposite partner (Wolter's *Gegenbegriff*) in the term 'wrath'. So it is 'peace' that is finely suited to serve as a transitional term between Paul's exposition of human need (1:18) and God's saving enterprise in the good news he proclaimed (Rom. 1:16-17: a programmatic statement, announcing what will follow). Up to this juncture in the statement of his argument Paul has pressed into service Jewish apocalyptic notions of divine retribution; he has used the 'pre-Pauline' soteriology of 3:24f. with its Day of Atonement language of expiation/propitiation and covenant renewal for Israel; and he has shared, with some modifications, belief in the forensic-covenantal promise of a new age that came with Israel's Messiah who ratified the pledge of grace to Abraham, David and their ancestors. The terminology of 'imputation' that runs through chapter 4 is such that Paul needed it to anchor redemption in the cross of Jesus and offer a rationale for God's justifying action. To cap it all, Paul has cited a pre-formed soteriological tag in the couplet of 4:25:

[He] was handed over for our trespasses,
And was raised for our justification.

The 'servant' language (Isa. 53:6, 11-12) and the presence of a credal formulation betray an origin elsewhere than in Paul's epistolary discussion. But he has chosen to use it as a final capstone to his sustained argument. Now he is ready to draw out some corollaries, and his linkage is the gift of 'peace with God' (*eirēnē pros ton theon*: the preposition highlighting the essentially relational character of the gift with the same thought reiterated in the noun for 'access', *prosagōgē*; it means a privileged introduction to a VIP) which is the present possession of those persons who are otherwise described as 'declared right with God' by faith. 'To be justified is to be at peace with God';[15] but to have God's peace as his gift for us to receive and enjoy (see Moffatt's translation[16]) is more than to be justified. It is to know God's 'reconcilement' in all that the Greek word with its derivatives and associations means in human experience *vis-à-vis* the God and Father of our Lord Jesus Christ, both in the present and for the future.

THE FORM OF THE PASSAGE

The interpretative connection between Romans 3:21ff. and this section which we have used above helps us to see more clearly the literary structure of the latter. There are two parallel participial clauses:

verse 1: Having been justified (*dikaiōthentes*) by faith
verse 9: Having been justified (*dikaiōthentes*) now at the cost of his blood.

The phrase 'by faith' in verse 1 matches Romans 3:22, 25-26, where the presence of a Pauline addition may be claimed. The phrases 'in his blood' and 'now' (*nun*) are carried forward from Romans 3:25-26, again incorporating Paul's own interpretative comment.

The verses that follow under these two main captions are written partly to explain what justification implies and partly to correct teaching that was content to stay simply with a Judaeo-Christian framework.

So the interpretative sequences in both instances are given in a matching way:

Justified
yet 'we have peace with God' (v. 1)
Justified
yet 'we are reconciled to God' (v. 10)

Each explanatory and corrective sentence is then followed by a phrase with an identical preposition:

verse 1: 'through (*dia*) our Lord Jesus Christ'
verse 10: 'through (*dia*) the death of his son'

The implicit subject in both cases is God but there is a more sharply focused meaning given in verse 10 which, as we shall see, carries Paul's atonement teaching to a point further on than in 2 Corinthians 5:18-21.

Finally, we should remark on the interrelation of the sentences regarding 'hope' (*elpis*):

verse 2b: 'we exult in hope'
verse 5a: this 'hope does not put us to shame'

The nature of Christian hope that reaches forward to the final consummation (Rom. 8:17, 23-25) is explained, following verse 2, in a series of 'chain' arguments. Paul resumes the thought of 'hope' at verse 5, and continues to renew his interest in a 'discussion by linkage'. The progress of his thinking moves by set pieces of logical deduction:

(*a*)   Why did hope not fail us?

(*b*)   Because God's love is ours in experience through the Spirit's presence.

(*a*)   How do we know God's love objectively?

(*b*)   In our weakness, ungodliness and sinful condition, Christ died for us. That is the sign of God's love — shown to abject specimens!

[Within this question/response is a parenthesis: For a righteous person one would hardly expect another to die/ Perhaps for an exemplary person one would be found to die]

(*a*)   Now (*nun*) set right with God, we are sure *a fortiori* (how much more) of deliverance at the final day of retribution.

(*b*)   Now brought from enmity (i.e. being displeasing to God) to friendship with God, we are sure *a fortiori* (how much more) of our continuance in salvation to the end-time.

Conclusion:

(*i*)   'we exult in our hope' (v. 2)

(*ii*)   'we exult in our trials' (vv. 3-4)

(*iii*)   'we exult in our present (*nun*) reconciliation' (v. 11)

Three deductions from this form-analysis may be made. First, it looks pretty evident that the centrepiece of Paul's whole argument is the celebration of God's love. Twice repeated (vv. 5, 8), that divine *agapē* is localised in both human experience and historical deed. Paul appeals to the realisation of God's love in the lives of his hearers, certified by the Spirit's witness; equally he grounds that love in the 'proof' or 'demonstration' that points to the death of Christ in whom the Father's gift of love for sinners is for him convincingly seen.

Secondly, justification and reconciliation are linked by a third term, 'saved' (twice, vv. 9, 10), but the pericope closes with a renewed emphasis on reconciliation (v. 11) whereas 'justified' in verbal form is not used except in an ancillary way, denoted by a participle.

Thirdly, the present reality of justification which brings with it peace and the gift of the Spirit (v. 5) as tokens of the new age of messianic blessedness and joy is never allowed to replace the future prospect of eschatological deliverance (v. 9) and continuing salvation (v. 10). Is it feasible to detect a polemical note here, warning against a false reliance on 'final justification' that would minister to a careless attitude in the present (seen in Rom.

3:8, 6:1f., 'Shall we continue in sin?') and based on a denial of futuristic eschatology?

E. Käsemann[17] uses the earlier verses (5:3-5) to argue for an understanding of the basic structure of Paul's eschatology as directed against those who thought only of a complete fulfilment of God's promises in a celestial life on earth here and now. This may be exaggerated; nor can we say with any confidence that Paul is tacitly appealing to a baptismal response in 5:5 when the Spirit was given and believers came to realise God's love poured into their hearts (cf. Acts 2:17-18, 33; Tit. 3:6 for the same verb, however). If Paul did have conversion or baptism in view at verse 5, it might just strengthen the personal appeal his section makes and call on his readers to live out their 'new life' promises as they break with past evil associations (a theme presented in 6:3-23).

THE APOSTLE'S TEACHING

We may now proceed to gather up the previous discussion on Romans 5:1-11 into something of a constructive statement. Then we shall set this example of Paul's kerygma in conjunction with our earlier studies of Romans 3, 2 Corinthians 5 and Colossians 1. Indeed, that will be the most interesting part of the exercise.

According to Paul, reconciliation postulates an estrangement. A rift in relations between God and man makes the repair of the breach and restoration of amity a prime necessity if ever God's purposes are to be realised and man is to be 'saved' from his plight and peril.

THE HUMAN CONDITION

(i) Paul is under no illusion as to the serious and hopeless state of man's condition. Subjectively considered, man is 'helpless', i.e. powerless to aid himself, 'ungodly', blighted with a malaise that recalls the exposé of 1:18-32, and a 'sinner', which is Paul's favourite term for man's lostness and sorry state. Romans 3:23 expresses the meaning of *hamartia* (sin) as both a missing the target of divine righteousness and a coming short of the divine *doxa*, God's splendour, seen in the first Adam and restored in the second Man, Jesus Christ (see earlier pp. 50,51).

On the objective side man stands under God's judgment, his 'wrath' (5:9). This term (*orgē*) is not an affective or emotionally charged disposition of God as though God bore personal malice or exhibited pique against offending rebels. Indeed Ephesians 4:26, 31 (Ps. 4:4; cf. Jas. 1:19-20) warns against precisely these outbursts of temper and bad feeling as well as indicting a settled attitude of hatred of our fellows. And God's love is the centre of Paul's thought (5:5, 8). Yet God's *orgē* is real in terms of his moral resistance to evil and his judicial indignation in its presence. Evil invites his judgment by calling down his condemnation and his edict of banishment.

Two other parts of our passage fit into this whole picture. If men and women find 'access' through Christ's reconciling work, it follows that outside of Christ, there is only alienation and separation from God; and this, we may suppose from the consistent Old Testament tradition, e.g. Genesis 3:24; Isaiah 59:2, is the essence of man's sinful state. He is distanced from God because God has declared him an outlaw and an exile.

(*ii*) But the obverse side of the picture is seen in Romans 5:10: 'when we were enemies . . .'. Interpreters are hopelessly divided over the question: does 'being enemies' mean 'while we were hating God' (active) as in Romans 1:30; 8:7, or 'while God was opposed to us' (passive)? Two arguments tip the scales on the side of the latter. In the total context of Romans 1:18-3:20 where God's righteous wrath is directed to the ungodly world and in consequence the world stands under his sentence, it must be an offence to God to view such a scene, Paul infers, and he can only meet it with a stern face of disapproval and opposition. Then, as Wolter has noted,[18] since the reconciliation spoken of in verse 10 — against which 'being enemies' is a foil — is said to be 'to God', it is logical to assume that Paul meant: once we were hostile *to God*, now we are reconciled to him. That sad state is the lot of Israel according to Romans 11:28 where no anti-semitism can be justifiably traced since the writer is himself a Jew, passionately involved in his nation's fate (Rom. 9:1-5; 10:1).

Divine displeasure and human alienation sum up the state of men and women who are the objects of reconciliation. In a previous discussion (pp. 33,34) we noted that as sinners such persons were placed 'in the wrong' forensically and needed to be cleared and 'set right'. That is the language of justification. At this point in his statement of the message Paul moves to another dimension of the human state. The gift of 'peace' (5:1) makes sense only as it is understood as coming to those formerly estranged and at enmity. On God's side that barrier is denoted by his 'wrath'.

'Wrath' combines both forensic and eschatological ideas corresponding to man's need as 'unrighteous' (*adikos*) and 'ungodly' (*asebēs*): both terms are found in Romans 1:18 and both call down the divine *orgē* as a present reality. Paul has taken a term in Jewish apocalyptic thinking where it connotes the 'day of judgment' and has brought it into the present where its effects are already at work (1 Thess. 2:16; Rom. 9:22). But the future aspect is not overlooked, as verse 9 reminds us. Paul is evidently using the conventional language of Jewish apocalypticism. 'Wrath' is replaced by 'eternal life' in Romans 2:5-8; and 'peace' in 5:1 has to be understood as a synonym in Jewish expectation for the new age of messianic bliss and favour. The term 'peace' (*šālôm/eirēnē*) is the relationship of acceptance with God based on eschatological salvation, not human feelings of inner harmony or tranquillity. But Paul has personalised it by relating to man's experience of 'access to God' and knowledge of his 'grace' (5:2: there may be an anticipation of this in Job 22:21; Isa. 27:5; 57:19; cf. 57:21). If, as E. Schweizer has said,[19] Romans 1:18-3:20 'deal with the eschatological outburst of God's wrath', the turning point comes at 5:1 with a celebration of the new age of God's salvation when 'peace with God' is both heralded and enjoyed by his people.

GOD'S ACTION

(*i*) At the heart of this passage is *the revelation of divine love*. The phrase 'the love of God' (*hē agapē tou theou*) is, perhaps contrary to popular expectation, used by Paul only rarely. In fact there are but two other references (Rom. 8:39; 2 Cor. 13:13). Nor does Paul use the verb 'to love' of the Christian's response to God very frequently (Rom. 8:28; 1 Cor. 8:3; note that 1 Cor. 2:9 is a borrowing from some Jewish source). It is just possible that verse 5 may be translated: 'our love for God has been poured into our hearts by the Holy Spirit', but the context is decisively against this rendering which Augustine promoted. The following verse clearly emphasises how Christ's dying for the ungodly is related to this love; and in verse 8 Paul writes unmistakably of God's *own love* for us (*tēn heautou agapēn*) as demonstrated in Christ's death for sinners.

So here is one clear datum in Paul's soteriology: he can bring himself to express the love of God in this way because he found the focus of that love in the cross of Christ. God's love was no axiom or postulate he could take for granted. The believer's own experience, while it confirmed the reality of that love, did not prove it. Rather its convincing proof was seen in what God did in the past event of the cross ('Christ died', vv. 6, 8), though the demonstration continues — Paul's verb *synistēsin* ('proves'; 'shows', RSV) is present tense — because the one historical event has given for all time the paradigm of what is always true of God, namely he is love. Yet his eternal nature once — and once for all — came into focus at Christ's cross and its image remains.

The love of God is set in contrast to several other items in the discussion. First, its remarkable character is brought out in the somewhat tortuous syntax of verse 7. Paul starts out from the premise of Christ's death for the ungodly (v. 6). He proceeds: to contemplate a person dying even for a righteous man is wonderful for it hardly ever happens. The inference would be drawn, that to imagine anyone dying on behalf of an unrighteous person is quite unthinkable, as it never occurs. Then the second half-verse seems to lessen the dramatic thrust of the argument by introducing a qualification: perhaps for a good man a voluntary death is thinkable, whereas the opening of verse 8 invites us to consider, as a climax, that the totally unthinkable has taken place. Christ died for us wretched sinners to manifest God's own love as distinct from man's, even when man's love leads him to surrender his life for a good person or perhaps a good cause (taking *hyper tou agathou* as neuter). The point of Paul's argument, if the text is not corrupt or has been left unrevised by its author as has been suggested, is that a signal display of human love would be seen in a person's dying for a good cause (e.g. patriotism); on the contrary God's love shines out in that he gives his son to death for the most undeserving of causes when those he died for were rebels and enemies. So that love is 'scarcely conceivable among human beings', but it actually did once take place.[20]

Secondly, Paul sees the divine *agapē* coming to expression in a concrete event — 'at the right time', 'at the appointed hour' (*kairos*) of prophetic destiny and eschatological hope when God's promises came to realisation (see Mark 1:15; 12:2; Ps. Solomon 17:21: 'Look, O Lord, and raise up for them their king, the son of David, at the appointed time [*kairos*] which, O God, you did choose'). That 'decisive moment' reflects the divine initiative in so choosing the time and place for his love to be made known

(Gal. 4:4); it also speaks to the desperate human condition, for it was when men were 'helpless', 'ungodly' and 'enemies' that the drama was enacted. No more compelling indication of God's taking the first step in man's recovery could be given, a fact reinforced by the twice repeated adverb 'still (*eti*) powerless', 'still (*eti*) sinners' in verses 6, 8.

Thirdly, references to Christ's 'death' (v. 10) and 'blood' (v. 9) seem to be there in the text as shorthand expressions or code-words for his self-sacrifice for human sins. We have tried to make a distinction between these words, and we note again how rarely Paul uses the description, 'the blood' of Christ (Rom. 3:25; Col. 1:20). The language is cultic-sacrificial, denoting the life laid down in death and as an atonement (i.e. a covering) for sins. The 'death' in verse 10 picks up the earlier references to the verbal form, 'he died' (vv. 6, 8), and expresses more the self-offering of Jesus in obedience to God's holy design in love (Rom. 8:32, with its reminiscence of Gen. 22 and the rabbinic ideas of the sacrifice made in the 'binding of Isaac'). The 'death' of Christ takes on deeper poignancy and saving value when it is viewed as the death of the son whom God loves (Col. 1:13; cf. Eph. 1:6).

(*ii*) *Reconciliation stands in some degree of tension with both 'justification' and 'wrath'*, both words represented in our passage. We have seen how Paul begins with the forensic idiom (v. 1), picks it up later (v. 9), but does not explore its significance at any depth. Instead, the immediate consequence of being set right with God is 'peace', a term synonymous with 'reconciliation', which then takes over in the discussion and which is used to denote both restored relationship with God (so reversing and nullifying the baneful effects of sin) and 'a real participation in the life of the risen Christ', a theme which is later worked out in chapters 6-8.

'Wrath' naturally is that which sets up the hiatus between God and man, and is given here its eschatological meaning, as in 1 Thessalonians 1:10; 5:9; Romans 2:5, 8; 12:19. If the verbs 'saved' in verses 9 and 10 are of equal weight, the hoped-for deliverance from God's final judgment is secured by Christ's 'life'. The last term would mean in context his advocacy of his people's cause at the last day and their preservation from divine retribution. Nothing is said about Christ's assuming their sin or enduring God's wrath on the cross, even if 'enemies' does carry the thought of 'hostile to God'. Paul again has left unexplained 'how' the reconciliation is effected except to make certain reportorial statements. These are:

(a) God's hostility to man the sinner is the essential background of Paul's doctrine. On man's side the sorry condition of his alienation is seen in his unrighteousness and inability to save himself.

(b) God's unconstrained initiative gives proof of his love, for which Paul can find no parallel since God is not dealing with 'righteous' or 'good' people but his 'enemies'.

(c) Man's part is to 'receive the reconciliation' or 'enjoy peace with God' as his present possession. In both cases it is the gift of God which no one can merit or earn. Paul's anti-nomistic strain is evident in the language he uses. 'Let us have peace' (reading *echōmen* in v. 1) is therefore inappropriate as a translation in this context, whatever the merits of its textual pedigree. On the other hand, while Paul certainly wished to stress the present availability of God's grace in reconciliation, it still remains that men and women must 'receive' it and for that to happen human responsibility is called into play. E. Dinkler[21] therefore puts his finger on a real concern when he suggests that the gift of God's peace is to be matched by our seeking to live in that relationship (Rom. 14:19; Col. 3:15; Phil. 4:7). The concurrence of the indicative ('We have peace') and the imperative ('Let us have peace') is typically in the Pauline manner, and there is therefore no real need to choose between the disputed readings.

(d) A person's 'exulting' (RSV 'rejoice'; other versions give 'boast' for *kauchasthai*) is a significant feature in this paragraph. As was explained earlier (pp. 26,60), Paul's pre-Christian life as a pious Jew was characterised by this outlook and attitude: he boasted of his compliance with the minutiae of Torah religion. By what happened in his conversion he came to a re-evaluation of this 'boasting', and saw it as a species of sinful pride. Henceforth he will 'boast in the Lord' (1 Cor. 1:31) now that he has been set right with God by his grace in Christ crucified and through meritless faith. All other boasting is excluded (Rom. 3:27) and even his missionary service is not suitable for this exercise (2 Cor. 11:12-30). He may only truly 'boast' of his weaknesses (2 Cor. 12:5).

Yet here we find him 'boasting' not only in his trials (5:3) but in God from whom, in Jesus Christ the Lord, he has

received the restored relationship (v. 11). It is a concluding·
tribute to his full reliance on God's free grace and strength
(*charis* means both) that has met and answered his deepest
needs as a sinner: as an ungodly person he has been forgiven,
as a powerless individual he has been reinforced by divine
power for his life as a Christian. And the gift of reconciliation
is thus none other than the Spirit in his life (v. 5) bringing the
privilege of filial adoption and joy.

ROMANS 5: I-11
IN THE SETTING OF THE PAULINE TRADITION

Our attention will now be directed to the question of how far
Romans 5:1-11 carries forward, confirms or modifies Paul's
earlier teaching on reconciliation as seen in the three places
where he has commented on the tradition. First of all, we may
note certain definite features that serve to crystallise his earlier
thinking.

(*i*) Paul has given a sharper profile to the love of God in
providing the means of reconciliation in the person of Jesus
Christ. The statement 'in Christ God was reconciling the world'
(2 Cor. 5:19) runs parallel with the previous verse, 'God ...
through Christ reconciled us to himself' (v. 18); but it says no
more than that Christ was the agent of the divine enterprise,
even if it does stress God's personal presence in what happened.
The passage in Romans 5 leaves us in no doubt that God's
personal involvement was one in which his love focused in a
single deed: 'Christ died *for us*.' 'Making peace (*eirēnopoiēsas*) by
the blood of his cross' (Col. 1:20) is certainly a strong statement
of God's activity in securing cosmic harmony by the cross, but
what that 'peace' entailed is left undefined, and so has been the
source of much diverse interpretation (see p. 126). Romans 5:1
re-phrases the term in an unmistakable way: reconciliation is
none other than 'peace *with God* through our Lord Jesus Christ'
who unites us to the Father and is not (in this context) described
as the unifying centre of cosmic forces in which men and women
are one unit out of several components.

(*ii*) Our present passage firmly and clearly anchors the
reconciliation in the historical event of the cross. Paul had
prefaced the citation of 2 Corinthians 5:18-21 with reminders of
Christ's love (v. 14) seen in his death 'for all', but a clearer focus
is given by assertions that he 'died for us' (Rom. 5:8) and that we
are 'reconciled to God by the death of his son' (Rom. 5:10). The

Father and the Son are more closely brought together; and this collocation gives added weight to what the death of Christ involved. Moreover, the beneficiaries of his reconciling work are made more personal: it was not only 'the world' or 'those who live' (2 Cor. 5:15) that are mentioned as including persons for whom Christ died. Paul writes warmly of Christ's dying 'for us', and 'our being reconciled'.

True, in Paul's redaction of Colossians 1:22 the death of Christ is prominent and an emphasis on his real bodily suffering serves to oppose any gnostic or docetic tendency to turn redemption into a divine charade. The reconciliation of 'all things' (1:20) is qualified by the insertion of 'the blood of his cross', and the more vivid idiom is not repeated at verse 22, whereas Romans 5:9 relates 'his blood' more precisely to what Christ did in securing our pardon and amnesty. Both Paul's editorial supplements in Colossians 1 and his teaching in Romans 5 emphasise by the use of past (aorist) tenses of the verbs that reconciliation is a historical event, complete in its 'having-happenedness'. 'He has now reconciled' (Col. 1:22); and 'we were reconciled' and 'now that we are reconciled' (Rom. 5:10, both aorist passive in verb formation) leave no room for misunderstanding as to the completeness and certainty of what God has done. 2 Corinthians 5:18 has the aorist participle, yet verse 19 with its periphrastic tense leaves the reconciliation more in the state of an ongoing process than a final deed.

(*iii*) The 'world' of 2 Corinthians 5:19 may well have been understood in a cosmic sense, and it is clear that the scope of reconciliation in Colossians 1:18-20 embraces all sections of creation, only to be applied concretely to human beings at 1:21-22. Romans 5 rules out any misunderstanding and possible confusion. Paul is talking throughout of the lives of men and women who are in need as sinners. The background is not so much one of 'trespassers' (2 Cor. 5:19; Col. 1:21) and 'estranged persons' in an alien universe (Col. 1:21) as 'enemies of God' who stand in need of being delivered from their exposure to 'the wrath of God'. And human impotence to secure deliverance is accepted here, since men and women are both 'powerless' and 'ungodly', an analytical judgment on the human situation which is deeper than that given in the other passages.

(*iv*) Paul's language of justification (in Rom. 3:24-26; 2 Cor. 5:18-21) and deliverance from the dark domain of evil powers (Col. 1:13) leading to the assurance of forgiveness (Col. 1:14) is essentially negative. It stresses that all impediments to reconciliation are removed and a new status is conferred. But in Paul's teaching, by using the language of 'reconciliation', he stresses that the positive side of man's restoration to God is really the goal of the salvific drama. Romans 5:1-11 therefore is not content to leave man as a 'justified' individual or a member of a new community, 'the kingdom of his beloved son'; it ushers him into God's presence (v. 2) and assures him of a welcome in the family of God where the Spirit is the Spirit of adoption (v. 5; Rom. 8:14-16).

These distinctive features obviously may be offset by a body of common elements that unite Paul's teachings which we have so far considered. In particular we should want freely to grant that this commonality of understanding is what counts in the long run. Paul's exposition of reconciliation reveals the following clear-cut statements:

(*i*) God is the provider of the new relationship he freely offers. The author of reconciliation is referred to consistently as God himself who initiates and carries through the process. And he does so in love. This feature, as we shall observe later, is *the* characteristic thing about both Jesus' recorded teaching on God as Father (e.g. Luke 15) and the way he saw his mission as God's messenger to the world. In each instance the picture of a seeking, caring and forgiving God who meets the sinner before he repents is one that has no parallel in Judaism.

(*ii*) At great cost, epitomised in Christ's blood or death on the cross, God has moved to deal with a situation only he could resolve. Here is a knot only God could untie, said Luther quaintly. The 'dilemma' is that reconciliation is not cheaply secured since God both 'justifies' (i.e. vindicates) himself and offers 'justification' (Rom. 3:26) as a ground on which he extends the grace of reconciliation. God's love and 'righteousness' in some mysterious way, never quite explained by Paul, come together in the cross of Jesus. That death is the focal point of the divine love; it is also a necessary event for God's concern for sin to be expressed, though Paul draws back from saying that Christ bore the divine wrath. He was 'appointed' (2 Cor. 5:21) a sacrifice for sin and took man's part over against God in a representative way. Since 'blood' and 'death' are words in the vocabulary of atonement, we may infer that his death was that vicarious sacrifice because of which barriers to reconciliation are now overcome, and it is that saving love of God seen in Christ's death, by God's appointing, that has power to reconcile.

If our previous discussion of the tradition-history of the texts has any validity, we now conclude that in the two places where Paul has expressions that give a rationale for 'reconciliation' (in the terms *hilastērion*, expiation/propitiation in Rom. 3:25 and 'Christ made sin' in 2 Cor. 5:21), he has drawn upon traditional teaching which he has not stopped to explain further. We may say that this fact certifies his agreement with what he quotes and that therefore the atonement teaching had a wider currency than Paul's use of it in these places since it was already in the church before Paul pressed it into service. It would equally be true that Paul's acceptance of the tradition *as far as it went* has to be seen in the context of his concern to draw out some matters that were not sufficiently prominent in the original formulation. In specific terms 'expiation' has to be lifted out of its cultic setting and related to divine salvific righteousness for the whole world. The sacrifice of Christ as a sin offering has to be reinterpreted in terms of justification and the new age of reconciliation that the cross and resurrection (2 Cor. 5:14-17) ushered in. The same principle of 'tradition' and Paul's 'redaction' which gave the old forms a new depth is seen in one other place where Paul stays to quote an interpretative text to answer the question, How did Christ save his people? We refer to Galatians 3:13, where the 'curse' that came on Christ is a prelude to the conclusion Paul is seeking to establish, 'that in Christ Jesus the blessing of Abraham might come upon the Gentiles'. That 'blessing' is the promised Spirit of the new age, available to all.

(*iii*) Human need is the dark canvas against which the divine love shines brightly. Alienation and positive wickedness make men and women unable to save themselves and lead to their being cast only on the free forgiveness of God. While Paul says that we are 'justified by faith', he does not say 'we are reconciled by faith'. The attitude to reconciliation is, on man's part, one of grateful acceptance (Rom. 5:11), not, we may contend, answering the call, 'Be reconciled to God' (2 Cor. 5:20), though that is the usual interpretation. Reconciliation is the concomitant of justification, but it is a larger term. It is 'peace with God' and a place not only in the new world now 'rectified' but in the new fellowship of the Spirit (Rom. 5:5).

(*iv*) Above all, reconciliation moves always on the plane of personal relationships. It expresses both the privilege of being in a happy relationship of friendship with God and the demand of so living in grace (Rom. 5:2) as not to frustrate that grace (2 Cor. 6:1). The relationship is, we may say, more fragile than the new standing suggested by justification. Paul never contemplates a reversal of justification or an overturning of either legal acquittal or royal amnesty (Rom. 8:33-34; Gal. 5:5). But the Corinthians, or some of them at least, can turn their backs on God's offer which they once received in the Pauline gospel. They can and in fact did range themselves with the 'unbelievers' (*apistoi*, 2 Cor. 4:4; 6:14-15) who must be reconciled to God by the message of the kerygma. Their failure to abide in 'righteousness' is seen in their acceptance of those whom Paul branded as 'servants of [counterfeit] righteousness' (2 Cor. 11:15) who are Satan's emissaries. They have put themselves back under the devil's jurisdiction by opposing his gospel. And they need to see once again the outstretched hand of Paul as he appeals to them, Be reconciled to God. And the Colossians are warned to abide in their new relationship with God by adherence to the apostolic teaching (Col. 1:22-23). So the category of reconciliation shares an existential quality, thus making it admirably suited to express the tension in Paul's theology between '*already* justified . . . *not yet* finally saved', as it is formulated (*die Spannung zwischen dem Schon und Noch-Nicht*).

(*v*) If it is true that justification and reconciliation are partners in being associated yet having each a distinct nuance, we may ask why Paul moved from justification (in chapters 1-4 of Romans) to the new vocabulary beginning in chapter 5. Part of the reason has already been before us in the consideration of Romans 3:24-26. There Paul, we suggested, expressed dissatisfaction with the forensic-cultic idiom that limited soteriology to covenant-renewal for the Jewish nation and sought to universalise the scope of Christ's saving deed to include the Gentiles on the basis of faith, not covenantal nomism.

The prominence given to reconciliation from Romans 5 onwards, together with the language of 2 Corinthians 5 (where justification terms in v. 19 are added to correct a possible wrong-headed idea) and Colossians 1:21-22, suggests yet another reason. '*Reconciliation' is the way Paul formulated his gospel in communicating it to the Gentiles*. The terminology is not restricted to the Old Testament-Judaic tradition; it has little if any cultic-forensic association; it relates to a universal human need, namely forgiveness and personal relationship; and it can take within its scope both personal and cosmic dimensions. For pagans newly won over to Christ there was this pressing need: to receive assurance that the Lord who had granted them pardon and had broken the entail of their sinful past was indeed the ruler of the spirit forces that held their erstwhile lives in the bondage of fear and cosmic dread.

With this theory before us, it may be appropriate to draw out an ancillary conclusion. Paul employed the 'reconciliation' imagery as a tool of communication to the Gentile world, but from all we have seen he was not the first to invent or use the term. 'Reconciliation' was already part of the Christian vocabulary before he adopted it. But in his hands it took on a new meaning. Its earlier setting was the cosmos as Christ was viewed as lord of all worlds and the central principle by which all the disparate elements of the universe were held together. That is clearly the sense of 'reconcile' in Colossians 1:15-20 in its first edition, and 2 Corinthians 5: 18-21 may have taught a cosmic salvation by divine fiat. Paul seized upon the term as altogether suited to express what the Christian kerygma meant to those unversed in Jewish thought-forms and whose 'needs' were not those of the world of justification/guilt/acquittal, represented by the Jewish-Christian credo of 1 Corinthians 15:3ff.

Paul's use of the hymn in Philippians 2:6-11 shows how he could adapt a pre-Pauline composition, edit it by the inserting of 'even the death of the cross' (v. 8) and possibly widen its scope by enriching verse 10, to make it express more clearly the kerygma for hellenistic society. We submit as a hypothesis that exactly this procedure has been applied to early Gentile-Christian hymnic celebrations of 'Christ the *cosmocrat*, ruler of creation', and that in Paul's creative hands the teaching is more securely anchored in the cross with the emphasis on a removal of all barriers that obstruct reconciliation with God, whether innate fear of demons or personal insecurity caused by alienation or human distress which the offer of forgiveness and new life was designed to overcome.

As we move on to consider the use of reconciliation in reference to Jew-Gentile relations, we can test this hypothesis and see whether, in fact, in the mind of Paul and his later school, 'Christ our peace' met the needs of Gentiles who were wrestling with the conundrum of Israel's role in salvation history (Rom. chs. 9-11) and seeking to find in a now multiracial church a rationale for Christ's reconciling work as it affected ancient society (Eph. 2:11-22).

PART III

PAULINE THEOLOGY IN A
NEW SITUATION

CHAPTER NINE

RECONCILIATION AND UNITY IN EPHESIANS

INTRODUCTION

In recent years a great deal of attention has focused on the setting of the letter in the Pauline corpus known as Ephesians. The significance of this document has been newly appreciated in the light of its teaching on the place of the church in the purpose of God; but the doctrine of Christ and his saving work in this letter has also been freshly examined to see how expansive is the presentation of the cosmic Christ in these chapters.

The result is that older concerns to do with the letter's authorship and authenticity — whether or not it represents the full flowering of Paul's theology occasioned by his prison experience in Rome, where Acts 28:30-31 leaves him — have given way to some newer interests. The issue really stems from a literary question that asks what kind of letter this Ephesian document really is. There is now a virtual consensus that (*i*) Ephesians is not a 'letter' in the usually accepted sense of the term, akin to, say, Paul's writing to the Philippians, and (*ii*) its destination is not the local Christian community in Ephesus in the province of Asia. These matters can almost be 'proved' by a simple comparison of the style and content of Ephesians with its long sentences (for example 1:3-14), convoluted syntax, and the absence of personal address and direct appeal to the readers, apart from the closing section of 6:21-22. What we are looking at in Ephesians is really a tract dressed up in epistolary form; or, more adequately, a liturgical document composed in such a way as to yield long paragraphs of sonorous cadences, extended descriptions, and somewhat abstract theological statements. If any part of the New Testament could claim to be a transcript of the church at worship, it would be Ephesians with its solemn, elevated, and rhythmic style, and a clear absence of those features that stamp other Pauline letters as obviously sent to cope with pastoral problems at Corinth or in Galatia.

It is difficult to believe that Paul would write in an impersonal

157

and indirect way to a Christian fellowship in a city where he had lived for some considerable time. Indeed, as far as the record in Acts goes, he stayed at Ephesus longer than in any other single place, including those instances when he was in prison (see Acts 19:10; 20:17-38). On the face of it, this 'letter' can only be regarded as a circular address sent out to churches in a wide area which Paul knew at a distance. The textual evidence in 1:1 where 'at Ephesus' in Authorised Version/King James Version rests on a much later and disputable reading and the words are not found in the early manuscripts and the testimony of the church fathers. The most likely theory is that our 'letter' represents one example of an encyclical document sent around a group of churches, presumably in Asia Minor (because of its several links with Colossians), and hand-delivered by a courier to a wide diversity of Christian congregations. If we are right in regarding the epistle as an 'open letter' addressed to Gentile churches in Asia (3:1), this estimate helps us to account for two puzzling features and brings us right up to the issue that is under active discussion today.

(a) For one thing, the writer has heard of his readers' Christian faith only through indirect channels (1:15), and he knows equally that they are acquainted with him and his ministry only in this roundabout manner (3:1-2). His bond with the readers is one of author to recipients (3:4) rather than one of firsthand acquaintance and intimate association. Paul had lived and laboured in metropolitan Ephesus for nearly three years, and it is passing strange that he should distance himself from his readers in this way — if 'Ephesians' was sent to the church in that city.

(b) Secondly, the classifying of Ephesians as epistolary catechism, or an exalted prose-poem dedicated to the theme of 'Christ in his church', helps us to approach the letter and its historical situation in a new light. The author breaks out into an elevated meditation (especially in chs. 1-3) on the great themes that fill his mind — God's purpose in Christ, his fullness in Christ, Christ's fullness in the church which is his body, the church's exaltation to share Christ's present glory. Concepts like these lift him on to a plane of rapture and contemplation which is betrayed in his language. The profusion of rare terms he uses (a total of 82 words not found either in Paul's other writings or in the New Testament as a whole), the parallelisms in his thought and sentence construction, the piling up of synonymous words

(1:19) and his fondness for relative pronouns (1:3-14, which is one connected sentence!) and the preposition 'in' (also 1:3-14) which is used in an exceptional way as C. F. D. Moule has noted[1] —all these characteristics are part of a style that is like that used in early Christian liturgy where words are chosen not only to convey meaning but to communicate feeling and to create a worshipful atmosphere.

THE SETTING OF EPHESIANS

This appreciation of Ephesians as a transcript of early Christian praise offered to 'Christ exalted in his church' has an immediate consequence: it sets the document in a period of church history when old battles having been fought are now regarded as belonging to the past, former tensions between Jewish Christianity and Gentile congregations founded by Paul are resolved, and the ethos of Christianity is subtly shifting to take on a new dress. The church is becoming increasingly ecumenical and accepted as a social institution in the world. The vision of an immediate and dramatic 'second coming' of Christ is fading as the church is becoming convinced of its place in history and adjusting to its destiny on earth (3:20-21) where its future lies. Indeed our writer can see the church under a double aspect: it is already exalted with its Lord (1:22; 2:5-6; 5:27), yet it lives an empirical existence on earth and faces trials (6:10-12). There are continuing struggles with error (4:17ff.; 5:6), but for the church of Ephesians, thought of as universal and transcendental, nothing can dissolve the unity it has with its now glorified head (1:22f.; 4:15f.; 5:30).

The new slant put upon Paul's teaching is clearly to be seen in several ways.

(i) The engagement between Paul as champion of Gentile liberty in Christ and the Judaizers who insisted on the necessity of circumcision for his converts is now over and done with. A first reading of Ephesians 2:11 seems to contradict this statement. But it is instructive to examine the word for 'Gentiles' (*ethnē*) in the letter. In the earlier letters Paul uses the term ordinarily of Gentiles in the sense of 'non-Jews', but in Ephesians it carries more a negative or pejorative flavour, meaning 'non-Christians' (3:6; 4:17) called 'the rest of mankind' in 2:3. 'Having no hope and without God in the world' (2:12) fits the Gentile world exactly. When the term is intended to mean 'non-Jews', as F. W.

Beare notes,[2] the writer adds the phrase 'in the flesh', 'Gentiles *physically*' (*ethnē en sarki*). A tell-tale expression like this suggests a certain distance in time from the Jewish controversies of Paul's active ministry — a distance indicated by the text of 2:11. His readers are those who were 'at one time . . . Gentiles in the flesh, called the uncircumcision', but this last word, like 'circumcision', is for him and the readers an archaic term. The separation of Christianity and Judaism is recognised; Jewish Christianity has passed into history as a once-posed threat to Paul's Gentile converts, but it has no continuing relevance to the audience of Ephesians. The great conflict, says Beare, 'which engaged Paul's energies all through his life, has ended in complete victory and leaves in this epistle barely an echo'.[3]

In a church predominantly made up of Gentile Christians the danger presented a new face. It was not that Gentile believers will succumb to Judaising practices such as circumcision (or the items listed in Ignatius, *Magnesians* chs. 8-10). Rather the threat was that Gentile Christians should want to cast off all association with the Old Testament faith and disown their origins in Israel's salvation history. This tendency was present in Romans 11:17-22, as we observed. Here it reaches its extreme form, and Gentiles need the salutary reminder (which the Gospel of Matthew powerfully conveys) that 'salvation is of the Jews' (to borrow a sentence from the Fourth Gospel) and Paul's 'salvation history' theology never displaced the significance of Israel as the people of God who have now come to full realisation in the 'one body' of a world-wide church in the author's day. And that recall is the theme in Ephesians 2:11-22, where the breaking down of 'the dividing wall of hostility' between Jews and Gentiles would take on significance if it was a reminiscence (as seems likely) of the destruction of the Jerusalem Temple in AD 70. In that world-shaking historical event, the balustrade which separated the Court of the Gentiles from the inner courtyards was destroyed, and the text of our letter is pointing out the symbolic meaning of that happening, in the light of Christ's death in AD 33. Messiah's death destroyed Jewish privileges in principle and hastened the end of the Temple religion for the Jews who remained unmoved by his death. In other words, it is the religious 'wall of partition' that is now broken down, and it is the religious disabilities which separated the Gentiles that are overcome. At the same time, the entry of the Gentiles upon new privileges of access to God by communion and covenant and their becoming a living Temple, 'a dwelling place of God in the Spirit', is a sure sign that Israel's hope is not destroyed but fully realised in a new community where Jews and Gentiles embrace one another as 'fellow citizens' (2:19). Neither has forfeited its identity except to have it transcended and subsumed under a higher name, 'one new person' (2:15).

(*ii*) Paul's apostolic ministry, often regarded in the early church as disputable and as often defended vigorously in his active life-time, is here seen in retrospect (3:1-13). Nothing is clearer in the apostolic record than the constant struggle Paul had to maintain the validity and credibility of his call to apostleship and his true standing as 'apostle to the Gentiles' (see 2 Cor. chs. 10-13 in particular). But this epistle sets Paul's apostleship apart in a way that defies challenge. The shift is greater than simply a distinction often noted between 1 Corinthians 3:10-15 and Ephesians 2:20; 3:5. In the first reference Paul is arguing for the way apostolic figures such as Apollos and others are to be regarded: they are servants who have the privilege of working together and building the foundation. Paul established the church at Corinth by his ministry of initial evangelism (Acts 18). Apollos came later (Acts 19:1) and consolidated the work. But, Paul goes on (1 Cor. 3:11), the laying of a foundation is really Christ's work, since neither Paul nor his fellow-missionaries are part of that foundation, which is restricted to Christ himself (1 Cor. 3:5). The verse in Ephesians 2:20, depending on its correct translation, envisages the foundation as the work of a corporate group, 'apostles and prophets', to whom was given peculiar insight into the 'mystery of Christ' (3:4). Paul's apostolate is held up to veneration in a way that seems to reflect a wistful looking back at the leaders of the primitive church as they are now seen as a specific number and the guarantors of the new society that rests on their witness (exactly as in Rev. 21:14).

(*iii*) We made reference earlier to the suggested background of Ephesians 2:14 in the Jerusalem Temple barrier. Since 1930, when H. Schlier's study on 'Christ and [the] Church in the Letter to the Ephesians' appeared,[4] a rival interpretation has been much canvassed, especially in Germany. The joining together of the several images in Ephesians 2:11-22 (the wall, the body, the new man, the building) seemed to Schlier to make sense only if the writer was deliberately drawing on a gnostic myth which features these images. This interpretation refers to the gnostic drama of a cosmic redeemer who breaks down the wall that separates the aeons that divide the heavenly *plērōma* from the earthly world. On this view, the allusion is to the gnostic redeemer's re-entry from the terrestrial zone (to which he has descended on his mission of enlightenment) to the celestial regions. He has gone back to the heavenly world, and his flight path — if we may use the modern term — necessitated a breaking down of all hindrances that stood in his route. He returns bringing with him his followers and members who had been imprisoned in the material world; they form now the new man, his body and they are sometimes referred to as a building.

But the author's use of this image of a barrier drawn from Gnosticism is part of his method of communicating the gospel to the people of his day. Unlike Paul who used the language and idioms of his opponents only to refute them, the author of Ephesians uses language of myth because it is part of his own audience's conceptual background, their mental furniture. Yet he does not share the gnosticising idea of the myth as a symbol of man's recovery of a divine destiny by ascent to the heavenly regions. On the contrary, his purpose is to proclaim an event in history, namely the abolishing of the Jewish law which divided Jews from Gentiles. These alienated peoples are now reconciled by an event in redemptive history. The author is using the myth as vehicle of communication but transcending its significance by a special application of its imagery.

There are other factors in Schlier's theory, interestingly discussed by W. Rader[5] who notes how the author of Ephesians was believed to have made common cause with Gnosticism in that both thought that the cosmological change had ontological effects. This conclusion marked a decisive turning point in Schlier's pilgrimage to the Roman Catholic church and its sacramental theology.

E. Käsemann[6] accepted Schlier's study of the setting of Ephesians 2:11-22 but without following his lead into Catholicism. Yet he also offered an understanding of the church as an ontological reality. He saw the significance of the gnostic myth as leading to an assertion that creation and redemption are joined in Christ. The effect on his doctrine of the church is to give a transcendental status to the body of Christ, suggesting thereby a type of ecclesiology removed from Paul who stresses repeatedly the earthly existence of the congregation which lives 'between the times' of creation and final redemption and anticipates its final glory in the future. In a later study[7] Käsemann has modified his view of the role of the church under gnostic influence, and yet he continues to see the ecclesiology of Ephesians as typical of an institutionalised Christianity which has subordinated christology to a 'high' view of the church. In this way Käsemann is able to acknowledge an important development in the ecclesiology of Ephesians, but also to relegate it to a post-Pauline era when a degeneration from the apostle's theology set in. Not surprisingly this position has been seriously challenged, notably by H. Merklein[8] who argued for the priority of christology in Ephesians and saw its teaching on the cosmic Christ who unites Jews and Gentiles in reconciliation by his death on the cross as its genius. So christology is expressed through Christ's saving work; only then is the nature of the church determined, in opposition to Käsemann's position.

The debate has raged on the possible gnostic influences on the author of the letter, with two major landmarks. (a) For writers such as E. Percy, Fr. Mussner, R. J. McKelvey, B. Gärtner, Markus Barth, and M. Wolter,[9] the Old Testament-rabbinic background to Ephesians 2:11-22 is adequate to provide an interpretative key. There is no need to go beyond the use of figures like Adam, the Gentile proselyte whose conversion to Judaism was regarded as his becoming a 'new man', and the new Temple in Enoch ch. 90 (and at Qumran with its restriction of the new age to the members of true Israel) as a sign of the new age for both Jews and Gentiles to explain how the writer's mind would and did work. The thrust of the argument in Ephesians 2:11-22 is most satisfactorily accounted for as leading to a conclusion about the place of Gentiles in the new Israel. The argument is based on rabbinic exegesis of the Old Testament and the hope extended to those 'afar off', to pagans that they may now 'come near', i.e. enter the new community. The breaking down of the barrier is most intelligibly understood, for these scholars, as an allusion to the Jewish law. The verb 'has broken down' (2:14) suggests a vertical barrier denoting a division between two groups of people living in this world rather than a horizontal division between the upper and lower worlds.

(b) E. Schweizer, in company with Schlier in his later commentary dated 1957, P. Pokorný and J. T. Sanders,[10] offered a mediating position with the reminder that already in the Jewish Dispersion of the first-century Judaism had become infected with gnosticising ideas. The figure of Adam in the biblical story, in particular, had become a cosmic idea, filling the universe, and this 'theology of the cosmos' is paralleled in what is known in Jewish speculation as it reinterpreted the traditional Jewish faith in terms borrowed from hellenistic thought-patterns. His chief argument against Schlier is that Gnosticism drove a wedge to set up an insuperable barrier between the higher and lower worlds. Ephesians, even when it uses this image, regards the two worlds as compatible, but its author moves decisively beyond Jewish-hellenistic 'cosmic theology' in relating reconciliation to Christ's death on the cross and the historical coming together of Jews and Gentiles. But these thoughts represent an advance on Paul's thinking and suggest a milieu where Christianity is more openly exposed to the influence of Judaeo-hellenistic speculation.

The gnostic 'cosmic man' hypothesis has suffered heavy criticism in recent years, and while there is still no consensus about the terms 'one new man' and the 'dividing wall' in our chapter, it looks certainly convincing to maintain that these terms can be viewed on an Old Testament-Judaic canvas. But it is an open question whether the situation they envisage is one that arose in Paul's lifetime or reflects more naturally a period in church history and growth when a multiracial church has appeared on the scene with the old distinctions of Jewish Christianity versus Gentile Christianity having dropped from view.

(*iv*) This brings us to a final section as we explore, however tentatively, the setting of Ephesians. One of the most fruitful contributions made by E. Käsemann arises from yet another way of accounting for what he regards as the use of gnostic language and concepts. We hope to show that his suggestion is not necessarily tied to his acceptance of Schlier's 'gnostic theory'.

Käsemann envisions a situation in which Gentile Christians were feeling a certain unease about the historical linkage of their faith with Israel and were rejecting the Jewish Christian emphasis of salvation history. To fill the vacuum created by this rejection of the Old Testament they were looking to timeless gnostic myths about creation and redemption. The net result was not only a severance of Gentile Christianity from its historical moorings but an effective dissolving of Christian community. Gnosticism as a religion had little room for the notion of a church. It spoke to the needs of individuals who were content to remain as enlightened individuals and be only loosely joined to others who shared their experience, but the church idea was alien to Gnosticism. This accounts for the author's insistence on the place of the church as the new creation, and also his bringing Jews and Gentiles into one body where each needs the other not only in the cosmos but in history. Ephesians, then, offers a sustained apologetic for the necessity of the church as a historical entity in which the Gentiles in particular have their place as part of redeemed creation with links connecting them to old Israel.

Even if we discount as unproven much of Käsemann's arguments that the author shows dependence on the gnostic 'redeemer myth' background, his is still a viable treatment of a suggested historical background to the letter. It would be hard to deny that the stress Ephesians makes on cosmic unity has in view the gnostic tenet that humanity is held in the grip of a relentless and pitiless fate. The letter states that God's plan embraces these cosmic powers — the aeons — which first-century man most feared (3:11). The divine purpose in Christ announces that those spiritual beings have lost their hold on men and women (1:3-10; 3:9f.) and that in raising his son from death's domain and placing under his feet the entire universe including these powers (1:20f.) God has given assurance that the secret of the universe lies in the cosmic Christ, not in timeless myths. The church too is exalted above these agents and need not fear their tyranny and malevolence (1:22; 2:1-10; 3:10; 6:10-12). The church as a universal society is freed from local restrictions and already glorified with a glory now bestowed on its head (1:21, which is logically connected with 2:1ff.). The eschatological dimension in Ephesians is more or less fully realised, and little remains of the 'reserve' or tension between 'already saved . . . not yet fully redeemed' which we have seen to be characteristic of Paul.

Yet certain Pauline problems, left unresolved in his lifetime as an active, pioneer missionary and church builder, are still with the author. The wheel of debate over Jewish-Gentile relations has turned to expose a new problem. In Paul's mid-career the issue was the Jewish acceptance of baptised pagans without circumcision; now it is the Gentile Christians' acceptance of the Jewish heritage of their new faith. Paul had to defend his kerygma against Jewish misrepresentation and distortion and the imposition of cultic practices; now his same proclamation is in danger of losing contact with history by the flight to timeless myths, and our epistle has to reinterpret Christ's work in the light of his cross and specific historical details, such as the emergence of 'one new man'. Paul had to deal drastically with the threat of a gnostic 'take-over' in Corinthians and Colossians as his gospel was in danger of becoming completely hellenised; now the Christian disciple has to reinterpret Paul's gospel to make it intelligible to men and women in hellenistic society and to take their language to convey the saving truth in Christ.

CONCLUSION

In sum, as we approach Ephesians 2:11-22, we should catch some undertones of controversy. Addressed to Gentile believers in a church now multiracial and transnational, this paragraph opens with a reminder that Jewish Christians are fellow-believers along with them (2:11). In a 'vigorous affirmation of the history of salvation', as Masson (see p. 181) calls it, this section states that formerly Gentiles were deprived of all that the messianic hope meant to Israel 'after the flesh'. 'But now' (the emphatic particle — *nuni de* — picks up a contrast with vv.11-12) they have been blessed through Israel's Messiah who has repaired and made good the deficiency of their uncovenanted and uncircumcised state (v. 13) and brought Jews and Gentiles together in a reconciled society (vv. 14-18) in which Gentiles suffer no lack (v. 19). The inference seems clear. The Gentiles who enjoy such privileges can never deny the Jewish heritage of the gospel without severing that gospel from its historical roots. We may suspect that this teaching is occasioned by wrong-headed notions entertained by Gentile Christians who, like those mentioned in Romans 11:18ff. but with greater vehemence, were 'in danger of absolutising their true and present situation, and beyond this, of forgetting the history of the gospel and of the promise', as Käsemann describes the situation. He goes on to illustrate the point by citing Ephesians 1:12*b*-14 which 'climax in the claim that the Gentiles participate in this redemption which properly belongs to Israel or to a holy remnant in Jewish Christianity'. The force of the author's argument is to insist that 'the church stands in continuity with the people of the old covenant; this continuity is demonstrated by Jewish Christianity'. So the main 'scope' of the passage (2:11-22) is to bring together two ideas. The writer has already established that the messianic hope has met all the needs of his Gentile readers who, though converted to Christ later in time than the Jewish believers (1:12-13), are in no way inferior on that account since they both share in the Spirit of messianic promise (1:13; 4:30). Now he must oppose and counteract any trace of Gentile arrogance and supposed independence by pointing to the creation of a new society in Messiah's reconciling work that respects both ethnic groups as mutually interdependent but lifts their relationship on to a higher plateau of something that either could not achieve without the other, by becoming 'one new man in place of two', a third race.

EPHESIANS 2:12-19

I

v. 12 Therefore remember
That you were at that time without Christ,
Alienated from the commonwealth of Israel,
And strangers to the covenants of promise
  [Having no hope
    and without God in the world].

II

v. 13 But now in Christ Jesus,
You who were once far removed
Have been brought near by the blood of Christ.

III

v. 14 [For] he is our peace,
Who has made both one
By destroying [the dividing wall of the fence]
  the hostility, in his flesh,
v. 15 [abolishing the law of commandments and ordinances]

IV

That he might create in him one new man [?making peace],
v. 16 And reconcile both in one body to God [through the cross],
Thereby killing the hostility in him.

V

v. 17   And he came and proclaimed peace
        To you who were far removed,
        And peace to those near.

VI

v. 18   For through him
        We both have access in one spirit
        To the Father.

VII

v. 19   Now then you are no more strangers and sojourners;
        But you are fellow-citizens with the (Jewish) saints,
        And members of the household of God.

THE LITERARY STRUCTURE OF THE PASSAGE

Set out in the way we have adopted, this section is seen to be cast in poetic and rhythmic form. This conclusion, with variations as to the exact details of arrangement of the verses, is generally conceded ever since G. Schille's pioneering study in 1965.[11] His discussion of Ephesians 2:14-18 as part of 'Early Christian Hymns' drew attention to many unusual literary features in the passage, especially the presence of several couplets and, above all, its confessional character. It traces the course of the redeemer's mission as a 'bringer of peace' by way of the cross to his triumph, and runs parallel with Philippians 2:6-11 which, like this 'hymn of the redeemer', ends with the Father's presence (v. 18). Schille paid tribute to earlier suggestions offered by Haupt, Ewald and Dibelius who labelled the section (vv. 14-18) an excursus, though the hymn-like character had been observed ever since Bengel: 'by the tenor of their words and a kind of rhythm [these lines] resemble a hymn or a song', Bengel commented as far back as 1742 in his *Gnomon*.

The setting out of the lines by Schille has been severely criticised, notably by R. Deichgräber.[12] As we have offered a variant form of hymnic structure it may be well to make some comment. J. T. Sanders sums up the essential features of a hymnic composition suggestively found in 2:14ff.

The hymnic elements here are prominent. Participial predications, as well as the opening predication on the pattern *autos estin* ('he is'), the heavy use of participles, the *parallelismus membrorum* [or couplets] . . . , and the cosmic language all lend support to the conclusion that this passage is a hymn. The beginning and end are clearly marked off by the frame provided by the quotation from Isa. 57:19 in v. 17 and the anticipation of this quotation by the mention of the far and the near in v. 13.[13]

Also we may observe the switch from the 'we-style' (in vv. 14-16 where the Christ-hymn is concentrated) to 'you' at verses 17, 19.

Deichgräber's objections are: (*a*) not every christological fragment is to be classifed as a Christ-hymn, a point to be granted since we are suggesting that only verses 14-16 may be a hymn addressed to Christ; (*b*) 'the completely prosaic character of the section' is evident, he maintains, but it is hard to justify that description, given the rare terms and rhetorical features present; (*c*) 'the inordinate length of the lines' is held to go against the classifying of a hymn here, but according to the analysis we have submitted, with later additions suggested — as distinct from Schille's deletion of phrases such as 'the hostility' (v. 14), 'having killed the enmity in him' (v. 16), 'you' (v. 17), 'both in one spirit' (v. 18) — the lines are much more uniform and symmetrical.

There is a suggestion, obviously the most ambitious of all proposals to be made regarding the literary form of Ephesians 2, that verses 11-22 are built up in an elaborate series of parallelisms. J. C. Kirby[14] argues for this as part of his overall thesis that in chapters 1-3 we should see a lengthy statement of thanksgiving to God (called by its Jewish name, *berakah*) offered as a transcript of a Pentecost festival celebration by the church at Ephesus. Within that liturgical framework, 2:11-22 is an independent unit, made up of an elaborate chiasmus where lines A to K are then reversed in the order K[1]-A[1] with verse 15 coming at the centre point. K. E. Bailey[15] proposes a similar arrangement but with seven divisions within the material; the centre is also verse 15 in his construction. Finally G. Giavini[16] follows the same pattern, noting that there is an inverted order of parallelism, while verses 14-16 interrupt this inverted pattern with an extended section of step parallelism.

Some of these arrangements suggest a fanciful structure and are known more for their ingenuity rather than for the straightforward reading of the text. This is not to infer that a poetic formation may not be seen in the way the lines are written. But we must have respect to the content of the lines as well to rhetorical features which are detected in some attempts at elaborate periodisation. It is a wiser course to base arguments to do with the literary form of a passage on the teaching in the section more than on the presence of rhetorical forms.

There are two questions before us in trying to reach a firm conclusion regarding the form-analysis of 2:12-19. The first matter is to know whether verses 14-16 (or 14-18) formed originally a separate hymn devoted to the theme of 'peace', or 'reconciliation', or in praise of the redeemer as Schille and Pokorný call it. This raises a related question: Was the section composed by another hand and inserted into the text by the writer of Ephesians, who added certain supplementary phrases, partly to augment and partly to correct the existing hymn?

(*i*) We may dispose of a prior question fairly easily. It looks evident that verses 12 and 19 go together since they are both full of step parallelism while, when they are set side by side, they offset each other in inverted order. Thus:

STANZA I	STANZA VII
1 That at that time you were *without Christ*	3¹ And members of the *household of God*
2 Alienated from the commonwealth of *Israel*	2¹ But you are fellow-citizens with the (*Jewish*) *saints*
3 And *strangers* to the covenants of promise	1¹ Now that you are no more *strangers* and sojourners

The author of Ephesians, if he borrowed this set of contrasts from a traditional source, has amplified the verdict 'without Christ' by adding 'having no hope and without God in the world' — a thought derived from 2:3 and repeated in 4:18 as an indictment of Gentile evils and penalties.

The question is still under debate whether, even if the unusual literary characteristics of a hymnic passage are conceded, it is necessary to see Ephesians 2:14-18 as a separate and cited hymn; or has the author of the letter formulated an 'excursus' as earlier commentators thought and as later writers such as R. Deichgräber, P. Stuhlmacher and M. Wolter have maintained?[17] The issue really turns on the prior question of whether an original hymn written in celebration of cosmic peace has been taken over by the Ephesian editor, either completely or with suitable modifications (so Käsemann, Lührmann[18]). Or does the passage stand in direct continuity with Paul's teaching with many of its features paralleled in the apostle's call to unity in the church (1 Cor. 12:13; Gal. 3:26-28; 5:6; 6:15; Col. 3:10-11; and especially Rom. 3:30f.; 12:5; 2 Cor. 5:17 — all cited and considered by Wolter who regards the chief emphasis to fall on the 'new creation')? The latter term is used of both Jewish and Christian conversion in traditional teaching and is given a sociological and racial application by the writer of Ephesians who, however, stays within the framework of Jewish presuppositions based on the meaning of Isaiah 57:16ff.

The list of agreements with Paul's earlier teaching looks impressive at first glance, but we shall have to query a simple development from Paul shortly. It seems more in line with the data to suppose that the writer has in fact taken over a pre-Pauline hellenistic hymn of cosmic transformation and in keeping with (*a*) a new situation in the church and (*b*) his perception of Paul's soteriology of the cross, recast it by important additions.[19]

(*ii*) Stanzas II and IV-V are linked by a common treatment of the contrast 'afar off/brought near' drawn from Isaiah 57:19. One of the most thorough expositions of the use of the Old Testament in this passage begins with the recognition that the contrast was first applied to the nation of Israel and then to Jewish proselytes who were 'brought near' to Torah in conversion; but our author in Ephesians has taken it considerably farther, as we shall see (pp. 188-191). The application, H. Sahlin contends,[20] is to the true Israel, the Christian church. The blood shed in the Jewish convert's circumcision is now replaced by Christ's blood shed on the cross (v. 13: see Col. 2:11) or possibly shed in his babyhood circumcision (Luke 2:21). So when a Christian receives the counterpart of Jewish circumcision, i.e. in baptism, he shares in all the benefits obtained by Christ's death. The upshot is that baptism renders the distinctive mark of Judaism, i.e. circumcision, obsolete; and the member of the 'true' Israel is brought near as part of the new community which supersedes Israel 'after the flesh' (2:11). The scriptural justification for this claim is a *midrash pesher*, or interpretative commentary, on Isaiah 57:19, modelled on the practice at Qumran of bringing old scriptures up-to-date by relating them to the contemporary scene. Proponents of this line of interpretation,

such as K. G. Kuhn,[21] rely heavily on the Jewish setting of the
text and oppose any recourse to gnostic imagery, as we saw.
They find many striking parallels in the texts of the Dead Sea
scrolls that speak of God's habitation set on a rock (1QS 8:4-10;
1QH 6:25-27, as in Eph. 2:20-22), the entrance of the community as a 'coming near' (1QS 6:16, 22, 11:13) and the exclusion of
'aliens' and 'strangers' from the new Temple (4QFlor 1:1-7; cf.
11Q Temple 29:8-10). The 'holy ones' or 'saints' are permitted
to dwell in the house for ever, in association with the angels (1QS
9:7f.; 1QH 3:21ff.). This background is very suggestive, but
there is no final proof that our author is consciously in debate
with Qumran exclusivism or even indebted to such traditions,
save as these contrasts may well have been part and parcel of
Judaic thought in his world-view and may reflect perhaps some
animosity to incoming Gentiles or even a reaction to Gentile
pride (see pp. 191f.).

(*iii*) Our chief interest focuses on 2:14-16 (= strophes III, IV)
for this is the heart of the message of reconciliation. Our
submission is that the author has taken over a pre-formed
hymnic celebration, called maybe a 'song of reconciliation' (so
Wengst) and adapted it to his purposes. The original version
centred on Christ the peace-maker who united Jew and Gentile
to God and destroyed in his flesh the hostility directed at God —
a sentiment quite in line with Paul's teaching in Romans 5:1-11,
where 'hostility' carries this sense. The establishing of 'peace'
(twice repeated, vv. 14-15) matches the achievement of Romans
5:1, 'we have peace with God'; but the reconciling ministry is
located 'in one body' which is left undefined. The Pauline author
has sensed the danger with this lack of concrete and specific
detail and has slipped in an addition — 'through the cross',
repeating what Paul did to earlier hymns in Philippians 2:8 and
Colossians 1:20. The reason for this suspicion about the phrase
'through the cross' being a later addition is that (*a*) the line is
already overloaded with awkward syntax; (*b*) the passage from
verse 15 looks to be dependent on Colossians 2:14-15 which has
supplied the reference to the cross; (*c*) the analogy with
Colossians 1:20 is close where, as we saw (p. 121), Paul has
added a characteristic corrective to ground the reconciliation in
the cross. Our author is recapitulating this emphasis, led to it by
reminiscences of 'peace' in both texts. He is making even clearer
the link between reconciliation and Christ's work on the cross,
and not simply as achieved by his incarnation (v. 14: 'in his

flesh', which if borrowed from Col. 1:22 omits 'by his death').

The two other suggested additions to an existing hymn are striking, since as we shall go on to see they orient the direction of the author's thought and argument in a new course. We shall discuss their significance in the next section, and include here simply the reason for believing them to be additions. The phrases in question are:

v. 14: and the dividing wall of the fence
v. 15: abolishing the law of commandments [expressed] in ordinances

The main point to observe is the way in which the term 'hostility' is used in a type of couplet (*parallelismus membrorum*) connecting verses 14 and 16. In both instances the immediate antecedent is the forming of two (groups) into one. The matching lines run as follows:

v. 14: he has made the two (*ta amphotera*) one . . . overcoming the hostility, in his flesh.
v. 16: he reconciled the two (*tous amphoterous*) in one body to God [through the cross] killing the hostility in him.

In the light of the preceding context with its mention of Christ's blood (a cultic-sacrificial term) it would be natural to interpret the hostility of verse 14 as man's enmity to God which Christ's coming in the flesh destroyed. This is then repeated in verse 16 as an act of reconciliation *to God*. The interpreting phrases 'in his flesh' (v. 14) and 'in him' (v. 16) go together. As we noted above, there is no specific reference to how the reconciliation is achieved. The allusion to 'the two'/'the both' has been taken to recall a vestige of a cosmic myth by which heaven and earth were brought together (so Schlier). N. A. Dahl[22] traces the term to a reunion of male and female, but of this myth there is little trace in the context and the discussion of Ephesians 5:31-32 is far removed from this section. The two parties are most likely God and humankind who, as typified in Gentile alienation (vv. 12-13), were opposed to God and are now united by Christ's taking human form.

A parallel thought is found in verses 15b-16. The object of redemption is to create — in the sense of Ephesians 2:10, 'created in Christ Jesus' — 'one new person' by reuniting the two, heaven and earth or God and man, in a way that produces peace between them. The necessary requirement was that the existing hostility should be 'killed' by being absorbed 'in him', referring to his incarnate body, as a line of interpreters from Chrysostom to Bengel and on to E. Percy and H. Schlier in the modern period has maintained.

We should emphasise that *this looks to be the original intention of the hymnic passage*. Its purpose is to describe the effect of cosmic peace, now wrought between God and humankind as by Christ's taking human nature the rift is closed in a reconciliation that now brings together the alienated parties. The 'one body' corresponds to 'the one new man', i.e. the redeemer who embodies both sides and neutralises the enmity in his own person, perhaps in the same way as is described in 2 Corinthians 5:18, 21.

The author's taking over this tribute to mankind's reconciliation has not left the text untouched. The signs of his additions seem to us to be clear, as evidenced by unusual and cumbersome syntax. His intention has been to achieve two goals: (*a*) to rewrite the hostility to make it include the human relations between Jews and Gentiles who were divided by all that is meant by 'the fence'; and (*b*) to state what the 'hostility' meant in an appositional phrase, 'the law of commandments and ordinances', which is thereby 'abolished'. 'Broken down' (*lysas*) and 'abolished' (*katargēsas*) are clearly parallel, and in the revised edition of the hymn these works of demolition refer specifically to Christ's removing the barrier that kept the races apart. That barrier is the legalism engendered by Israel's devotion to Torah as its own peculiar privilege and its consequent separation from other nations. The upshot of these insertions is to turn the 'first version' of the hymn into a proclamation of the redeemer's work in uniting disparate human groups by removing the offensive item that kept them apart

How far the author believed that in their being reconciled to God (a pre-Pauline conviction) they would thereby become reconciled to each other (the author's novel extension of Paul's earlier teaching) is not clear. Certainly his attitude to the law moves beyond that of Paul in two ways. He has a more sinister understanding of Torah as an alienating force driving Jews and Gentiles into mutual animosity. And he has a more radicalised view of what Christ did to destroy the law. Paul, to be sure, regarded Torah as a stumbling block on the road to God (e.g. Rom. 11:32), and he wrote emphatically of Christ's saving obedience unto death as bringing the law to its end or goal (Rom.

10:4; cf. Gal. 3:24-25). But the law is not undermined (Rom. 3:31), and it is still required of Christians to fulfil it, in spirit at least (Rom. 13:8-10; Gal. 5:14; 6:2). Our author, given a new situation in the church, urges on his readers the reminder that the day of Jewish particularism is now over and that access to the Father is open to 'those who were near' (Jews) and those who were once 'at a distance' (Gentiles). Both receive the same message of peace (v. 17) and both — now 'one body' in the church (as in Eph. 1:23; 3:6; 4:4; 5:30) — are co-members of the same community that shares privileges formerly known only to one member (vv. 18-19).

On literary grounds, therefore, stanza III is complemented by stanza V, with common catchwords such as 'peace'/'proclaimed peace' in corresponding lines. The baneful effects of division are replaced by a union of the two parties. Stanza VI carries forward the story of the benefits received; it is based on Romans 5:1-2 but reinterpreted to include both Jews and Gentiles in their free access to the Father.

The author evidently also knows well the text of Colossians as is clear from his indebtedness to Colossians 1:15-20; 2:14-15. Finally, one provocative study sees in Ephesians 2:14-16 a third section of a Christian hymn whose first two strophes have been preserved in Colossians 1:15-17 and 18-20.

The arrangement runs like this:

Strophe I: The unity of all things in creation (Col. 1:15-17)
Strophe II: The unity of all things in redemption (Col. 1:18-20)
Strophe III: The unity of the races in the church (Eph. 2:14-16)

E. Testa suggests an overarching title for the entire composition, called appropriately enough: 'Jesus the Universal Peacemaker'.[23]

Such is the nature of the evidence at our disposal that this theory as to the genesis of a single christological statement, of which we have three parts surviving, can neither be proved conclusively nor denied outright. The attractiveness of the theory is that the threefold statement did set a pattern for later credal and liturgical praise, as we see in 1 Clement and the Apostolic Tradition of Hippolytus (c. AD 215) where the great eucharisitic prayer celebrates God's acts in creation, redemption and the church. The difficulty comes in imagining the creation of such a unitary composition when it seems clear that the focus on God's reconciling activity in the three areas was produced only by some response to misunderstanding and wrong emphasis — and that needed emerging historical circumstances. To investigate such proposed conditions that led to the composing of Ephesians 2:11-22 in the light of traditional forms and the author's redacting of them to meet current needs is our next task.

THE RECONCILIATION BASED ON UNITY
INTRODUCTION

The centre of the section's argument is in verse 14: 'He is our peace, who has made [us] both one' ('us' in RSV is not in the Greek). This is a single programmatic statement, since it combines within itself a number of elements drawn from the surrounding context. These may be tabulated: (*i*) the underlying alienation of men and women as human beings *coram Deo* has been remedied in the death of Israel's Messiah; (*ii*) the enmity between Jews and Gentiles has thereby been overcome and neutralised; (*iii*) these disparate segments of the first-century world are now called to a harmonious amity within the fellowship of the Christian church; and (*iv*) both Jews and Gentiles in losing their ethnic privilege gain something in return which our author regards as far better, namely a place in Christ's body, and as Christ's body this society forms a new race of men and women. Their newly acquired privileges are given as reconciliation to God which includes access to God through Christ, a place in God's family and a future as the eschatological Temple of God.

But these benefits are to be enjoyed only in the mutual society of all God's people, and this confirms our earlier statement that what comes to the newly created society is richer than what was possible while Jews and Gentiles were separate and divided. Not only do Gentiles find in their 'reconciliation' a change from hostility to friendship in the vertical dimension as they are 'brought near in the blood of Christ'. They come to share on the horizontal plane the inheritance of Israel but at a deeper level; and together with Israel they enter into a new relationship with God by uniting with Israel. This is implied in the terms 'one new man in place of the two' (v. 15) and 'we both (*amphoteroi*) have access in one Spirit to the Father' (v. 18), as well as by the announcement of a 'mystery' hitherto not known to either Jews or Gentiles but now evident in Pauline Christianity: 'that the Gentiles are fellow-heirs, members of the same body, and partakers of the promise in Christ Jesus through the gospel' (3:6). This new order of relationship has been well set out in recent discussion. We may select one example which states the matter with unusual clarity. Karl Martin Fischer writes:[24]

> The thesis of the Ephesian letter is both clear and unequivocal: Israel is God's people and had the covenant promises, which the Gentiles did not have. But the astounding miracle has happened in that Christ has pulled down the wall between Gentile and Jew, which is the law with its commands, and in this way he has opened for the Gentiles a way to God in the one church. But the church is not simply a continuation of Israel, 'a Judaism without restrictions' (*ein entschränktes Judentum*); rather it is something completely new, a 'new man' (2, 15). It is the heir of Israel in both its promises and covenant. The history of Israel is also the church's history. We should think of both continuity and discontinuity in equal measure. There is the continuity of the promise but discontinuity of its realisation. Not that there are two covenants, one old, the other new; but there are two partners in the covenant, old and new. . . .
>
> The Christian is indebted for his existence, his passage from death to life, above all to God's grace (Eph. 2, 7). That means for the Gentile as for the Jew a truly new beginning . . . [not only] for the erstwhile Gentile but implicitly also for the erstwhile Jew . . . since circumcision and the law cannot any longer be conditions of salvation.

The steps by which this new network of relationships both with God and with each other was attained may now be considered.

(i) *The Double Structure.* This phrase is helpfully used by both Stuhlmacher and Wolter to indicate the two-dimensional interest of this writing. The author wants seemingly to run together the 'reconciliation to God' and the merging into one body in Christ, the church of two early Christian groups who otherwise were kept apart by ethnic and religious barriers as well as by sociological and racial divisions. The primary question is, Which thought of reconciliation has priority not so much in time as in importance and theological weight in his mind? In other words, is the 'hostility' (v. 16) which makes the reconciliation necessary an enmity between men and women and God or between Jews and Gentiles? A number of commentators refuse to commit themselves in answer to what they believe to be an unreal question. W. Foerster in regard to one aspect of the passage's 'double aspect' concludes:

> We hardly do justice to the passage if we do not perceive that the Law plays a double role, dividing the Gentiles from the commonwealth of Israel and also Israel from God.[25]

And it follows that there is a twofold cause of alienation. Gentiles are separated from God (v. 12; referring back to 2:1-3); and the law both keeps non-Jews from Israel, as 3 Maccabees 3:3-4 illustrates: 'The Jews continued to maintain their goodwill towards kings . . . yet worshipping God, and living according to his law, they held themselves apart in the matter of [kosher] food; and for this reason they were disliked by some,' and also acts as a barrier to fellowship between God and man as a sinner (Rom. 7:7-25; Gal. 3:19ff.) — so the restoration is double-sided. Peace is established in the church as the body of Christ produces a new fellowship between God and man and at the same time a new fellowship which forgiven and reconciled people may enjoy with one another. The paraenetic or hortatory sections in Ephesians chapters 4-6 show how the latter works out in the life of the congregation and in the attitude of the congregation to the world.

If we recall the earlier suggestions made as to the historical setting of the letter, then this teaching on reconciliation between Jews and Gentiles would have a particularly pointed application in the period of post-AD 70, characterised as it was, in Stuhl-macher's words,[26] by 'ancient anti-semitism' on the one hand, and 'Jewish contempt of pagans' on the other. The overcoming of this animosity *on both sides* through Christ the reconciler in the church would serve as a model to the ancient world of the 'real' reconciliation between God and humankind typified in the contemporary society's yearning for 'peace'.

When the matter of priority — racial harmony or soteriolog-ical relation to God — is pressed, it seems clear that the Ephesian author's basis is God's action in Christ the reconciler of sinners. He has apparently anchored an earlier tribute to world redemption firmly in the cross and sacrifice of the human Jesus; and from that event he extrapolates the teaching of its effect upon society. For all his interest in the church as an ecumenical and cosmic reality he never permits its origin in salvation history to be obscured or minimised, and salvation history implies the death of the reconciler.

A writer's attitude to the interpretative and form-critical issues will tip the scale in the direction of what he decides regarding the primary intention of the passage. E. Käsemann, following H. Schlier, is not involved in that particular debate and categorically declares that the hymn represents a product of 'that particular segment of the church which created hymns in praise of Christ as cosmic Victor'.[27] Earlier in his essay he had located the precise life-setting of these hymns: 'For the NT hymns are predominantly witnesses of the unbridled enthusiasm which is characteristic of the earliest Hellenistic community and the beginning of its world mission.' He wants to see in the message of cosmic reconciliation and the (gnostic) message of global peace a starting point from which Christians drew conclusions to do with the unity of mankind and so to see the 'unity of the church' as an example of that oneness. For Käsemann the hymns of Colossians and Ephesians say little about personal or ethnic reconciliation and are dedicated to the (false) enthusiastic notion of world dominion entrusted to the hands of the exalted Lord; their accent is doxological and celebratory, not soteriological or ecclesiological. So the quesion of the author's use of tradition or the influence of Isaiah 57:19 does not arise; and 'the reconciliation' is a gnostic term. Wolter[28] points out that Käsemann has overlooked that in 2:16 the teaching is one of reconciliation *to God*. In an earlier discussion (pp. 75-9) we have sought to show disagreement with Käsemann's thesis and the reasons for such a negative verdict.

So the question remains: Is it sinners who are primarily the subjects of reconciliation or Jews and Gentiles in racial and religious tension? That issue can only be fully commented on once we have moved on to consider the other parts of the exegetical problem.

(*ii*) *The Wall of Separation*. We are building on our previous discussion and conclusion that in the earlier version of the hymn or the tradition known to the author the hostility was man's animosity to God which Christ's incarnation overcame by 'killing' it. The writer gives a horizontal application of this reconciliation by relating to the 'dividing fence' which kept Jews and non-Jews in separate compartments of religious and social life. Three possibilities are suggested for the author's meaning.

(a) He may have had the Temple wall in mind, as his phrase parallels Josephus' description of a notice posted on the wall around the Court of Women. In 1871 M. Clermont-Ganneau found one of the pillars mentioned in *Ant.* 5:417/*Jewish War* 5:194 (cf. Acts 21:27ff.); the inscription reads:

> No man of another race is to enter within the fence (*dryphaktos*, Heb. *sôreg*) and enclosure around the Temple. Whoever is caught will have only himself to thank for the death which follows.

This fence and its pointed warning served to remind the non-Jews that they must keep their distance from Israel's sacred shrine. The fear of trespass was very real, as we can see from Paul's difficulty in Acts 21; and the Romans respected the right of Jews to retain the sanctity of the enclosure on the Temple mount.

The obvious advantage of this background is that it picks up the early designation of the Gentiles as 'alienated from the commonwealth of Israel' (2:12), and accounts for the highly emphasised liabilities belonging to the Gentiles as 'strangers and sojourners'. These restrictions (in v. 19) are reversed as the Gentiles are brought into the 'house of God' and made sharers in the new Temple (vv. 21-22).

The 'historical interpretation' would find endorsement in Charles Perrot's theory[29] that at the back of Ephesians 2:11-22 as a whole lies a synagogue lectionary reading of Exodus 21:1-22:23. This 'book of the covenant' passage treats the theme of the Gentiles who come to live in Israel's land. A corresponding lectionary reading from the Prophets is Isaiah 56:1-9; 57:19, which relates also to the Gentiles and Israel. Exodus 21:8 and 22:21 specify two groups, 'foreigners' and 'strangers' — the same titles given to Gentiles in Ephesians 2:19, and the same words applicable to non-Jews who enter the Temple mount area. The Isaiah lectionary (56:3) has the Gentile exclaiming, 'Yahweh will surely separate me from his people'; and the sight of the Jerusalem sanctuary would remind any observant pagan that here was a place from which they were excluded and where they were not wanted.

With the fall of Jerusalem in AD 70 all this dramatically changed, and our text is offering a *midrash* on the lectionary readings in the light of the new age that came with Israel's

Messiah and the new historical situation that followed on the quietus of Israel's liturgical worship in the second Temple. The barrier, both in its visible symbol of the fence and what gave the fence its validity, 'the law of commandments and ordinances', is now broken down and abolished. But of course even if we are correct in supposing a situation post-AD 70, the law was not then abolished. Judaism lived on, to be reconstituted at Jamnia and to be reborn in Pharisaism. All the text is saying, therefore, is that access to God is no longer restricted to the Jewish cultus since for both Gentiles who were never in Israel's fold and Christian Jews who have witnessed the official 'end' of their most venerable institution in Torah and Temple, religion is set on a new basis of a free approach to God 'in the spirit' (vv. 18, 22). So in a real way restored fellowship with God for both groups means a new beginning in their mutual attitudes. Out of the two segments of humanity emerges a new people. H. Chadwick's description[30] of the situation, that 'Gentile Christianity emerges as universal Judaism' hardly takes the matter far enough. 'A new creation by God' builds on the past but speaks of a reality greater than and different from either antecedent in the Gentile world or in Judaism.

(b) M. Dibelius asked a question of this interpretation: Would the Gentile readers living in Asia Minor have understood the allusion? We can return a more confident answer to his query than Dibelius' contemporaries were free to do, because since the publication of the Dead Sea scrolls we know how widely Jewish sectarian influences, seen in the scrolls and paralleled in documents circulating in Roman Asia (e.g. Colossians, the letters of John, the Apocalypse, Ignatius' letters, Odes of Solomon), had spread. The presence of a strong Jewish contingent in Asia since the time of Antiochus III (early 2nd cent. BC) is attested by Josephus (*Ant.* 12:147-153) and seen in tomb inscriptions. It is not improbable that any intelligent pagan in Asia would have contact with Jewish matters, and would be aware that the Temple area contained an inner shrine not accessible to any but worshipping Jews (cf. Antiochus' decree, reported in Josephus, *Ant.* 12: 145, 146). On the other hand, there is no certainty that such an illusion would have been known to — or appreciated by — the readers of this letter, living in Roman Asia. For that reason this specific background has often been denied (by Haupt, C. Schneider in Kittel's *Dictionary*, Ch. Masson[31] following Dibelius) and the emphasis placed elsewhere, namely on a removal of the enmity between God and man.

So the question lingers, and it has given rise to an alternative suggestion regarding the meaning of the wall. This is the theory that Ephesians 2 makes use of a myth which describes the ascent through the heavenly regions of the gnostic redeemer to the Father of All. The bold outline of this mythical saga has already been referred to, but it should be mentioned here in view of Karl Martin Fischer's recent attempt to set it on a firmer basis in the light of the Nag Hammadi texts from upper Egypt.[32] Fischer's entire treatise seeks to understand the message and purpose of Ephesians in this way, namely as drawing on the same world-view as was later (2nd cent. AD) documented in these newly-published Gnostic texts. The common denominator is a christianised syncretism in which Christian (= Pauline) elements mingled with current ideas drawn from hellenistic and oriental religious experience.

Fischer makes four points by way of comparison. (*a*) *The cosmic division*. In his view the 'separating wall' parallels what is basic to gnostic thought, namely 'the absolute division between the upper world of light and the lower world of darkness. Between the true heaven, the home of the gnostic, and the earth . . . lies a clear division'. The return of the gnostic to his true home is made possible only as he 'passes through' — as did the redeemer — the regions, where 'passwords' give the right of access. The myth of a redeemed redeemer is found in no one place, but Fischer appeals to *The First Apocalypse of James* as evidence of an ascent to heaven, with 'passwords' found in *The Gospel of Thomas*, 50 (cf. Origen, *Against Celsus* 6:31). (*b*) *The return to unity*. Again we are in touch with a typically gnostic idea. The beginning of man's fall was his 'division', seen in Eve's separation from Adam (*The Gospel of Philip*, 68: 'When she (Eve) was separated from him death came into being. If he again becomes complete and attains his former self, death will be no more.'). In a later section of *The Gospel of Philip*, 70, Eve's mortality is traced to her separation from Adam, and it is said that 'his separation became the beginning of death'. Then a Christian flavour is given to the myth of gnostic Adam: 'Christ came to repair the separation . . . and again to unite the two, and to give life to those who died as a result of the separation and unite them.' Chapter 71 goes on: 'He (who was) redeemed [the gnostic Jesus] in turn redeemed (others).' Fischer appeals to the tractate *The Thunder, Perfect Mind*, 19, where in a fractured text the redeemer announces, 'I am the union and the dissolution.'

(c) *The cancelling of enmity.* The overcoming of hostile spirit-powers is part of the drama of the redeemer's return to heaven as he pierces the dividing wall. Sometimes, as in the tractate *On the Origin of the World*, 126-127,

> the aeons are overthrown . . . they will fall (down) to the abyss and the [abyss] will be overthrown. The light will [cover the] darkness, and it will wipe it out. It will become like one which had not come into being. And the work which the darkness followed will be dissolved . . . And the glory of the unbegotten will appear, and it will fill all the aeons . . .

the end of cosmic disturbance is put in highly dramatic language. The redeemer's enemies are defeated in a final confrontation and overthrow.

(d) *The near and the far.* Ostensible as is the citation from Isaiah 57:19 in our passage, the idea of 'a bringing near' — a movement by which chaotic elements in the universe were pacified and subdued by the gnostics — also has its parallels in 'Naassene-preaching' (quoted in Hippolytus, *Ref.* 5. 7. 9-20). Fischer grants that in Ephesians the cosmic setting of the redeemer myth has been applied to the church and its unity; but his main point is to assert that the death of Jesus is used not in a Pauline, soteriological sense but in a way that simply overcomes man's mortality. So it carries a virtual docetic sense, as in the famous passage of the 'laughing Saviour' in *The Second Treatise of the Great Seth*, 56. There Jesus only appears to suffer on the cross, Simon of Cyrene dies in his place, and Jesus stands by 'laughing at their ignorance'. To be sure, the author of Ephesians opposes this blatant denial of a real death, but unlike Paul for whom the cross was the centre of the Christian soteriology, the Ephesian author uses the death of Jesus simply to correct the mythical cosmology and to do so in the direction of a highly developed piece of ecclesiology. 'The near and the far' contrast relates to the church, Fischer contends, and not to the reconciliation of sinners to God.

Reaction to Fischer's theory from those who deny at base the validity of the gnostic redeemer story as a key to New Testament christology has been predictably vigorous. We may single out one such response.

M. Wolter has levelled two serious criticisms against this

refurbishing of Schlier's and Käsemann's theory of the gnostic 'barrier' broken down by the heavenly Man. First, it is selective of the evidence it appeals to, rewriting the Ephesians text to suit its own purpose and (it may be added) overlooking the elements of distinctively Christian content that are essential to the text. Secondly, Fischer has not really reconstructed a gnostic hymn from the text but only individual sentences for which he finds parallels in the Nag Hammadi documents. Nowhere are these brought together to form a compact 'myth' or drama. The argument is by inference, not direct evidence. These criticisms seem cogent, and would have the net effect of eliminating any direct dependence of our passage on the later gnostic heavenly Man myth — assuming that it *did* exist, as R. Reitzenstein confidently asserted. But his reconstruction has been seriously questioned ever since C. Colpe's review of the 'history of religions school'.[33] Not even the more recent data from the Nag Hammadi library, especially *The Apocalypse of Adam* tractate, give positive evidence of a pre-Christian redemption myth untouched by Christian influences.

(*c*) In its place Wolter and others such as Mussner, Masson and Stuhlmacher turn back to an understanding that stays within the framework of the rabbinic Judaism. This view has the merit of combining the phrases 'dividing wall of the fence' — itself an unusual compound (*to mesotoichon tou phragmou*) — with 'the law of commandments (expressed in ceremonial) ordinances'.

The text of verse 15 is just as obscure. 'Abolishing in his flesh the law of commandments (contained in) ordinances' has several ambiguities. There is an obvious link with Colossians 1:22 ('In his body of flesh by his death' Christ reconciled believers, a reference that may be explained by 2:11, if that means that Christ's 'circumcision' was his surrendering his 'flesh' (= mortal nature) to evil powers; see p. 41). The 'flesh' (*sarx*) of Christ was then more than his incarnate existence (Rom. 1:3; 1 Tim. 3:16; cf. John 1:14; 1 John 4:2); it implies his identity with sin on the cross, as in 2 Corinthians 5:21; Romans 8:3.

'The law (*nomos*) of commandments' evidently refers to the Jewish Torah and its *miṣwôt*; it is important to remember that this word 'law' is lacking in the entire Colossian letter, though Jewish legalism is often thought to be part of the Colossian threat (based on 2:14, 16). 'Ordinances' (*dogmata*) comes from Colossians 2:14 rendered 'legal demands' in RSV but implying not so much Torah requirements as cultic prohibitions based on the ascetic way of life (Col. 2:20, 'Why do you submit to regulations?' [*dogmatizesthe*]). It looks as though the Ephesian writer has taken over words used pejoratively in Colossians and applied them to the Torah seen as a barrier to Christian experience.

The Jewish law and its scribal interpretation then acted as a protection of Israel from paganism and syncretism but also served to drive a wedge between Israel and her pagan neighbours. Mussner combines the metaphorical reference to 'the dividing wall' (= the law) with the historical allusion to the Temple notice, and others such as Ewald suggested the barricade of ghetto walls. But it is conceded that the metaphorical application has the advantage of being able to gain support from documentary evidence which used the term 'fence' of the law. In specific terms, 'the dividing wall' matches 'hostility' as the 'fence' is explained by 'the law of commands contained in rules' — if these verses are not simply another example of piling up synonyms, as Percy suggests.

The three passages in the second-century BC *Letter of Aristeas* are germane to this matter:

> When therefore our lawgiver [Moses], equipped by God for insight into all things, had surveyed each particular, he fenced us about (*periephraxen hēmas*) with impenetrable palisades (*charaxi*) and with walls of iron (*sidērois teichesis*) to the end that we should mingle in no way with any of the other nations, remaining pure in body and in spirit . . . worshipping the one Almighty God above the whole creation (139).
> And therefore, so that we should be polluted by none nor be infected with perversions by associating with worthless persons, he has hedged us about on all sides (*pantothen hēmas periephraxen*) with prescribed purifications in matters of food and drink and touch and hearing and sight (142).
> We must perform all our actions with discrimination according to the standard of righteousness — more especially because we are separated from all men (151).

At face value the points of contact between Ephesians 2:14-15 and this description of Jewish particularism, using a metaphor of the law as a protecting fence, seen also in Mishnah Aboth 1:1,2 ('make a fence for Torah'), 3:18 ('Tradition is a fence for Torah') as well as Isaiah 5:2, LXX; Proverbs 28:4, LXX: 'those who love the law surround themselves with a wall' (*teichos*), as understood by the rabbis, seem impressive. The *Aristeas* passage looks to be a defensive statement against charges of Jewish separation evidenced in Esther 3:8 and 3 Maccabees 3:4 where, as we saw, 'living (*politeuomenoi*; cf. Eph. 2:12: 'alienated from the commonwealth [*politeias*] of Israel') according to God's law' was an occasion of pagan contempt of the Jews.

In the context of Ephesians 2:11-19 the following points of identification are made, thus connecting the 'wall' with Torah religion in Judaism. (*i*) The Gentiles were indeed cut off from Israel's status as God's people (*politeia*) and devoid of messianic hope.

(*ii*) Christ the peace-bringer united Gentiles and Jews by demolishing the barrier erected by Jewish Torah piety and practice in such matters as *kashrut* or dietary laws which forbad Jewish contact with pagans. The basis for this clear separation was already laid in Maccabean times and in what developed in both rabbinic and hellenistic Judaism as a response to paganising encroachments on the Torah faith. The attitude to Torah hardened, and it was tantamount to apostasy for God's law, Israel's glory (*doxa*), to be given to any alien people (Baruch 4:2ff.). Israel's pride and privilege was to be retained within her borders and not communicated to non-Jews, as M. Hengel has illustrated in support of his thesis of 'Torah ontology'.[34] H. Braun has called this process the 'sharpening of the Torah', with its double edge: (*a*) on Israel's part Torah is apotheosised as a divine attribute or even a hypostasis, gathering to itself the cosmic and creative functions attributed to Wisdom in Proverbs 8, Sirach 24, and the Wisdom of Solomon. Torah became a perfect model on which creation was based. And Torah became the mediator of creation and revelation between God and the world. With the axiom accepted 'the whole Torah is from heaven', Israel's determination to 'live according to Torah' as God's special people was confirmed, and the rabbis (with the exception of Diaspora Judaism with its stress on missionary emphasis) contended for the exclusive revelation of Torah to Israel. 'Happy are we, O Israel, for we know what is pleasing to God' (Baruch 4:4) expresses the sentiment of pride (cf. Aboth 3:19). The other side of this teaching is that (*b*) the Gentiles are severed from all hope. They are the peoples of the world who had once been offered Torah by God and had refused it. Henceforth the Gentiles would be known, with some notable exceptions, as 'law-breaking' (Ps. Solomon 17:24) or 'despisers of the law' along with apostate Jews 'who had made themselves as Gentiles', and excluded from God's mercy. The result of this twofold process was to accentuate the difference between Jew and non-Jew; to blind the Jew to any self-criticism by Torah itself and to give Torah a status of ontological and cosmological force which effectively made its practice an impossible ideal; and equally to arouse feelings of deprivation, hatred and suspicion among Judaism's pagan neighbours. The term 'hostility' (Eph. 2:14, 16) is the exact description of this double effect of a notion that expresses God's gift of the law as the erection of a fence. The fence metaphor served both to minister to exclusivist pride and to drive away all who would approach.

Christ's self-offering was made in his 'flesh' (v. 14). Perhaps his incarnate presence is meant as an antithesis to Torah, if the idea runs parallel with another idea in Asia Minor Christianity expressed in John's prologue, 1:1-14, 17. But more probable is the meaning of Christ's submission to the law's penalty as he endured vicariously its 'curse' (Gal. 3:13) and 'condemnation'. See earlier, p. 62. His self-giving was that of his 'one body' (v. 16, but the term spills over into ecclesiology) on the cross and it spells the final dissolution and destruction of Torah exclusivism. The verbs are emphatic, going far beyond Paul's earlier position: the fence is broken down, the law's validity is destroyed (v. 15; cf. 2 Tim. 1:10), and the hostility is killed off. The writer can further adopt the Pauline vocabulary and word-usage by citing the hymn in which Christ 'reconcile(s) both to God'. Where the earlier Pauline teaching had uniformly ascribed the reconciliation to God with Christ as the agent or means, this hymn attributes the reconciling power to Christ because (a) in the hymn's first draft it is God and man who are brought together and (b) in the author's adaptation the new man is nothing less than Christ's body, the church.

(iii) There emerges 'one new man' replacing the two, and that new company is assured of both proximity to God in worship (v. 18) and a new standing as members of God's reconstituted commonwealth (v. 19; 3:6). The neuter object 'both' need not be played off against the masculine of the adjective (amphoterous) in verse 18. Paul had used the neuter noun when he had characteristics of a group in mind. Here the sense would be: the two groups, divided in their racial qualities, are brought together into one, and as persons have access in one spirit to the Father.

Nothing can now separate believers from God, not the law (vv. 14c, 15a) nor his wrath (2:3), as they have filial confidence to approach the Father. And nothing can separate them from one another since they come to the Father 'in one spirit' who is rightly regarded by Masson as the unifying Spirit of Ephesians 4:4: 'There is one body and one Spirit.'

THE NEW CREATION

The above discussion has put us on a promising track to elucidate the other pieces of terminology in our passage. Two parts remain to be considered.

(a) The 'one new man' expresses the language of conversion. The precise term may be without parallel in the Pauline corpus where the nearest approximations are: 'all one (masculine) in Christ Jesus' (Gal. 3:28); 'one body' (1 Cor. 12:13; Rom. 12:5); 'a new creation' (2 Cor. 5:17; Gal. 6:15; cf. Col. 3:10-11); 'newness of life' (Rom. 6:4); 'created' (as a keyword in Eph. 2:10, but with a difference in Gal. 6:15; 2 Cor. 5:17; Col. 3:10-11; Eph. 4:24). And we may add 'the laver of rebirth' (Tit. 3:5) and the 'born anew' terminology in Ephesians 2:1, 5; John 3:3; 5:24; 1 John 3:14; 5:4; 1 Peter 1:23; 2:2; James 1:18 (?) *Barnabas* 6:11; 16:8. It seems obvious that here is a rich seam of material used to denote the passing from death to life which results in the new creation (*Barn.* 6:13: 'in the last days he made a second creation').

The vivid contrast of death/life derives from the Old Testament, especially with its insistence on the two ways, one leading to life, the other to death (Deut. chs. 27ff.). This has been justifiably claimed as at least one source for Christian ethical admonitions found in both the New Testament paraenesis and the early pastoral manuals (*Didache* chs. 1-3; *Barn.* chs. 18-20). It is a contrast that comes directly from Judaism with its promise to the pagan convert who, on 'coming over' by circumcision, *tebilah* washing and sacrifice, was regarded as a new-born child of Abraham, a new creature. The language of the romance *Joseph and Asenath* describes graphically (chs. 49-50) the experience of the proselyte Asenath who from the day of her conversion is 'made anew, freshly created, and brought to new life' (61:4f.). Cf. Philo, *On Special Laws* 1:51: 'These last he call "proselytes", or newly-joined, because they have joined the new and godly commonwealth (*politeia*)'.

The verb 'to be renewed' is a technical term in the literature of conversion. The association with baptismal renewal is close, and the promise of forgiveness in cleansing is a prelude to the entry into new life with a fresh start and a high status (Acts 26:18; Heb. 6:1-4; *Barn.* 6:11; 16:8).

Our writer clearly has this type of experience in view; and this background may well be defended, whether W. Nauck's theory that verses 19-22 contain a 'baptismal hymn' is cogent or not.[35] The setting is that of emergence from alienation to family relationship on the part of disadvantaged Gentiles who now come to share in the new creation of the 'perfect man' (4:13) who is growing into maturity as he grows into the head, who is Christ in his fullness (1:23; cf. 4:15-16). The hortatory calls to 'put off the old man' (4:22) and 'be renewed' by 'putting on the new man' who is created after God's image (= the exalted Christ, 4:24) fit exactly into this scheme. In other words, the language of proselyte baptism, conversion and renewal is lifted out of a narrow mould and given this widest application to Gentiles who become not converted Jews but a new humanity as part of God's cosmic plan to place all things under the rightful headship of Christ (1:10). The renewal (*anakainōsis*) language borders on that of restoration (*apokatastasis*) of a reconciled universe. But the author is guarding against the drawing of false conclusions by insisting that reconciliation and renewal in the 'new man' comes about only by a return to God made possible through the cross. For all the emphasis on the church as exalted with the enthroned Christ as world-ruler who reigns in the 'heavenly places' (1:3; 2:4-7), the epistle historicises the 'mythical' language that betrays its place in a baptismal liturgy; the author calls on his readers to manifest their unity on earth (4:1-4). He does not discard the 'mythical' language, but domesticates it . . . by pressing upon it an 'eschatological reservation', says W. A. Meeks,[36] citing the fact that the Christians are not yet in heaven; the Spirit is only 'the down-payment on the inheritance' (1:14). He might have added the call to continuing watchfulness and warfare in 6:10-20 as evidence of the church's existence in this world. We will return to this side of the matter shortly.

And if baptism lies in the background of verses 19-22, as it does most likely in verse 11 which functions as a 'baptismal *anamnēsis*', calling the readers to act out their new life received in conversion – baptism as the hymnic pieces embedded in the text recall to them their baptismal profession, it underscores the need for personal response, repentance and forgiveness as much as does the proselyte conversion terminology of verse 15. The making of 'peace', in the sense of the bond uniting Jews and Gentiles in the one church, depends on the 'peace' wrought by Christ, the *śar šālôm*, 'prince of peace' (in Isa. 9:6: a messianic title according to the data in Strack-Billerbeck, III, p. 587) and proclaimed by the peace-bringer of Isaiah 52:7 who 'publishes salvation' as the gift of God. The underpinning of the author's argument for 'one new man' who cements Jews and Gentiles in one body is the appeal to scriptural promises, now seen to be fulfilled in Christ. That idea brings us to the use of Isaiah 57:19 which is explicit in verses 13, 17. But with a mind such as belonged to the author and conceding the subtle ways he appeals throughout the letter to the Old Testament (e.g. 4:8-9; 5:31-32) there is one other allusion that may be mentioned in support of his teaching of 'one new man in place of two'.

The sentence recalls Ezekiel's vision of the two sticks (37:15-23), symbolising Judah and Israel.[37] Yahweh's promise is 'I will join with it (the first stick) the stick of Judah, and make them one stick, that they may be one in my hand.' The symbolism is applied to dispersed Israel which will become regrouped and then, 'I will make them one nation ... and they shall be no longer two nations, and no longer divided into two kingdoms' (v. 22). Pledges of cleansing are given, to be followed (vv. 24ff.) with the announcement of David's heir as their king, obedience to God's ordinances and statutes (v. 24), and the establishing of 'a covenant of peace' (v. 26) as 'an everlasting covenant' in a 'sanctuary' (vv. 26, 28) which will be God's 'dwelling place' with them (v. 27).

The cluster of ideas with its links to Ephesians 2:15-22 is striking; and when is added the reminder that the preceding section of Ezekiel 31:1-14 has described the theme of resurrection and the gift of the Spirit (v. 14), we are left to wonder whether the sequence 'resurrection — renewal — 'one nation' — new 'covenant of peace' — God's dwelling place, his shrine in the Spirit in Ephesians 2:1-22 does not run artistically and theologically along lines already set in the Ezekiel prophecy as the author's fertile imagination meditated on it.

(*b*) So much is speculative; what is not in doubt is the use made of Isaiah 57:19 in our text. What is of great interest is the surprising and novel way it is used.

Rabbinic exegesis brought to bear on the Old Testament texts in this connection starts from Psalm 148:14: 'the people of Israel ... are near to him (Yahweh)'. Various comments in the Midrashim pick out the theme that 'no nation is near to God save Israel', and Israel is referred to regularly as 'a people near to him' ('*ām q'rôḇô*). From this promise the contrast is made: Israel is a nation close to God, the Gentiles live afar off. In Jewish terminology the phrases are frequently used *q'rôḇîm* (the 'near ones' = Israel), *r'ḥôqîm* (the 'far away' ones = the nations of the world; see Strack-Billerbeck III, pp. 585-7; cf. I, pp. 167, 215f.). But Isaiah 57:19 as a proof-text is restricted to a difference within Israel of 'righteous' and 'sinners' and is not applied to Gentile proselytes, even though the 'near'/'far' language occasionally is so found. In the Mekilta on Exodus 18:5 the proof-text is Jeremiah 23:23: 'Behold, I am a God that brings near (*qrḇ*) and not a God that repels (*rḥq*).' Rabbi Eliezer is quoted as saying of God, 'I am he that brought Jethro near (*qrḇ*), not keeping him at a distance (*rḥq*).' The result is that Isaiah 57:19 which *does* have the 'near'/'far' contrast was not applied to proselytes, probably since the wording of the Old Testament passage would indicate a preference for proselytes over natural Jews. The text mentions the 'far ones' before the 'near ones', and this precedence would create an embarrassment for the rabbis. The prophetic statement was confined to a distinction within Judaism. The 'far ones' are Jews who have become ritually defiled, the 'near ones' Jews who are justified by Torah.

A second observation is based on the above data. Since the language 'near'/'far' is drawn from Jewish missionary terminology, the introducing of Isaiah 57:19 into the discussion serves to exalt the status of Gentile proselytes, and so by transference the position of Gentile converts to Christianity. The fact that Ephesians 2 explicitly uses the prophetic statement at both 'ends' of the discussion (vv. 13, 17) suggests that Isaiah 57 was a text being claimed by Gentile Christians. They were exploiting this verse to enhance their newly-found privilege over Jewish Christians. The author of Ephesians enters the debate by recalling their proof-text, but he adds the reminders that (*i*) Gentile privilege rests on redemption 'through the blood of Christ', that is, he is in the Pauline tradition with its emphasis on unmerited grace (2:1-10), and (*ii*) both Gentile and Jewish Christians share a common access to the Father (v. 18). In these ways the false claims of Gentile superiority and Gentile arrogance are refuted.

Thirdly, we can investigate a little more closely the ground of this Gentile pride based on their use of Isaiah 57:19. Christ's death 'in the flesh' (v. 15) looks back to verse 11: the Gentiles 'in the flesh' were known as uncircumcised by those who were circumcised 'in the flesh'. This suggests that 'flesh' means the rite of circumcision — a usage that looks back to Colossians 2:11 as precedent (and similarly in Phil. 3:3-5). Then Christ's 'blood' and his circumcision 'in the flesh' add up to the same meaning: to be reconciled to God 'by his blood' means to have received the benefit of Christ's being circumcised. That may account for Gentile disdain of circumcision, since the readers were claiming that the uncircumcised state was superior to the circumcised. The readers may have heard of the teaching of Jewish allegorists (referred to in Philo, *On the Migration of Abraham*, 89f.) who thought of themselves as already in heaven and 'without bodily existence' (*asōmatoi*). In such bodiless existence they had no place for circumcision which by definition is a physical act, and they looked down on those Jews who continued to practise it.

If the author's readers had been influenced by this type of speculative Judaism, evidenced in their use of Isaiah 57:19 as referring to themselves, it is easy to see how they — as persons both uncircumcised pagans and claiming to be in an ethereal state of spirituality as 'risen with Christ' — would disparage the body (like the enthusiasts at Corinth and elsewhere who had 'come into the kingdom' already on their own admission, 1 Cor. 4:8; see Phil. 3:12-21; 2 Tim. 2:17-18; Polycarp, *Phil.* 7). These claims were grounds for their superiority as well as their minimising of the cross-'side' of Paul's kerygma and their advocacy of a 'realised eschatology' which was forgetful of the church's present duty on earth.

Philo (*On the Life of Moses* 2:288) speculates about Moses who departed this life and on his return to the Father gained a 'single unity' as the duality of soul and body was resolved. Elsewhere (*Quest. Exodus* 2:29) Philo comments on the attainment of unity by Moses as he ascended and so 'come(s) near to God': 'He is changed into the divine, so that such men become kin to God and truly divine'. It is suggested that the teaching of this epistle is couched in language that partly reflects and partly refutes this 'Ephesian heresy' — as Derwood C. Smith calls it.[38] The author accepts the current Asia Minor teaching in the Pauline assemblies that the church is raised with Christ (Col. 3:1-4) but places against the overspiritualised belief in a 'baptismal resurrection' the reminder of what is still future for the church (Eph. 2:7: 'in the coming ages' . . .). He recalls what is the church's present fate on earth as a people committed to the soteriological basis of their faith ('in Christ's blood' . . . 'through the cross' . . . they are reconciled to God) and to a way of life utterly opposed to ethical permissiveness (4:17-5:20) such as disfigured the Corinthian church with its mistaken belief in a celestial life begun on earth.

Finally, it looks as if the quest for unity was much debated in the Asian churches. Only thus can we account for the heavy concentration of interest in this theme on the part of our author. The simplest way to regard his teaching is to see it as a corrective to fissiparous tendencies at work in the congregations. The idea of Gentile Christians displaying vaunted superiority over the Jewish Christians has already been mentioned. Perhaps from the unexpected use of Isaiah 57:19 we may add to this the presence of a false idea of oneness, as these Christians converted to mainstream Pauline Christianity in their province out of an earlier proselyte status — the language of verse 19 which speaks of 'strangers' (*xenoi*) and 'sojourners' (*paroikoi*) looks to be patterned on the Jewish proselyte terms *gēr* and *tôšāb* — were lording it over their brethren and claiming that as 'the far off' members they were specially privileged; and as 'already risen' with Christ to heavenly life they were free to indulge their passions (cf. 5:3-7) as part of a mystical body of Christ already divinised. As their pure spirits were saved, nothing on the physical level had any relevance to their religion. Seen in this light the author's rebuff of their wrong-headed claims to oneness takes on fresh significance. We can just as well understand his paraenetic warning: 'No longer live as the Gentiles do' (4:17; cf. 2:2-3 for what that way of life entailed) and encouragement to serious moral endeavour (2:10: 'created in Christ Jesus *for good works*').

CONCLUSION

What has emerged from our study of Ephesians 2:11-22 is indeed an assertion of both personal and ethnic reconciliation. The picture of 'one church', resting on a firm apostolic base (2:20; 3:4-6) and dignified with descriptions that idealise its role and life (2:19, 21-22), comes into view as a result of that reconciling work of God through Christ's blood and cross. Contact with historical redemption is always retained in spite of the exalted status of the church which 'sits in the heavenlies' in Christ (2:6), where there is also enduring conflict (6:12).

The paradoxical nature of the church's status may arouse our curiosity as why the author has allowed these two strands of ecclesiology to remain side-by-side. We recall two facets of our previous investigation: (*a*) we are dealing in Ephesians with a liturgical document that in doxological and other-worldly idioms sees the church *sub specie aeternitatis*, as God sees it and will one day make it to become (5:26-27); and (*b*) we are reading the work of a man who is both Pauline theologian and Pauline polemicist. He is a faithful exponent of Paul's theology as seen in the pastoral letters sent to Corinth, Rome and especially Colossae. There Paul had outlined his teaching on reconciliation, partly in dependence on liturgical and catechetical forms and partly in correction of some potentially dangerous tendencies. The author of Ephesians borrows from this repository of Paul's materials and draws heavily on the liturgical traditions which were known and used in the Asia Minor congregations. Among these were baptismal liturgies and christological hymns that celebrated the praise of God as the author of new life (e.g. 1:3-14; 5:14) and reconciler of the world. It may not be fanciful to see one specimen of the latter in Colossians 1:15-20 and one example of the former in Colossians 2:13-15. In both instances doxological materials have been edited to bring Christ's cosmic victory as unifier of the spiritual powers into a salvation-history framework, with the focal point illuminated as the cross of Jesus and his death are pictured as the means of the forgiveness of sins. In other terms, the reconciliation was reinterpreted under Paul's hand in strictly personal terms. Of this emphasis Romans 5:1-11 is the classically-formed model of Pauline doctrine. The place of Israel is determined by Paul's abiding hope for his compatriots who will be saved and united with the now reconciled Gentile wing of the church to form ultimately one complete family — or, to use Paul's own imagery, one olive tree composed of different branches. This realisation of the divine purpose is described as 'all Israel' being saved (Rom. 11:26) when God will have mercy 'upon all' (Rom. 11:31-32), i.e. Jew and Gentile alike.

But in the course of the few decades that followed both Paul's martyrdom in AD 65 and the end of the Jewish commonwealth with the fall of the second Temple in AD 70 new situations developed and surfaced. And these are reflected in what we read in Ephesians. The author has to meet, in a way available to him and to that extent different from that of his master, several threatening problems in the Asian province. His letter with its teaching on reconciliation provides the data for what follows.

(*i*) The formulation of Christian liturgy leads to an even more exalted and ethereal concept of the church under gnosticising influence, partly Jewish and partly occasioned by the increasing hellenising of the gospel. The Pastoral Epistles confront the same Asia Minor scene with its threat of a gnostic take-over and controversies of a speculative nature (1 Tim. 1:3-4, 6:20, 21). The answer is sought in a firmer grasp of the institutional ethos of the church, 'the pillar and bulwark of the truth' (1 Tim. 3:15). Notions of baptismal resurrection, 'realised eschatology' — see 2 Tim. 2:18 — replacing the Pauline 'reserve' that locates a tension in Christian living between the two Advents of Christ, and a slide into antinomian freedom are countered by a reliance on credal, liturgical and ministerial forms and a recall to the authentic Pauline message. This is precisely the stance of the Ephesian continuator of the apostle's kerygma.

The doctrine of reconciliation is exposed to the danger of evaporation into a gnostic myth of the universe, with the figure of a 'mythical' Adam filling the world as a cosmic body. The high-flown liturgy would give endorsement to that idea. But the author repels all such ideas by anchoring reconciliation in the historical Jesus who by his 'circumcision' (= death) 'in the flesh' (= in a mundane circumstance) broke down the barrier that separated God and man. 'By the blood of Christ', denoting his sacrificial death, as the author learned from Romans 3:25f., God has brought the former alienated pagans near to himself as well as sealing the end of the cultic religion of Judaism.

(*ii*) Those readers of his tract would be reminded of their 'baptismal confession' (2:11) as they reflected on their former state and the steps God took to rectify it. But their newly-discovered freedom from evil ways and from Jewish cultic rules — even if as half-way proselytes they had come to Christ by way of the synagogue — should not mislead them. They are not reconciled to God to form a new people of God independently of Israel, a kingdom of 'saints' (2:19 is picked up at 5:3). They may have received in baptism the counterpart of the Jewish puberty rite, but the sign of the covenant still impinged on their lives, for they are heirs of the old covenant along with faithful Israel. Judaism may no longer be a live option for them; anti-semitism and a proto-Marcionite attitude of severing the faith from its Old Testament roots are less feasible if they want to remain 'the people of God'. The 'enmity' that Paul had seen as existing between God and man (Rom. 5:10) is applied to the former antagonism between the races and now overcome in Christ's death, and the resultant unity made real in the 'one body' of the church has, as Wolter rightly calls it, 'a new foundation of existence'.

It is God's design to create Gentiles along with converted Israel as one new people. There are links that connect both groups with their past but in the 'one new man', 'one body', a new entity is born that is not a revamped Judaism nor a patched-up paganism; it is the new creation that presages the 'reconciliation of all things' in God's kingly rule over all creation. Of this rule Christ's reconciliation of the men and women who are his body is a microcosm and foretaste.

(*iii*) Israel's role in preparing for that new order has come to an end. The author speaks in terms of the fate of the 'dividing fence', with its Torah piety and prescriptions already torn down in Messiah's death and the destruction of the Temple. More emphatically than Paul — since his historical perspective is from a later time — he sees that the age of Torah is fully over. It has given way to a new freedom of approach to God in the new Temple where both Gentile Christians and Jewish believers find their place as partners on equal footing as reconciled sinners. What Paul had envisaged as 'all Israel' — believing Jews and Gentiles — at the end-time is seen now to be a present reality in the creation of a new people. This is the author's reply to Gentile claims to superiority at a level deeper than Romans 11:21, 25, since in his day Jewish Christianity has become more of a museum piece and Gentile Christianity is more assertive and powerful.

(*iv*) The Pauline theologian shows his kinship with his mentor nowhere more obviously than in his refusal to surrender Paul's teaching on reconciliation as the setting up of a network of personal relationships. The church, reconciled to God and to itself as a multiracial community, must show by its life and in the most practical terms the integrity and quality of its new life. The ethical summons of Ephesians 4:1ff. sets the tone for what is to follow (chs. 4-6) where the themes are: interdependence within the body; the claims of new life displayed in a corporate identity, the new Adam; dissociation from all that would stain the image and lower the high ethical standards of the new community; and the 'household code' teachings on social relationships within the various 'stations' in which God has placed the members.

It is interesting to observe how the section 2:11-22 may have provided something of a groundplan for the rest of the epistle:

(a) 'both' made one (2:14) is picked up in 3:6; 4:3-5, 16 ('the whole body'); 5:31 ('The two' in marriage shall become 'one', but in v. 32 applied to 'Christ and the church' in a synzygy).

(b) 'one new man' (2:15) is related to the church's relationship to Christ (4:13) and its corporate existence (4:24).

(c) 'former aliens now reconciled to God' (2:12, 16) are recalled in 4:18 and in the 'soteriological contrast' ('once'/'now') of 4:8.

(d) 'access to the Father' (2:18) is developed in 3:11-12, 14-15; 5:20.

(e) 'fellow-citizens with the saints' (2:19) is linked with 5:3b; 6:18.

(f) 'members of God's household' (2:19) is carried forward to the 'household code' (5:21-6:9), with the 'membership motif' in 4:16; 5:30.

(g) 'foundation of apostles and prophets' (2:20) is repeated in 3:5.

(h) 'whole structure is joined together and grows' (2:21) — exactly as in 4:15-16; and 'the body of Christ' is built up in 4:12.

(i) 'God's dwelling place in the Spirit' (2:22) is linked to 3:16-17 ('Christ may dwell in your hearts' as 'his Spirit' strengthens the 'inner man'); there is 'one body and one Spirit' (4:3), who is not to be grieved (4:30).

(j) the link between Christ and the church is further developed from the statement that Christ 'came' — presumably in his ministry through the church — to 'proclaim peace' (2:17). That good news is then entrusted to the church to share with the world (6:15; cf. Rom. 10:15). The gospel calls men and women to God's new world of 'righteousness and peace' (Rom. 14:17), a phrase that neatly combines the promise of justification and reconciliation.

(k) Christ as peace-maker by his blood and cross (2:13, 16) reappears in 5:2, 25. The initiative in the cross rests with Christ, not with God's sending or giving his son which is

Paul's main emphasis on *Christus traditus* (though cf. Gal. 2:20). In the earlier teaching it was the work of God; here Christ's voluntary self-giving is the focus. The response to his sacrifice is the church's maintaining the unity of the Spirit in the bond of peace (4:3).

One or two verses seem to epitomise the spirit of the paraenesis: 'we are members one of another' (4:25); 'we are members of his body' (5:30). Together they form the phrase 'one body' (4:4), which is exactly the thrust of the liturgical and polemical passage of Ephesians 2:11-22 where the Pauline teaching on reconciliation gains a fresh dimension by being applied to persons-in-community.

PART IV

JESUS AND PAUL

CHAPTER 10

VARIATIONS ON A THEME

INTRODUCTION

To set Jesus and Paul together with a view to comparing their respective teaching is to enter a treacherous minefield. Paul is known to us across the centuries as a thinker and missionary whose dominant concerns emerge in a pretty clear picture as we inspect his letters. There will always be dispute as to his chief emphases, and our task in the previous chapters has been to sketch the leading ideas in one area, reconciliation. Certain patterns have come to light.

(a)   Paul's use of the terminology has been made in conscious dependence on traditional teaching which was already present in the church, mainly in hymnic forms. It apparently contained some motifs that Paul found either inadequate or potentially dangerous, e.g. a celebration of Christ's cosmic work in terms of automatic process or other-worldly fiat. In taking over such notions Paul corrected these by additions that anchored God's reconciliation of the world in historical events and especially in the atoning cross of Jesus.

(b)   Pervading the apostle's teaching was his desire to express reconciliation in personal terms. For him the Christian life arose out of a knowledge of God's grace that takes the initiative and meets men and women in their alienation with the offer of transforming forgiveness. Categories of justification by faith were useful to express the rationale of the new life in salvation to Jewish audiences. But once Paul's mission moved out to confront the cultured hellenistic world the expression of his kerygma changed with the diversity of dominant needs. To men and women in Graeco-Roman society the prime need was to experience deliverance from bondage to superstition and demonic forces that were thought to hold human life under its sway. Paul's adaptation of the message of reconciliation was admirably suited to meet that need and to communicate the good news of God's saving power in the cross where Jesus overcame the spirit-powers and delivered the church in a victorious engagement that both proclaimed the end of the old order and offered forgiveness of sins as a sign that Christians belonged to the new world.

(c)   The followers of Paul remained true to his 'insight into the mystery of Christ' (Eph. 3:4), while deepening and extending his teaching in response to several changes in historical circumstance. The demise of institutional Judaism spelled out more clearly than in the period before AD 70 the end of Jewish Christianity as a viable alternative to Pauline social egalitarianism as expressed in his letters (Gal. 3:28; 1 Cor. 12:13; Col. 3:10-11). Gentile Christianity in Roman Asia moved dangerously near a hellenising of the gospel (as we can see in church situations in Rev. chs. 2-3, as well as the influence of false teachers who threatened the church at Colossae). The rise of this type of gnosticising teaching may be in evidence in the opposition to Paul's disciples ('All who are in Asia turned away from me', 2 Tim. 1:15; cf. Acts 20:28-35, where there are warnings directed to leaders in the province) as well as resistance to Ignatius' form of Christianity in a later decade. The slide was one into a gnosticising, docetic christology and moral laxity.

Paul's school met the challenge with a restatement of the master's teaching that applied his message to new areas. In particular, the unity of Gentiles and Jews in 'one church', already expressed in the 'capital epistles', is extended to incorporate Christ's reconciling work as its cause. What he did in reconciling sinners to God is given a new dimension. The church's oneness as a new creation, replacing its earlier ethnic groupings, becomes itself part of redemption, just as the Pauline creed is reshaped to include the church as one of the credal articles confessed (so Eph. 4:4-6; cf. 2 Clem. 14). The institutionalising of Pauline Christianity, seen in the liturgies, baptismal confessions and hymns that underlie Ephesians as they do Ignatius' letters, has proceeded to the point where the emergence of the church out of its Jewish matrix following on Paul's Gentile mission is established as part of salvation history; hence 'reconciliation' — one of Paul's soteriological terms — may be claimed for it. And the trajectory is complete.

A term that began its career to emphasise the scope of God's salvation was taken up into Paul's vocabulary as ideally suited (with modifications to accentuate his theology of the cross and the personal ramifications that theology involved) to communicate the kerygma to his Gentile mission churches. When its cosmic sweep is again in danger of leading to false triumphalism, the term reconciliation is recovered and reminted by the Pauline school in Asia and put back into circulation as a way of expressing the new phenomenon of the church, with renewed emphasis on the cross and personal response. The setting of reconciliation in the Asian churches' baptismal catechesis is a powerful reminder (Eph. 2:11) that unity in the church rests on a soteriological base.

The above reconstruction, of course, has to be tested by the data in the extant letters of Paul and his disciples. It is much more problematic to show that this 'leading idea' has its roots in Jesus' teaching — and more foolhardy still to try to trace it back to Jesus' experience. There are two roadblocks that stand in the way of this enterprise. The question is whether they are insurmountable.

JESUS' MISSION: THE GOSPEL PICTURE

(*i*) One obstacle is *the nature of the Gospel material itself.* Our sources of information to do with Jesus' attitudes and recorded teaching are the gospels, mainly the first three; but by general consent in modern research they are not biographies of Jesus designed to tell us all we wish to know about 'who Jesus was' or 'what motivated Jesus'. The synoptic Gospels are records of the literary deposits of early Christian preaching and worship. To be sure, they claim to incorporate historical reminiscences of Jesus and his first followers, and Luke's witness (Luke 1:1-4) clearly establishes some link between the evangelists and the eyewitnesses and preachers of the word. But their purpose is both kerygmatic and faith-building (John 20:31, a verse that speaks for all the Gospel writers' purpose). That is, they contain interpreted history, expressed and angled so as to enforce the church's claim that in Jesus of Nazareth God was personally present in a new way and that in the now exalted Lord he offers his salvation, wrought out in the historical ministry of Jesus, to all.

When the Gospel accounts are examined and analysed even with rigorous criticism there is a remarkable consensus of opinion and agreement as to the central core of Jesus' message and impact. The picture that emerges has the following clearly authenticated traits.

(*a*) Jesus announced the imminence of God's rule (Mark

1:15 puts the thought in its own idiom, but the announcement underlies Luke 11:2; Luke 22:18 = Mark 14:25; Luke 17:21). With his coming 'the turning point of the ages' occurred, dividing God's salvation history into before/after (Luke 16:16). This eschatological dimension is seen in the way Jesus called on men and women to prepare for the coming of the Son of man (Luke 17:22-37) and promised an entry into the messianic realm (Mark 10:15, 17, 23). As a sign of the kingdom's presence and power he exorcised demons (Luke 11:20: cf. Mark 3:27; Luke 7:22; 10:18) and shared the 'messianic banquet' with unlikely guests, the poor and despised in Israel, as a token of 'eschatological reversal', namely 'the humble will be exalted'. (This saying has a wide distribution in the Gospels and other Christian sources: see Matt. 18:4; 23:12; Luke 14:11; 18:14; cf. 2 Cor. 11:7; Phil. 4:12; 1 Pet. 5:6; James 4:10.) Implicit in these statements is the claim that the age of God's kingdom has superseded the age of Torah with its scribal interpretations (Mark 2:18-22).
(b) Jesus issued a demand for radical obedience which entailed a call for allegiance to himself. Parts of the great sermon illustrate the first summons (Matt. 5:21-48; 6:19-24) as his call, Follow me (Mark 1:17; 3:14; Luke 9:59), does the second.
(c) His characterisation of God was in terms of *Abba*, 'dear father' (Luke 11:2; Mark 14:36), with its related teaching of God's providence, care, and provision for human needs (Matt. 6:25-34; Mark 11:22; Luke 11:9-13).
(d) Jesus' conduct exemplified his teaching in several ways: he himself trusted God (Mark 4:35-41) as he called for a like faith on the part of his hearers (Mark 9:23); and he reached out in conscious seeking to the dispossessed in Israel, the poor and the needy, the 'people of the land' whom the Jewish pietists rejected (Luke 15:4ff., 8ff., 11ff.). See Matthew 21:28-32; Luke 18:9-14; Luke 14:7-24; 13:28ff. The token of his interest is seen in his sharing a meal with outcasts, and his calling disciples precisely from this stratum of the 'people of the land' (Mark 1:16ff.; 2:13-17; Luke 14:28-33). The call to discipleship illustrates much of the above teaching as he called for radical decision and offered rewards for risk-taking (Mark 10:21; Matt. 5:29f.; Luke 9:57-60; Matt. 13:44-46). His possessing the Spirit in baptism (Mark 1:9) prepared for his role as 'baptiser in the Spirit' (Mark 1:8) — another sign of the

new age, now proleptically at hand.

(e) Jesus' destiny is a corollary of what is said about his mission in statements such as 'I came not to call the righteous, but sinners' (Mark 2:17), and rests on his obedience to God. He, early or late in his ministry, became aware of his role in history as one who would 'sum up' the fate of Israel; hence his mission to Jerusalem (Luke 13:31-33) with its challenge (Mark 11:1-11, 15-19) and the ensuing tragedy of rejection (Luke 13:34-35). His self-chosen title, 'Son of man', drawn from Daniel's picture of a faithful remnant (7:13-27), reflects an awareness of his destiny to embody Israel in suffering as a prelude to glory when the kingdom of God will come 'in power' (Mark 8:38-9:1). At the last supper he interpreted his death as an atoning sacrifice by which the kingdom would come (Mark 14:22-25); and he was executed on a political charge because at a deeper level his religious claims were disowned (Mark 14:61-64).

(f) His vindication beyond death was already foreseen (Mark 14:28; 16:7) and arose out of his filial awareness of being God's son (Mark 12:1-12; cf. Matt. 11:25-27 = Luke 10:21-22) to whom the future kingdom will be entrusted and whose rule will embrace the Gentiles. Signs of Jesus' wider concerns to extend God's rule and blessing to non-Jews were already there in his public ministry (Luke 4:16-30; Matt. 8:5-13 = Luke 7:1-10) and were a main cause, along with a critique of Torah piety and Sadducean privilege, of his death, as historically regarded.

The above summary statement would need several qualifications if it were to come anywhere near a well-rounded synopsis of what the mission of Jesus involved. For our purposes it will suffice because it highlights the salient features that stand out when the rigorous techniques of Gospel criticism are applied to the data. The overview we have just given may also serve as a groundplan of Jesus' teaching, and alongside it we can set the results of our foregoing study on Paul.

JESUS AND PAUL AS HISTORICAL FIGURES

(ii) The other difficulty with our comparison between Jesus and Paul arises from a set of obvious facts regarding *the ways Jesus is distinguished from Paul*. These can be quickly enumerated.

(a) Jesus was a Palestinian Jew, whereas Paul was a Jew

who belonged to the larger world. Both teachers came out of the same Old Testament-Jewish family life and religious matrix, but they did not have the same exposure to Graeco-Roman culture. Jesus never left the land of Israel (*'ereṣ Israel*) except for occasional visits to Tyre and Sidon (Mark 7:24) and to Caesarea Philippi in the north (Mark 8:27). Paul was born in Tarsus in Cilicia and perhaps raised in Jerusalem (see earlier, pp. 16, 17); but after his conversion he became a world traveller not only in Asia, Greece and (modern) Yugoslavia (Rom. 15:19) but in Italy and, it may be, Spain (Rom. 15:24, 28). Jesus as a Jewish rabbi stands in contrast to Paul the apostle to the nations (Rom. 1:5).

(*b*)   Jesus had a different audience from Paul. In the main Jesus directed his preaching of God's rule to Jews in Galilee where Capernaum was his headquarters (Matt. 4:13, 23-25; Mark 1:14-15) and people are said to have come to him. The layer of Matthew's Gospel that restricts Jesus' earthly ministry to Israel (Matt. 15:24: 'I was sent only to the lost sheep of the house of Israel') and similarly delimits the mission of his disciples (Matt. 10:5, 23) raises some considerable historical problems. But there is some ground for credibility in that no later missionary church as Matthew's (28:19-20) would have invented such a limitation if there were no firm basis in the tradition of the historical Jesus. After the resurrection, of course, the scope of the disciples' outreach altered, as the various mission charges illustrate (Matt. 28:18-20; Luke 24:47; Acts 1:8 — all having the Gentile mission in mind). Paul stands in direct contrast if we take the Acts narratives of his conversion at face value (e.g. Acts 9:15; 26:17-18; different in Acts 22:17-21, which records a later vision in the Temple). His autobiography endorses the sequence of a 'conversion' leading to a 'call' to evangelise the Gentiles (Gal. 1:16; cf. 1 Cor. 9:1) as their apostle. He was entrusted with a ministry (Gal. 2:8) to a polyglot, cosmopolitan group called 'the Gentiles' (Rom. 1:13-14), or the 'Hellenes' (Rom. 1:16), i.e. non-Jews. While he never renounced his concern for his fellow-Jews, his missionary strategy was geared to reach out to the non-Jewish elements of society. Two titles, interestingly in the same passage, mark the extent of the contrast:

Christ became a servant to the circumcised (Rom. 15:8)
[Paul is] a minister of Christ Jesus to the Gentiles (Rom. 15:16).

(*c*) So far the distinctions have been somewhat superficial and some qualifications will need to be entered especially to do with Jesus' reaching out to non-Jews and Paul's sense of enduring debt to Israel. But in the main the lines of demarcation hold. The most important and fundamental difference, however, lies elsewhere: it is that the two persons lived in contrasting ages, separated by the resurrection of Jesus. The Fourth Gospel is plain in its witness to the clear division in God's salvation history: 'before Jesus was glorified' things were different from what they are after his exaltation (John 2:21-22; 7:39; 11:51-52; 12:16). Specifically 'the Spirit had not been given', before Jesus' triumph over death released the powers of a new age. After Jesus ascended to God, a new world was born (John 20:17).

Paul rejoiced to live in that new era, whose inception was marked by Jesus' resurrection and his gift of the Spirit (as in the pre-Pauline credal fragment he quotes in Rom. 1:3-4). In Jewish terminology 'this age' had given place to 'the age to come', at least in a way that showed that the two ages ran concurrently (1 Cor. 10:11) and that in Paul's experience the energies of the new age were already being exerted in what God was doing through his ministry and in anticipation of the end of the old aeon at the parousia of Jesus (1 Cor. 15:24-28).

Certain well-established consequences followed for Paul based on his conviction and experience, both his and that of his converts, that in Christ a new beginning to world history had dawned.

(*i*) The understanding of Jesus as Israel's national Messiah, while still regarded as true (Rom. 9:5; 15:8; 2 Cor. 1:20, 'all the promises of God find their Yes in him') in confirmation of God's pledge to his people, gives way to a richer and fuller conviction, namely that he is Lord of all nations. The lordship of Jesus is Paul's way of answering the question, 'Is God not the God of the Gentiles also?' (Rom. 3:29). 'Yes, of the Gentiles also', since the person of his son is greater than can be contained within the limits of the Jewish messianic hope. This is most likely the meaning of Paul's enigmatic words in 2 Corinthians 5:16. Paul rejects a knowledge of Christ 'after the flesh' which he once had; yet 'now we know him in this way' as nationalist Messiah 'no longer'. 'The basic meaning is that Paul, with others, had a new, fuller understanding of the "whole Christ" by the Spirit and by faith; and he sees others [as he saw Jesus] . . . in the new eschatological situation, in the "new creation".'[1]

(*ii*) Old Testament passages, once obscure in meaning and limited in scope, have taken on a fuller significance appropriate to the new age of the Spirit to which they refer (2 Cor. 3:6). A good example is found in 2 Corinthians 3:12-18 where Old Testament references to Yahweh as Israel's covenant God became reapplied to the new covenant of eschatological fulfilment in the new age introduced by Christ's coming and the Spirit's presence. The result is that 'the veil' of delimiting and obscuring Jewish exegesis that fails to perceive the temporary function of Torah-religion as it prepares for Christ (Gal. 3:24) is lifted whenever a Jew turns to 'the Lord'. What was true of Moses, who 'went in before Yahweh to speak with him' (Ex. 34:34), is lifted out of its original setting and made to apply to the Christian believer — 'every Christian has become a Moses' (as Héring comments[2]), and new scope is given to an Old Testament verse. Paul's interpretative comment, in a *pesher*-like comment similar to the practice at Qumran, is made in reference to Moses' turning to God's presence: 'Now the Lord whom Moses approached means *for us* the Spirit who will also transform us all into the image of God's perfect man, Christ Jesus, whether we are Jews or Gentiles' (3:17-18). This is one of the clearest instances of Paul's spiritual exegesis whereby the Old Testament is boldly appropriated and carried over into the age of Christian experience of new life in Christ.

(*iii*) The 'mystery' of one church including believing Gentiles along with faithful Jews was not known until Paul's day (so tribute to this effect is given in Eph. 3:4-6, based on Paul's teaching in Rom. 11:25, as we observed, pp. 194-6). This plan was hidden even from the spirit-powers (Eph. 3:9-10), and Paul can write mysteriously about their ignorance of who Jesus was as a fact that led to their undoing (1 Cor. 2:6-8). 'But now' — in a way that has become a standardised form of teaching, suggesting the pattern 'once it was hidden, now it is revealed' (Rom. 16:25f.; 1 Cor. 2:7f.; Col. 1:26f.; Eph. 3:4f.) — the *Heilsplan* or saving design of God that lay in obscurity has come to light in the new age; and it is an open secret for all to see and accept. The 'revelation' entrusted to Paul and his followers as their treasure to share with others is that Christ is living among the non-Jews (Col. 1:26-27) and is the universal Saviour whose grace and forgiveness are freely available to all persons without restriction. This is that 'gospel to the uncircumcised' (Gal. 2:7) for which Paul expended his missionary life and labours and by which he soon became known among the circle of his followers (Eph. 3:1-6) as its 'preacher and apostle and teacher' (2 Tim. 1:11; 1 Tim. 2:7: 'a preacher and apostle . . . a teacher of the Gentiles in faith and truth').

(*iv*) The widened embrace of God's saving plan meant that Israel's privileges had changed. Ethnic Israel are still 'beloved' (Rom. 11:28) and have first claim on Paul's gospel (Rom. 1:16). But their only hope of salvation is in Christ and by faith (Rom. 11:23), for there is 'no distinction' between Jew and Gentile (Rom. 10:12), and membership of God's family is open to all who exhibit faith in Israel's Messiah and so become the progeny of Abraham who is the father of 'many nations' (Gal. 3:7-9, 28-29). 'In Christ', therefore, Abraham's blessing of being set right with God is available to the Gentiles (Gal. 3:14), an acceptance that is confirmed in experience by the receiving of the Spirit who is the author of new life (Gal. 3:3). Paul's threefold appeal to scripture (Gen. 12:3, cited in Gal. 3:8; Gen. 15:6, cited in Gal. 3:6), to Christ's act of universal salvation (Gal. 3:13), and to Christian experience shared by all who come to faith (Gal. 3:14), spells the end of particularistic religion and opens the gate to a world-wide Christianity.

These innovations that were so obvious a feature of Paul's mission raise the question of their rationale. We are bound to ask for Paul's own justification of his apostolic ministry. What made Paul certain of his missionary vocation and gave him assurance as he claimed the Old Testament prophecies as 'fulfilled' and widened the scope of Christ's salvation to include the Gentiles? The most important reason he appealed to as his authority was Jesus' resurrection and the onset of the new age of messianic blessedness in him. He can bring together the twin realities of his vision of the risen Lord and his call to apostolic service (1 Cor. 9:1), and interrelate them as cause and effect (Gal. 1:16). Nothing should displace the centrality of the resurrection as the ground of Paul's apostleship, and the new era of salvation that dawned with Jesus' triumph and enthronement as world-ruler provided him with ample reason for all the characteristic features of his gospel for all nations. But there is more to Paul's kerygma than this stress on novelty and originality might imply. There are several important links that bind Paul's message to the ministry of Jesus in its impact on the men and women of his day. Admittedly Paul does not appeal in great measure to the traditions of Jesus' Galilean mission, and the modern interpreter would be hard pressed to construct anything like an outline of Jesus' ministry from Paul's few references to Jesus' earthly career. Nonetheless as we set the two teachers side by side certain important lines of unity and agreement stand out and, provided we make allowance for the difference the resurrection brought, these items of common emphasis do appear.

JESUS AND PAUL: WHAT THEY SHARED

In three particular ways Jesus' ministry has left a legacy on which Paul in the formulation of his message of reconciliation, whether consciously or not, has capitalised.

(1) *Jesus' concern for the outcasts and sinners* stands out most visibly in the Gospel of Luke. It is classically stated in the parables of chapter 15. For some interpreters the common theme in these three stories is one of 'rejoicing' which, to be sure, is a frequently repeated emphasis (vv. 6, 10, 32). There is equally a rebuke of harsh and censorious attitudes at least in the parable of the two sons, as the unbending disposition of the elder brother is held up to condemnation. Again, the picture of God as a loving person, whether as a shepherd, woman or father, has been made the focus of those three stories, an image drawn from God's love for Israel (Jer. 31:10-20). In this view Jesus is appealing back to the noblest sentiments of Old Testament theology and restoring its picture of God, obscured by legalistic religion, to full prominence.

It is better, however, to set Luke 15 within a broader context and see it as part of the section contained in chapters 15-19 which takes as its theme, 'The Gospel of the Outcast', in T. W. Manson's phrase.[3] There are at least four leading themes picked out in these chapters.

(a) God's love is expressed for the unloved and unlovable; the second term is not superfluous since both the younger son and the two tax collectors (18:11-14; 19:1-10) *are* rogues and tricksters who deserve all the nasty things that are said about them. No attempt is made — except when the parables are either allegorised or moralised — to whitewash their bad characters; they stand self-condemned, and we should refuse to exonerate them. They were rotten specimens of humanity — and they admitted it. Yet God's love, seen in Jesus' attitude to their contemporary counterparts, reached out to them not only in pity but in active goodwill and desire to reclaim and restore them.

(b) Judgment is passed in all these chapters on the critical and censorious attitudes of the 'righteous', whether we find them in the elder brother or the various rich men (16:1-13; cf. 16:14-15; 16:19-31), who seem to typify both Pharisaic irresponsibility to their trust (16:11) and Sadducean luxury (16:19), as well as the haughty pietist in the Temple court (18:9-14). The same spirit of criticism evoked the parables in chapter 15, according to 15:1-2, and is seen again levelled at Jesus' treatment of Zacchaeus in 19:7 (the same verb is used: 'they grumbled').

(c) The 'righteous' fail from lack of kindness and sympathy and they spoil themselves by pride (16:1-8, 14f., 19-31; 18:9-14, 18-24). Their disdain of 'tax collectors and sinners' (15:1; 18:9-14) is mirrored in the slighting and patronising attitude shown to Lazarus (16:21) as well as to the widow (18:1-8) and the children (18:15-17) as to the beggar outside Jericho (18:35-43). All these allusions serve only to mark out Jesus' attitude to the socially unwanted, including the Samaritans and lepers (17:11-19), as novel to the point of causing offence within the community of Israel as Jesus transcends barriers and reaches out to those beyond the pale.

(d) Nor can we fail to notice how even the unpromising folk in his society yield a genuine response (17:11-19 ; 19:1-10) and put the self-styled 'pious ones' to shame. The net effect of Jesus' revolutionary behaviour and teaching is to reverse the accepted standards of 'who is righteous' and 'who is one of the "people of the land" (*'am hā-'āreṣ*)' for whom no salvation is possible.

Jesus' conduct, seen in this Lucan section, is so utterly contrary to all that was expected of a teacher in Israel that modern scholarship has little hesitation in accepting the utter credibility of this trait of his ministry. His 'table-fellowship' with sinners (Luke 15:1-2) reflects his offer of friendship (Luke 7:34) and love (Luke 7:36-50). But that is only one side of the picture. The more remarkable and offending part of his attitude was that Jesus offered not only his concern to these people but also God's pardon and acceptance (Luke 15; 18:9-14; cf. Mark 15:31).[+] This disposition and pledge that effectively communicated the assurance of God's favour in the present and the promise of a share in the future messianic feast (Luke 14:12-24) was rightly understood by Jesus' enemies. They saw it as the end of all ethnic privilege (Matt. 21:43) and the collapse of Torah-religion with its focus on the minutiae of negative rules and prescriptions. Mark 2:18-22 with its denouncing of the rules of fasting is set artistically next to the pericope which relates Jesus' meal with 'tax collectors and sinners' in 2:15-17; cf. Luke 5:30, 19:1-10; Matthew 11:16-19.

Here Jesus and Paul are in striking agreement. They concur, not only in proclaiming the quietus of the notion that God has favourites (cf. Matt. 3:9) but in presenting the picture of God as one who overrides religious and racial barriers to meet human beings at the place of their need. This presentation of the divine character is remarkably the same in both sets of teaching. Jesus, acting in God's name, holds up the faith of the Gentile centurion (Matt. 8:5-13||Luke 7:1-10) with a call (reminiscent of Paul's 'by faith alone', *sola fide*) in Matthew 8:8 that undercuts the basis of all nationalist privilege by opening the door of God's kingdom to all believers (8:11; Luke 13:28-30); at the same time Israel stands self-judged (8:11-12) while faithful Jews who 'walk in the steps of our father Abraham' (Rom. 4:12) are indeed present at the last banquet. The same disposition of concern and care is extended to compromising Jews (like Matthew/Levi, Mark 2:13-17) and the women of Matthew 21:31-32 — the 'publicans and prostitutes' — and they are assured of a place in God's kingdom.

While Paul does not, for reasons that are still uncertain, draw upon these Gospel traditions of Jesus' welcome to sinners in Galilee, it still remains a fact that he has enshrined the distinctive elements in Jesus' whole ministry of outreach and compassion in his picture of the gracious God who takes the initiative and 'justifies the godless' (Rom. 4:5) when they are yet sinners and subject to righteous condemnation (Rom. 5:6). Paul is just as insistent that (*a*) ethnic heritage can be positively harmful when it is claimed as a way of seeking to influence God (Phil. 3:4-9; 2 Cor. 11:22ff.); in Christ such distinctions as grounds of merit are done away (Rom. 2:28-29; 9:30-33); yet (*b*) there is still a place for faithful Israel whose prototypical ancestor Abraham set a pattern of belief and confidence in God's promises that still holds for the believer, whether Jew or Gentile (Rom. 4:1-25; Gal. 3:6-14, 28-29).

Above all, both Jesus and Paul with equal firmness and equal novelty, build their teaching on the free grace of God that underpins all his dealings with men and women. The parable in Matthew 20:1-15 — 'the parable of the good employer' — has rightly been praised by J. Jeremias[5] as containing the essence of Jesus' 'kerygma' and vindicates that preaching against his critics; it speaks of a God who gives freely, not as a payment for services rendered nor as a reward for acquired merit, but who is good and generous in the face of human need. The owner's 'generosity' (20:15) is the key to the story, with the inference to be drawn that God will deal on this basis with all who enter his realm, whether early (as national Israel) or late (as the Gentiles who were streaming into Matthew's congregation). The murmured complaint of 'unfairness' (v. 12) fails to see that God is good to all who in any case have no claim on his favour, and his unvarying attitude is one of goodwill in response to human need that utterly transcends and cancels the nice distinction between a 'payment' and a 'gift'. Where God is concerned, all his dealings are in the nature of 'gift'; and this is once more a remarkable anticipation, utterly out of character with current Jewish teaching on merit and reward, of Paul's statements in Romans 4:4-5: 'Now to one who works, his wages are not reckoned as a gift but as his due. And to one who does not work but trusts him who justifies the ungodly, his faith is reckoned as righteousness.'

God's freedom in grace is at the heart of Paul's soteriology, as we have seen. We may with some confidence believe that, while he saw it most evidently at the cross of Jesus and in his own experience as a converted rebel to whom God's mercy was shown, this understanding of the way God saves men and women had been already anticipated and played out in the earthly career of Jesus of Nazareth.

(*ii*)   Jesus acted as he did *because of the new age he heralded and embodied*. The centrepiece of his preaching lay in the announcement of the 'kingdom of God' which is proclaimed as 'at hand' (Mark 1:14-15). The degree of imminence of that rule of God, itself an eschatological picture-word for the new age of divine sovereignty exerted over the affairs of men and nations in the Jewish tradition, is a matter for some continuing discussion, though certain proposals are now generally rejected as inadequate. Any satisfying solution has to hold together the ideas of God's rule as 'already arrived' in Jesus' ministry, as C. H. Dodd maintained in terms of a 'realised eschatology', and as imminently near in the future (so A. Schweitzer and R. Bultmann) with a 'parousia' to intervene between present and future. Mediating positions are offered by E. Haenchen and J. Jeremias who coined the expression an 'eschatology in the process of realisation', or better, 'eschatology becoming actualised' (*sich realisierende Eschatologie*); and W. G. Kümmel wants to clamp together the two aspects of the kingdom of God as 'both a present and a future power'.[6] The last-named view holds most promise since it manages to deal seriously with this double strain in Jesus' recorded teaching. We are faced with the paradox of an 'anticipatory' or 'proleptic' presence of the kingdom that still offers the promise of its future and fuller realisation on the further side of the cross and vindication of Jesus. It is a present reality working towards a future consummation.

What is important for our purpose is to remark on the data that speak of the kingdom's reality, whether in its full force or, more likely, with its premonitory signs, in Jesus' ministry. He boldly claimed that with his ministry that kingly power of God was already at work, 'in your midst' (Luke 17:21). The result is that a person can 'receive' it (Mark 10:15) since it is 'near' (Mark 12:34) and has already entered the realm of human experience (Luke 16:16; cf. Matt. 11:12). It would be wrong to deny elements of futurity that still belong to these notions, and Conzelmann has correctly noted how a saying that looks clearly to describe the kingdom's immediate presence may still have futuristic overtones (e.g. Mark 10:15). It seems clear, however, that Jesus did make one feature of his public ministry and enterprise *the* sign of the kingdom's imminent reality; he drove out demons, and 'therefore the kingdom of God has come upon you' (Matt. 12:28∥Luke 11:20). His presence among the people of Israel and his exorcisms which are attested as phenomena within the main synoptic strata (there are six or seven accounts of Jesus exorcising demons from individuals as well as 'generalising summaries' scattered throughout the Gospel tradition) and the Talmudic witness (Jesus 'practised sorcery', the rabbis agree; B. Sanh. 43a) are tangible tokens of God's nearness in power by which the kingdom of evil is stirred to hostility and resistance (Mark 3:22-27 and par.).

In the apocalyptic literature there is the promise of the new age: then Satan will be no more (*Assumption of Moses* 10:1). It is the arrival of the new age of God's rule on earth that provoked opposition which in turn was put down by his power. In that sense, with Jesus' promise that he has 'bound the strong man' and shackled Satan's might, it is more correct to say with R. Otto[7] that it was not that Jesus brought the kingdom of God; rather it was the kingdom of God that brought Jesus into the arena of salvation history and engaged him in a conflict that led inevitably to the cross and beyond.

The notion of an 'antagonistic motif', setting God's realm over against the domain of evil represented by demons at work in 'demoniacs', sick and dying folk, and malevolent foes, as the synoptic stories record, runs like a thread through the Gospel tradition and poses an inescapable challenge to the modern interpreter.[8] The other side of the issue is that Jesus seems never to have had a merely speculative interest in the world of Satan and demons; for him the power of evil presented an opportunity for God's kingdom to show its superior power as the lives of men and women were rescued and restored (Mark 5:1-20 and par.). 'I saw Satan fall like lightning from heaven' (Luke 10:18) matches the entire mood of Jesus as seen elsewhere, where Satan as an evil force is a challenge to be met and overcome (Luke 13:10-17) both by his ministry (Luke 7:21-23) and that of his followers (Matt. 10:1, 8; Luke 9:1-2; cf. the Marcan appendix, Mark 16:17).

The conclusion stands, therefore, that Jesus announced the presence of God's rule in his ministry of healing and deliverance and in one strand of the tradition at least likened that presence to an invasion of the kingdom of evil. The powers of Satan's kingdom would close in around him as his ministry moved to its climax (Luke 22:53) and prove seemingly victorious. But the end would be one of victory for Jesus and his cause as he emerged in the role of *Christus victor*, since the powers of the new age, already at work in him, were shown to be stronger than the forces of the dark dominion Jesus came to destroy. At this point we are already on ground familiar to Paul with his teaching on Christ's engagement with spirit-powers and his triumph over them in the resurrection, exaltation and parousia.

The 'christology of conflict' that sees Jesus and superhuman forces engaged in combat is now familiar to us through the contributions of Scandinavian scholars such as A. Fridrichsen, R. Leivestad and G. Aulén.[9] They have endeavoured to recapture what they call the 'classic' theory of the work of Christ, seen in terms of a dualistic confrontation between the powers of good and evil. Whether the precise formulation Aulén gives will have a permanent effect on Christian thinking is open to question. What is clearer and more solid as a result is that both Jesus and Paul shared the same Judaic world-view, and both treat evil in its personified form as a deadly serious threat. Yet neither teacher enters into a discussion of the so-called philosophical issues relating to the presence and influence of nonhuman evil in the world. Both sets of teaching, on the contrary, address concrete human situations and relate God's triumph to the potential for human restoration in a personal and practical way. For Jesus, as for Paul, the chief need is not to resolve metaphysical conundrums or to provide a reasoned apologia for God's omnipotence in the face of moral evil. Rather for both the key lies in the forgiveness of sins (e.g. Mark 2:1-12; Luke 5:17-26) and that experience is predicated upon an entry into the realm of divine grace, called 'the kingdom' (Col. 1:12-14) which God has established in the mission of Jesus whose victory over spirit-powers 'opened the kingdom of heaven to all believers'.

'Reconciliation' in both Jesus and Paul is a theme much greater than the presence or absence of the actual term would imply. Jesus' mission, as enunciated in his Nazareth sermon (Luke 4:16-30) was spelled out in the language of the overthrow of alien spiritual powers and the consequent setting free of the prisoners. The latest evidence from Qumran in the texts from Cave 11 which treat of the atonement wrought by the highpriestly figure Melchizedek looks in the same direction, and has a distinct bearing on how the work of Jesus was conceptualised in the Jewish-Christian world (cf. the epistle to the Hebrews).

Paul carried forward the same, or similar, notions regarding a conflict that issued in the overthrow of spirit-powers and the establishing of God's sovereign control over human lives. 'Reconciliation' implies deliverance and the restoring of human wholeness. In Jesus' ministry this is seen in his healing ministry and his forgiving acts; for Paul it is localised in membership of the new society living under Christ's dominion. The common link that unites the two teachers is the fundamental assertion that human lives can be released from thraldom to evil, forgiven and rehabilitated, and reordered in the will of God.

(*iii*) Jesus' announcement of the kingdom of God as inaugurated in his ministry rests upon the premise of his messianic vocation, even if his self-chosen description was 'Son of man' not 'Messiah of Israel'. It is difficult, however, to see how the historical events culminating in his Roman crucifixion are to be accounted for unless some veiled or implied messianic claim was thought to be associated with Jesus, as Otto once more perceptively noted.

The distinctive claim of Jesus was, however, to do with his filial office, which is implied in his statements at the trial (Mark 14:61-62), his parables (e.g. Mark 12:1-12), and the more explicit teaching attributed to him (e.g. Matt. 11:25-27‖Luke 10:21-22). This is an aspect of his message where the theology of the later church has been suspected of having formulated the manner in which it is presented. High-sounding statements as in the *Jubelruf*, the 'cry of joy', of Matthew 11 have increasingly come under suspicion, though J. Jeremias, A. M. Hunter and others have put forward an impressive case for the view that in these verses we hear the accent of Jesus' *ipsissima vox*, or 'authentic voice', reflecting his own original way of speaking[10]. Discussions to do with Jesus' filial awareness centre on two matters: his prayer life and his consecration to the public ministry, which in turn is focused in his baptism.

(*a*) Jesus' characteristic name for God was *'abbā*, an Aramaic word meaning 'my father' and based on the word for 'father' (*'ab*). The emphatic ending -*a* with a doubled '*b*' is now traced to a propensity of children to make phonetic sounds out of 'simple' forms of words by doubling the consonant; thus *'abbā* is one of the nursery vocabulary words (*Lallwörter*) associated with the child's name for his earthly parent (*'ab*). In English we see the connection in 'dada'/'daddy.' The homonym *'abbā* is thereby traced back to the babbling of infants and small children in Aramaic-speaking families and represents the caritative form of 'father'. The best modern rendering is 'dear father'.

Though *'abbā* is found only three times in the New Testament (Mark 14:36; Rom. 8:15; Gal. 4:6), and in each case a translation into Greek is provided in conjunction with the Greek letters which transliterate the semitic form, there is evidence of a wider usage. The data are as follows:[11]

1. The accompanying translation into Greek with verbs of speaking suggests a fixed liturgical setting. We can instance our use of semitic phrases now habituated in Christian liturgical or prayer speech, e.g. Amen, Hosanna, Hallelujah.

2. Jesus had the invariable custom of calling God by this name in his prayers. Out of 175 places where the four Gospels record Jesus as referring to God as Father, sixteen examples are in the setting of his prayers; if parallels are reckoned the number rises to twenty-one times. But the title for God in Jesus' prayer speech is exclusively that of Father. The sole exception of his recorded prayer without the name Father is Mark 15:34 = Matthew 27:46, both citing Psalm 22:1. Moreover this distribution is spread across the spectrum of the sources of the canonical

Gospels: Mark (once); Q (3x); Luke (2x); Matthew (once); John (9x).

3. The variation of usage shifting between 'father', 'the father', and 'my father', suggests that all references go back to the Aramaic *'abbā* as the original form of the address. We can see one obvious modification in the direction of ecclesiastical usage by comparing 'Father' (Luke 11:2) and 'Our Father who art in heaven' (Matt. 6:9).

4. The frequency of occurrence stands in contrast to the fewness of Old Testament references to Yahweh as Father of Israel or individuals within the nation. Old Testament theology and its development suggests a movement towards making God more remote and inaccessible. With the end of the first Christian century, however, 'Father' came into prominence, possibly as an anti-Christian counter-thrust.

5. The argument of Jeremias that *'abbā* as a name for God as distinct from one's human parent suggests something 'quite new, absolutely new' has been recently challenged by Sandmel, Vermes and other scholars.[12] Yet Jeremias's original premise was so cautiously framed and hedged about that no far-reaching claim to the uniqueness of the title may be rightly drawn from the evidence. In any case, Jesus not only called on God as *'abbā*; according to Luke 11:2 (cf. Matt. 18:3), he invited his disciples to invoke God in an identical way. So 'uniqueness' is hardly the correct word. What has emerged from Jeremias's full treatment and discussion of the background is that Jesus claimed an extraordinary intimacy with God and we are probably justified in asserting, with Jeremias, that 'in this term *abba* the ultimate mystery of his mission and his authority is expressed'. The term carries us back, by the use of the combined criteria of distinctiveness (at least in part), language, and homogeneity (in that Jesus' whole life was lived in a filial attitude of trust in and love to God), to Jesus' authentic words and contains in a nutshell both his message and his claim to have been sent by the Father and to have come from him.

The important result surfaces that here is a designation of God that sets relationship with him on a basis altogether personal, intimate and loving. Whatever anticipations there may have been in rabbinic Judaism (for example, in Aboth) or charismatic Jewish piety (in the case of Honi the Circle-Drawer), there is nothing by way of certain evidence to sustain the view that any other Jew so consistently set the loving Father at the centre of his teaching before Jesus. This stands out as the hallmark of his message, conveyed both publicly (Matt. 5:45-48) and privately to his own disciples (Luke 12:32); and it provides a window of access to his 'religious experience', his filial self-understanding set in a father-son relationship.

(b) The precise 'inner' meaning of Jesus' boyhood and adolescence is largely unknown to us. We may dismiss as either blasphemous or irreverent the pictures offered in the 'apocryphal' Infancy gospels: Jesus appears in these accounts as either a bully or a child prodigy. Stories of his making birds from clay and bidding them fly away or striking dead a youthful playmate in a fit of rage only show how far such information as we possess in Luke's Gospel chapter 2 is from these portrayals.

The visit to the Jerusalem Temple (Luke 2:41-52) provides us with a more substantial understanding of Jesus' youth with its frank admission of the boy's human development (2:40-52), which did not exclude an inquisitive mind that needed to be informed and taught (2:46). In any 'christology from below' this pericope finds its natural setting as reminding us that Jesus 'increased in wisdom' by what we must believe were the normal processes of education, training, growth and experience. All the more remarkable, then, is the dawning consciousness of a special relationship to God as Father that is mentioned as belonging to this episode (2:49: 'in my Father's house' is preferable as a translation required by the context. Joseph and Mary are seeking his whereabouts).

'The effect of the saying is to show that Jesus is indeed the Son of God, thus confirming 1:32, 35.' The phrase, as Marshall notes,[13] is more than a claim to be chosen by God; rather it suggests a personal consciousness of God in such an intimate way that the earthly parents are mystified (2:50) at a confession that betrays, if in a fleeting glimpse, Jesus' secret relation to the Father. How far that 'awareness' persisted and whether it grew with Jesus' advancement 'in favour with God' are hard to say, and a veil is drawn over the 'hidden years'.

At his baptism the veil is once again lifted, with a new dimension added (Mark 1:9-11; Matt. 3:13-17; Luke 3:21-22). This feature of the awareness of divine vocation is described in the heavenly voice, 'You are my dear son. In you I am well pleased' (Luke 3:22 = Mark 1:11; Matt. 3:17 is slightly different in its wording but the key words are the same). We focus our single line of enquiry on the nature of this appointment.

Obviously Psalm 2:7 is being used, and it is possible that the
setting of the psalm as a coronation text for the king carries over
into the baptismal narrative. Then Jesus' designation as God's
son will be the occasion of his 'institution into the office of the
eschatological king', as E. Schweizer regards the event.[14] The
title is above all functional and is related to a 'call' experience
preparatory to Jesus' public ministry. The alternative reading of
the text (even without an acceptance of the Western evidence
which supplies after 'You are my son' the additional sentence,
'Today I have become your father' taken directly from Psalm 2:7
in the Greek Bible) places the meaning of the heavenly voice in
Jesus' filial awareness. On this view, Jesus' sonship is conveyed
in terms of a personal relationship to God as his Father more
than a call to messianic office. To be sure, both relationships —
personal and functional — are mutually involved; the question
is, which is prior and foundational. I. H. Marshall has offered
cogent reasons in support of the priority of Jesus' self-
understanding as unique son of God, loved by his Father as
Isaac was (Gen. 22:2, 12, 16) by his earthly father Abraham, and
well-pleasing in his sight as his 'only' son.

The mention of 'well-pleasing' evidently drawn from Isaiah
42:1 raises the issue of Jesus and the Spirit. The link between
Messiah and the *'ebed* (servant) *Yahweh* figure in 2 Isaiah is
interesting not only because it is the 'spirit of Yahweh' that joins
them but also because the linkage is made in a way without
precise parallel in Judaism. Jesus moreover is eminently qualified for his 'office' as Messiah of Israel and servant of God
because he is uniquely related to God as his (only) son. The
tangible — and for Luke, visible — proof of this is seen in the
descent of the Spirit on Jesus in concrete form as a dove. Thus
sonship and the possession of the Spirit are intimately associated, and this 'experience' of Jesus will lay the groundwork for
his claim to be the bearer of the Spirit and the 'model' believer,
especially in the Lucan tradition. J. D. G. Dunn[15] points to Luke
11:13 as an important datum; there the pre-eminent gift of the
Father to his children is precisely the gift that came to Jesus at
his baptism: the Holy Spirit (cf. Matt. 7:11).

This section has been designed to indicate the close, even
causal, relation between Jesus' filial self-awareness, his receiving
the Spirit, and his teaching on the intimacy of that knowledge of
God which he himself enjoyed and which he believed it was his
mission to communicate (cf. Matt. 11:27c‖Luke 10:22c). Above

all else, it is the character of God that stands out as that of a loving, caring Father to whom his children matter and for their needs he has particular regard (Matt. 6:25-34 and par.; Luke 12:4-7, 32). It is this deep awareness of God's providential care and control that pervades the Gospel story; it surfaces as much in Jesus' behaviour whether he is in peril (Mark 4:35-44) or faced with human need (Mark 9:14-29) as in his public and private utterances. We may trace this confidence in God as Father back to his own filial relationship that dawned on him at his baptism, if not earlier in his boyhood.

All this matches with some preciseness Paul's picture of the Christian believer's relationship to God. The most intimate name is 'Father' (*'abbā*), conveyed by the Spirit probably in a context of worship (in Rom. 8:15-17; Gal. 4:4-7) but not restricted to that setting. Paul's often repeated title is 'the Father' (1 Cor. 8:6) who is uniquely the 'Father of our Lord Jesus Christ' (2 Cor. 1:3; 11:31; Col. 1:13) as well as 'our Father' (Phil. 1:2; 2 Thess. 1:1), and so descriptively 'the Father of mercies' (2 Cor. 1:3, patterned on the Jewish liturgical model both in the synagogue worship and at Qumran [1QH 10:14]). In the Pauline tradition this centrality of the divine fatherhood is considerably enhanced: he is the 'Father of glory' (Eph. 1:17) and it is his fatherly relationship to his children in grace that sets the pattern for all angelic and human fatherhood (Eph. 3:14-15).

The hallmark of Pauline Christianity on its experiential side is, as we have seen, the deliverance from dark evil powers and a transference to the realm of light. Colossians 1:12-14 expresses this movement in a clear fashion, and indicates that at the centre of the experience is the forgiveness of sins.

Not unexpectedly, in view of the presence of several terms that belong to the synoptic account of Jesus' baptism and early Christian baptismal language, a similar setting for Colossians 1:12-14 has been claimed. At the time of a person's initiation into the body of Christ and the community of faith the Spirit was active in certifying to that individual an awareness of filial relationship and joy. The witness of the Spirit was communicated in ways the Pauline believer knew well: the gifts of the Spirit in prayer speech and deep emotion, the joy of pardon and new life that followed on a right relationship with God by faith, and a sense of belonging to the family of God where Christ is elder brother as well as Lord, and all the members enjoy a fellowship (*koinōnia*) that transcends the divisions of sexual separation, social status and ethnic pluralism. But the Spirit's chief gift — we may infer from the cumulative data at our disposal — was a setting free from distrust, fear, and inhibition that made God a remote and fearsome being. For the first time, in the Pauline congregations, men and women came to see God as focused in his son Jesus Christ and were admitted to the freedom and intimacy of a family relationship with him otherwise unknown. This was indeed 'reconciliation' since it implied the initative of God who made the first move to reclaim sinners from their alienation; it proclaimed the end of an old age of cosmic fears and pagan superstitions; and it gave a new face to God as Father. This message rested firmly on historical circumstances — that at a point in time God had demonstrated his love in his son who died on the cross and vicariously acted to bridge the gap between sinners and the righteous God. But it had present potential in offering as a living experience the assurance of forgiveness and a place within the family of God where all the inveterate barriers were lowered. In short, Paul's 'message of reconciliation' (2 Cor. 5:19) offered a network of personal relationships to God and one's neighbours in society that answered the deepest yearnings of contemporary men and women, just as Jesus in his day had called and claimed men and women in a Palestinian life-setting to be his followers. To both groups the invitation was basically the same: 'Be children of your Father' (Luke 6:27-36): 'I will be a Father to you, and you shall be my sons and daughters' . . . 'Be imitators of God, as beloved children and walk in love' (2 Cor. 6:18; Eph. 5:1-2).

There is a nice summing-up of this aspect of Paul's theology in one place of his quoted material. At the climax of the *carmen Christi* (Phil. 2:6-11) the universal reconciliation is attained when all throughout the universe acknowledge that 'Jesus Christ is Lord' to the glory of God the Father. E. Lohmeyer[16] comments that the hymn's last word is 'Father' as though to betoken the fact that the 'reconciliation' (*Versöhnung*) of the world has been executed and is now celebrated through the one who came from God's presence, was obedient to death, and is now enthroned at the Father's side. And this person is none other than his son (*Sohn*) who is 'the first-born among many brothers' who will at last share his sonship in the filial homecoming of the family of God (Rom. 8:17, 29).

CONCLUSION

The three ways in which Paul's gospel of reconciliation stood in continuity with the ministry and message of Jesus of Nazareth underline that the former is no novelty bursting unheralded on the scene nor is it an importation from Paul's alleged indebtedness to the hellenistic mystery cults and redemption sagas. On the ground of a threefold commonality that (*i*) exposes God's concern for the outcast and sinner, and (*ii*) marks the transition to a new beginning in salvation history, and (*iii*) introduces a filial awareness of being a member of God's family, Paul is expressing in a fresh idiom what is implicit in Jesus' life and achievement.

These conclusions are far from academic, though we have at least hinted that they rest on a basis in recent scholarly investigation. One immediate consequence is to lay once more the ghost of that misunderstanding of Paul that rises to haunt each successive generation. The spectre of Paul as the archcorrupter of the simple gospel of Jesus appeared, for example, in the writings of George Bernard Shaw. He wrote in 1913 in his preface to *Androcles and the Lion*:

> There is not one word of Pauline Christianity in the characteristic utterances of Jesus ... There has really never been a more monstrous imposition perpetrated than the imposition of the limitations of Paul's soul upon the soul of Jesus .... Paul, however, did not get his great reputation by mere imposition and reaction. It is only in comparison with Jesus (to whom many prefer him) that he appears common and conceited .... He does nothing that Jesus would have done, and says nothing that Jesus would have said.

The picture of Paul as a second founder of Christianity and a perverter of what Jesus taught and lived by is one that will not go away. To many of our contemporaries Paul is a person to be despised and even hated exactly for this reason. Their sentiments are captured in the words of the Pardoner in Sir David Lindsay's *Three Estates*:

> By him that bore the crown of thorn,
> I would Saint Paul had never been born;

or in the allegation of the British political figure Lord Boothby, who regarded Paul as the sworn enemy of true religion.[17] With equal disdain some Protestant and Jewish religious scholars, while professing admiration and respect for Jesus of Nazareth, dismiss Paul as a 'vulgar revivalist' or 'morbid crank' or worse. To have Paul's message of reconciliation analysed in a way that reveals its essential oneness with Jesus' total impact is, we may say, one antidote to this kind of hostility which is so often based on misrepresentation in our modern world.

The objection to Paul along these lines is unnecessary. The modern mentality may continue to be disturbed and scandalised by Paul's message of the cross and his clear affirmation that only in Jesus Christ crucified and risen from the dead in a spiritual body is there hope for a flawed world. As we know him from 1 Corinthians chapters 1, 2 and 15, Paul would not have expected any other attitude from those who could not appreciate these emphases. The unnecessary resistance to Paul occurs when he is alleged to be the purveyor of a message at odds with his Lord. For, as the previous pages have tried to demonstrate in several ways, Paul's proclamation aims to call men and women into a network of personal relationships with God and with one another that may be described under the single rubric of reconciliation. Even if Jesus' reported teaching used the word 'reconcile' only once (Matt. 5:24), it may be said that his announcement of life under the rule of God as his children, formerly outcasts but now reclaimed and restored to God's family, is exactly expressible in terms of a personal relationship to God as Father and king. Both Jesus and Paul are at one most clearly and cogently in their insistence on the human predicament and what God has accomplished to welcome truant children from their disgrace into a new relationship with himself that then becomes the paradigm and model for life in society, whether such model is called the kingdom of God or the church. This single observation, we may claim, is what really binds Jesus and Paul together, and provides a justification for our study of reconciliation shown to be the shared ingredient in both Jesus' and Paul's ministry.

POSTSCRIPT

The task we set ourselves was to survey the main lines of the theme of reconciliation in Paul's theology. That enterprise has been done, though the adequacy and correctness of the approach we have followed must be left for others to assess. Obviously no two interpreters of Paul in this modern period will agree in matters of method and exegetical findings. What has been attempted may be offered as one student's effort and submitted to the evaluation of his readers.

What seems beyond dispute is that the New Testament syllabus of reconciliation covers matters as extensive and far-ranging as human thought can imagine. Such concerns embrace the mysterious plight of the universe, now fractured and broken but one day to be restored to its pristine harmony within the design of its creator and with added lustre. 'Man' — if such a generic term is still allowable as a shorthand abbreviation for the teeming mass of humankind, past, present and to come — is at this stage of his long pilgrimage estranged from God and alienated from his fellows. He cries out for deliverance from the *Angst* of bondage to evil and meaninglessness and from the results of social disorder and cosmic isolation.

1. The plight of men and women in Paul's day was understood by him in several ways. In Romans 1:18-32 he can trace back human disobedience and misery to an addiction to idolatry (1:23) in keeping with his Jewish heritage (compare Wisdom of Solomon 14:8-12), and it had become traditional in rabbinic circles to classify idol worship as one of the cardinal sins along with incest and murder (Aboth 5:9).

Sexual aberrations and social disorders were believed to stem from man's initial lapse into the practice of idol-making. This practice in turn reflected his desire for independence from God and his pride in wanting to be free from all authority. Paul's debt to the story in Genesis 3 is not far away in his analysis of the human condition. To that extent he speaks to that condition present in every age since men and women today as then are still proud at heart and innately want to be lord in their own right. The symptoms of the disease may change over the centuries though, to be sure, there is also a remarkable persistence in the character of the human malaise as Karl Menninger's racy report *Whatever Became of Sin?* (1973) illustrates on almost every page. The root cause remains the same, however. It is human arrogance expressed in defying God, in setting up a rival throne and in claiming opposition to God's rightful demand upon us to live as his loving obedient children. Sin — and Paul, we may believe, would not have disagreed — is 'my claim of my right to myself', in Oswald Chambers's words.

The more difficult part of Paul's analysis of the human predicament comes when we look at his teaching on man's servitude to 'the elemental spirits of the universe', a phrase found in his letters to Galatia and Colossae. It is commonplace that we do not and cannot share the powerful fear of Paul's contemporaries that the stars exercise a malign influence and that personal demonic forces contaminate food and drink and render the normal physiological and reproductive functions of life unclean. The question is whether Paul also saw the demonic powers as so much superstition from which Christ had come to set men and women free. His thinking seems to oscillate between a recognition that demons do not 'exist' (1 Cor. 8:4: this sentence may well be a quotation from the Corinthians themselves) and an admission that their influence is evil and must be resisted (1 Cor. 10:19-21). Not much of a transposition is needed when it comes to our relating to Paul's healthy attitude to the creation, to God's gifts, and to an ethic of responsible freedom. He is at pains to safeguard his gospel from the twin dangers of legalism, whether in terms of bondage to law or to a false asceticism (as in Col. 2:21, again he is quoting what others have said) or an antinomian disregard of all moral standards and discipline. Paul's entire ministry, at least during the time of his letter-writing period, was a constant engagement with these tendencies, both of which he judged to be equally pernicious.

One way in which we today can translate Paul's confidence in Christ's victory over the spiritual powers is offered by F. F. Bruce.[1] He appeals to the lure of astrology and the occult in modern society which in spite of its confidence in technocracy and claim to sophistication, is often plagued by superstition and the spell of age-old taboos. There are also powerful socio-economic and political forces that are raised to the level of demonic structures against which we as individuals struggle in vain. Atomic physics and electronic gadgetry have spawned a complex system of weapons and data-recording controls that threaten either to obliterate human life on the planet or to submerge the individual in a sea of serial numbers and algebraic codes. 'They may be Frankenstein monsters of [man's] own creation; they may be subliminal horrors over which he has no conscious control'. To such a modern predicament, Paul's answer is the same as that given to the Colossian threat:

To be united to Christ, he would say, is to be liberated from the thraldom of demonic forces, to enjoy perfect freedom instead of being the playthings of fate.

The hermeneutical knot is thus deftly severed by an appeal to 'demythologising'. Paul has used language, to us archaic and 'old world', which is capable of being transferred to a new scene. The lords which governed the planetary spheres are 'demythologised' by Paul 'to stand for all the forces in the universe opposed to Christ and his people'.

Given the legitimacy of this transfer, we have inherited from Paul the basic confidence that there is no force in the world — 'demonic' or human, impersonal or personal, structural or individualistic — that can separate us from God's love in Christ Jesus our Lord (Rom. 8:39). The key to the mysteries of the cosmos as well as the ills and tragedies and perversities of human life is offered in what Paul called his 'gospel', addressed to his contemporaries — and to us in our sorry state of bondage and alienation.

2. The good news proclaimed by Paul and his associates was that God in Christ had already taken the decisive step to promote that emancipation and recovery. Invariably, as we have tried to reiterate in company with some recent insights, Paul's thinking moves from solution to problem; from what God has already achieved he reads off a diagnosis of the scene where that action is played out; from God's deed he reasons back to man's need. At the cross of Jesus which becomes the focal point of the divine 'rescue and recovery' operation the eschatological deed, meaning that it enshrines within it both past hopes and fears and a potential for turning history in a new direction, was done. The consequences of that deed, 'once-for-all' wrought out and completed, still need to be renewed in a proclamation and a contemporising that is called by the apostle, 'the ministry of reconciliation' (2 Cor. 5:18).

We may sum up Paul's main contribution to the theme of the church's proclamation in the following manner. Paul's statements on reconciliation clearly define both the desperate human situation and the scope of God's action in history to make his aid and saving power known. In his discussing these two 'sides' Jesus Christ is presented as the criterion. He provides the standard by which human life in society and individually is tested just as his cosmic role and destined office as Lord of creation provide correctives to free-thinking gnostic ideas that

reduce his status to the level of one intermediary and then resort
to a veneration of the angels, as at Colossae (Col. 2:18). In the
light of the centrality of Jesus Christ the true image of God (Col.
1:15) and the last Adam (1 Cor. 15:45) Paul can see the cosmos
as having fallen away from its true relationship to its creator, and
humankind as having succumbed to the idolatry of worshipping
the creature in place of the creator (Rom. 1:25). Men and women
have lost their true identity as God's children — Paul has the
story of Adam in his sights throughout Romans chapters 1-3 —
and 'sinned', i.e. missed their way by coming short of God's ideal
for humanity set in the perfect man Jesus Christ (Rom. 3:23).
More than that, the human propensity to independence and
pride has turned the race into a generation of rebels and outlaws,
caught in the guilty act of defiance and meriting the deserved
sentence of judgment. Cosmos and the human creation alike
stand apart from God by some sort of voluntary choice and cry
out for restoration (Rom. 8:19-23).

For Paul it is the same figure of Jesus Christ who certifies
God's desire and design to mount an operation of deliverance. It
began in the incarnation, with God sending his own and only son
who not only came from God but as God. So Paul can use the
stately words of 2 Corinthians 5:19: 'God was in Christ
reconciling the world to himself'. The ultimate sign of this
self-giving was set up at the cross where God's love for the world
and Christ's love for his people came together in overlapping
images as they are focused on a background of human plight and
rebellion.

Acting in a representative way as the obedient son, Christ
identified himself with human alienation and man's lost condition. He died the sinner's death, voluntarily and vicariously
accepting the penal consequences of sin in such a way that sin's
strength was exhausted on him and lost its power to hold any
longer the new race of humankind that was born at the cross.
Notions of a divine-demonic 'conflict' are so inextricably woven
into Paul's teaching on the work of Christ that it is impossible to
ignore them. The emerging of the divine hero from apparent
failure and weakness into triumph, even on the cross (Col. 2:15),
proclaims a new day of hope and deliverance for the world; and
those who are identified with the crucified and risen Lord come
to participate in his breaking of the stranglehold of sin.
Categories that derive from the Old Testament sacrifices and
ritual are present in Paul's writing, mainly in places where he is

indebted to Jewish-Christian tradition. His own chosen vehicles of expression, it would seem, are more concerned to show the essentially personal nature of human wrong (sin is personified) and God's way of righting it — by triumphing over it and ushering in a new age, 'apart from law' (Rom. 3:21). The hallmarks are plain for all to see as they experience a release from sin's tyranny in forgiveness and a place in the family and fellowship of God as his children. Nothing is more characteristic of Paul's gospel of life-in-Christ, his 'ministry of reconciliation', than the assurance of pardon and release and a new freedom and confidence, heard in the cry, Abba! Dear Father. In terms such as these Paul's teaching on reconciliation bequeaths a legacy to the church, its ministers and teachers and members. It is the task of proclaiming both the bad news and the good news, so uniting man's need with God's deed.

3. That task is extended and its purpose, spirit and goal clarified by the life of the apostle who himself fulfills his ministry under God as a reconciling agent notably at Corinth, though his entire ministerial and apostolic vocation is one of linking God's power to the needs of men and women in his society. Paul insists that an understanding of the cross must lead to a life-style that is shaped by the message. The burden of his counsel to the Corinthians in 2 Corinthians chapters 4, 10-13 is exactly this: reconciliation must be seen in the congregational life of this fractious community just as it is made concrete and tangible in his own proffered forgiveness of those who had offended him and in his pastoral solicitude for their restoration to friendship with himself as God's apostle (2 Cor. 6:11-13; 13:5-10). 'Be reconciled to God' is Paul's message with enduring relevance to the Christian community as much as to the estranged pagan world. And he not only proclaimed 'reconciliation'; he embodied it.

Because reconciliation is above all a term of personal relationship, it can serve adequately to sum up the sense of mutual obligation or 'fellowship' (*koinōnia*) that A. M. Hunter[2] and others regard as the basis of Paul's ethical teaching to the churches. The dimension of reconciliation is as much horizontal as vertical. Paul's message was addressed to those who in being reconciled to God and continuing by loving obedience and firm commitment in that relationship to him were held responsible for the quality of their ongoing life in the Christian society of the church. The call of Paul's gospel was to live 'in peace' (1 Cor. 7:15; 14:33; 2 Cor. 13:11; Rom. 12:18; Col. 3:15; 1 Thess. 5:13).

The scope of such a term is wide. It ranges from the initial entry
to a new status with God in Christ to a concern for the interests
and well-being of one's neighbours (1 Cor. 8:7-13; Phil. 2:1-4)
and to an active desire to promote the growing together of all
members of Christ's body (1 Cor. 12:12-26; 14:12; Eph. 4:13-16).

Reconciliation is more than a theological code-word for God's
work of restoring men and women to himself. It marks the way of
life to which those people are summoned by the fact that they are
reconciled and share in God's continuing ministry of reconcilement in the world. The life of the Pauline congregations was for
the apostle one of the most telling methods of evangelism since
that corporate life was meant to reflect both the character of God
and the outworking of the message as it applied to the human
context. As Christians loved one another, forgave and were
compassionate to one another, and showed forth in their mutual
attitudes that they shared a new spirit which was not self-
centred, hard-hearted or spiteful but one that made for unity and
harmony, so they were giving expression to the authenticity of
the message of reconciliation. Evidence for this side of Paul's
practical teaching comes in his letter to the Philippians and his
note to Philemon. It has ramifications for the church in our time.

Set in an outpost of the Roman empire and beset by many
enemies (1:28; 2:15), the Philippian congregation was meant to
be a 'colony of heaven' (3:20, Moffatt) as it answered the call to
'lead a life that is worthy of the gospel of Christ' (1:27: the verb
means to 'live as citizens'). What that implied in the pastoral
context of the church situation is seen in the following section
(1:27-2:18) rightly called 'what Paul expects from the church'.
At the heart of the section is the great confessional statement of
2:6-11 with its climax, 'Jesus Christ is Lord'. More than likely
the reason for Paul's citation and use of the hymn was to
summon the readers to accept a way of life based on Christ's
lordship over those who claimed to be 'in Christ'. The detailed
application of that privileged status is seen in such down-to-
earth counsels as 'do nothing from selfishness or conceit . . . do
all things without grumbling [i.e. against God who has permitted the church to suffer, 1:29-30] . . . shine as lights in the world,
holding forth [as a light-bearer] the word of life' (Phil. 2:3,
14-15). These terms and counsels bear directly on the church's
influence on society and, as the Philippians respond to Paul's
calls, they will demonstrate their true life-in-Christ as reconciled
people and as those whose impact on their world extends the rule

of Christ and makes visible his presence in the church where he is acclaimed (2:9-11). They will thereby act as reconciling agents.

Paul's recommendation to Philemon describes the Christian as one who exercises an individual reconciling role. The apostle acts as a go-between intent on bringing together the runaway slave Onesimus and his master Philemon. Each person in that three-cornered relationship was called upon to do something difficult and costly. For Paul had to forgo Onesimus' service and company, which he prized (v. 11) and to take some responsibility for the loss incurred (v. 19). Onesimus must return to his master and accept the consequences of his wrongdoing (vv. 12, 18). Philemon is called upon as a Christian to forgive and to welcome Onesimus back as a 'beloved brother' (v. 16) and even, it may be, to grant him his freedom (v. 21). 'And each of the three [is to do] what he was called upon to do as a Christian'.[3] Here we see a picture of reconciliation in action on the horizontal and social plane. Paul is responding to the dictates of his conscience in parting with his friend when he would have preferred to keep him at his side (v. 13). Onesimus must follow the path of social convention and justice even when it meant accepting the consequences of his past, and stay within the framework of the contemporary order which included the institution of slavery (see 1 Cor. 7:17-24; Col. 3:22-4:1). Philemon is prompted to the Christian course of action by Paul's letter which is tender in its appeal (v. 14) yet firm in its insistence that there is a right thing to do (v. 8). Each individual, however, is left to discover the will of God for himself and be guided by the overarching principle of 'what is fitting' (v. 8; cf. Col. 3:18; Eph. 5:4) in a given context, yet with due acknowledgment of the lordship of Christ (v. 5) who has reconciled us to God (v. 19). 'For love's sake' (v. 9) is a guiding axiom, uniting both the Christian's desire to please God in all he or she does and the sense of gratitude we all share for what has been done for our redemption and reconciliation.

As Philemon is a member of the divine family, which is the tacit basis of Paul's appeal, he is now given a chance to show reconciliation in a most tangible and realistic manner: to forgive and welcome back the runaway thief and slave; and to give him a new standing in his household, since he too is now a member of the same family of faith (v. 6). As Paul is a Christian leader bound by cords of love and respect to both parties, he is here viewed as exercising a reconciling or intercessory ministry not so much in the customary way of public proclamation as by representing each man in the encounter to the other. He touches both lives and so brings them together in a true *koinōnia* as each party in the troika has been individually led to take his place in God's family and fellowship. A more realistic picture of what reconciliation involves at the horizontal or personal level could hardly be imagined. It is clear that this 'letter' of some 335 words is specially valuable for the light it sheds on practical Christianity that has a strong theological underpinning and that contains the promise of being worked out in a later time in a statement of the unity and equality of all humankind.

4. The application to ethnic problems in the later church results in a clear statement of reconciliation as ensuring the breaking down of racial and cultural impediments that are now antiquated in the 'new age' of Christ's kingship. The emerging of a new concept in the form of a society of men and women united to one another by the same bonds of love that first joined them to Christ the Lord and gave them free entry to the divine presence is the vision that fills the horizon of the author of Ephesians. Bound up with this far-reaching prospect of a transnational, multiracial Christian community as a novel entity on the world stage is the promise that this society mirrors as in a microcosm the hope of the world and the universe, at present divided and at odds with its creator. The author can reach out in his vision to the coming into being of a cosmos under the headship of Christ (Eph. 1:10; 4:15-16) in which all refractory elements in the universe are gathered together in such a way that they have lost their surdlike power to disturb the tranquillity of a created order in which God is 'all in all' and from which evil is forever banished. The earlier anticipation of this cosmic triumph of God had related the destruction of evil to the events of Christ's death on the cross and his resurrection (Col. 2:15; 3:1); the logical outcome of that historical victory is made by the Ephesian writer as he sees how all the supermundane forces are brought under the lordly control of Christ and 'reconciled' by losing their dysteleological power to thwart the age-old plan of God. They disappear as though they had never been; and in the end the author looks for a universe *sub specie Dei* — in its real 'form' — in which 'all things' are restored to how they were 'in the beginning' as part of God's design for universal wholeness.

5. Finally, we may set the above statement against the criteria for a New Testament theology offered in chapter one (pp. 2,3). There selected tests were proposed as 'conditions' which any

full-rounded theology would need to fulfil. In specific terms we suggested that its scope should include (*a*) the divine initiative and supremacy in grace; (*b*) an addressing of the cosmic and human predicament of alienation, brokenness and distress; (*c*) a centrepoint in the cross and victory of Jesus which offers the divine remedy and involves both an 'interchange in Christ' (2 Cor. 5:21) and a satisfying basis and a moral dynamic for the new life of reinstatement in God's favour; (*d*) the place of faith as response, which includes both a grateful acceptance of all that God has done and a pledge of new ways of living; (*e*) a rationale in a deed of historical 'is'-ness (God has reconciled the world in Christ) for a continuing obligation of ethical 'ought'-ness (Christians should show in their personal, social and global relations that they are both reconciled persons and reconciling agents); and (*f*) a missionary mandate which involves the church in its ongoing commitment to the *missio Dei* — the divine enterprise — in the world.

It is 'reconciliation', we submit, that measures up to most, if not all, of these standards, and fits neatly into one defined task of Christian theology as 'that activity of men struck by the biblical story, in which they undertake to revise continually the ways in which they say how things are with their present circumstances, in the light of how they read that story'.[+]

APPENDIX

The reprinting and republication of this book under a new imprint has given the author a welcome opportunity to take a fresh look at his earlier writing. Over the seven years since the book first appeared, Pauline studies have continued with unabated interest and have engendered a continuing debate. It is not our purpose to review—or even to chronicle—the more recent publications. The task of this Appendix is more modestly designed. It proposes to examine briefly some of the leading contributions, to restate the chief thesis of the earlier book with a degree of fine tuning, and to make a limited response to those who have been good enough to write reviews of the first printing of *Reconciliation: A Study of Paul's Theology*.

SOME RECENT PROPOSALS REGARDING A PAULINE "CORE"

The endeavor to ascertain whether there is a central organizing principle in Paul's theology has been pursued actively in scholarly circles. All researchers agree that Paul's thinking is not systematic, but rather, is directly related to the pastoral needs of his congregations. Most interpreters also believe that Paul's responses to community needs have been dictated by—and fashioned under the influence of—the adversary role he adopted to repel what he regarded as mistaken views and to expose deviant behavior patterns.

J. C. Beker's *Paul the Apostle*[1] has put the first of these assumptions beyond a cavil, with his dictum (restated in his 1984 preface) that "Paul's hermeneutic is shaped by the complex interaction of coherence and contingency," and the coherent center of Paul's thought is believed to be apprehended only through linguistic expression in its application to contingent situations. Christopher Rowland's *Christian Origins*[2] speaks of a Pauline correlation between "system and situation" to express the interconnection between Paul's gospel and the needs of his congregations. The term "system" is not well chosen because it has overtones of a rigid and unadaptable set of ideas and this is hardly descriptive of Paul's pastoral response to varying needs.

The second assumption, that Paul is constantly in debate with opponents, is not so universally approved, and indeed has been challenged. But there is considerable evidence for it, whether drawn from direct sources such as Philippians and 1 and 2 Corinthians (see my recently revised books and articles[3]) or indirect sources such as the setting of James 2:14–26. At first glance the neglected epistle of James may seem an unpromising source of information for Pauline theology, yet recent studies have taken a fresh look at the debate underlying James 2 in an attempt to see the position not only of a Jacobean opponent but also of a misguided Pauline enthusiast.[4]

But there the agreement stops. When we ask about a "Pauline center" or the underlying principle of coherence in Paul's theology (to use E. P. Sanders's expression,)[5] we are faced with a bewildering variety of answers. Usually the suggestions made range from being too narrow to being too wide. Proposals that say no more than that Jesus Christ is the center of Paul's life and thought, or that "he saw life under the lordship of Christ"[6] are of course obviously true[7], but they hardly touch on the complexity of this man's mind. Nor do they account for the flexibility of Paul's sensitive response to situations he met, as Henry Chadwick's essay "All Things to All Men"[8] has made clear.

At the other extreme we encounter suggestions that have been too far-reaching. Three recent proposals, I submit, belong to this category.

E. P. Sanders[9] draws attention to "two readily identifiable and primary convictions which governed Paul's life: (1) that Jesus Christ is Lord, that in him God has provided for the salvation of all who believe . . . , and (2) that he, Paul, was called to be the apostle to the Gentiles." Again, both statements stand out as clearly demonstrable, but they do not bring us *directly* to the heart of Paul's message.

C. J. A. Hickling[10] accepts the two statements as essentially accurate but goes on to add a rider: "God has already brought about in Christ a decisive and final *transformation of time*." The basic idea is that of the "turning point of the ages" (*Aeonenwende*)—an announcement believed to be so fundamental to Paul that Hickling can write[11]: "Here, surely, is the centre of Paul's thought, and indeed of his religion: not simply, or even principally, in the content of his assertions about God and Jesus and his own calling, but in the sense of fundamental and paradoxical contrast, as of one standing at a cosmic frontier with which this content was perceived." This slightly complex statement—if I understand it aright—brings us nearer to the Pauline center, since it recognizes the new age and the new life that came into the world through Christ; and Hickling rightly praises[12] the novelty of divine grace. Nonetheless the dualistic framework remains somewhat of an abstraction, requiring it to be filled with personal content and application. J. Christiaan Beker adopts a similar apocalyptic framework and regards "apocalyptic [as] the indispensable means for [Paul's] interpretation of the Christ-event,"[13] and in his 1984 preface confesses that "this question touches the heart of the matter."[14] He matches this schema, however, with an interface of Paul's use of "symbolic" terms in applying the conviction he had about the cosmic triumph of God to particular contingencies in the situations of his readers. This "interaction between coherent center and contingent interpretation" is offered as the key to Paul's hermeneutic, and indeed his theology. The outstanding question remains, however: How can a series of events on a cosmic scale be made normative to and binding on various human situations?

E. F. Osborne,[15] on his own admission, reduces Paul's theology to one "simple theme," namely the unity of God. Such unity is expressed in what God has done to reveal and convey his righteousness, which is thought of as a saving power; and it embraces the cosmos within its scope. The divine righteousness "provides a basis for ethical and political action,"[16] he rightly comments at the close of a sustained argument based on the flow of the apostle's thought in the epistle to the Romans. But confining his attention to that one letter is a drawback; it fails to gather into a synthetic statement both the pre-Pauline and post-Pauline traditions regarding that term. Beker's refusal to consider the interrelations of "Tradition" and "Redaction" in the Pauline corpus shares this same weakness. Also even if "the righteousness of God" is seen in this dynamic way, it still remains an open question how Paul expected what God once did in saving action to provide a model for the Christian's ethical endeavor.[17]

Clearly, before we enter the field with any further suggestions as to a *centrum Paulinum*, we need to ask about the criteria by which any proposal may be justified. There is here the obvious danger of a hermeneutical circle, because the criteria are drawn from the same body of data that *ex hypothesi* contains the organizing principle; and it may well be objected that we are selecting criteria that we know in advance will serve the interests of our proposed term. There seems to be no way to escape this dilemma unless we are prepared to abandon the quest and treat Paul's theology as fragmentary responses delivered *ad hoc*. Yet, provided we continue to test the criteria by the data as they are uncovered, and provided we are willing to revise the initial theoretical proposal in the light of the reconstructed criteria, the enterprise is worthwhile and may be honestly and conscientiously pursued. The better way of putting the process, then, is to speak of a "hermeneutical spiral" by which we rise from one level to a more adequately framed hypothesis as new data are fed into the inquiry and it moves upward and forward.

The basic patterns of Paul's theological teaching, derived, from his generally undisputed letters, are as follows: (1) The primacy of God's grace takes the initiative and promotes human recovery. (2) Such an operation, while entering human history in the person of Jesus of Nazareth and at a given point in time, has repercussions that affect the cosmic scene and involve even the mysterious spiritual intelligences often referred to in Paul's world view. These cosmic forces are regarded as both created by God and alienated from him. (3) The cross remains crucial to Paul's salvation teaching both as an event in time[18] and as related to man's need as a sinner. But with equal insistence Paul regards the cross as the instrument of self-denial by which the "flesh" is overcome and a new life, cruciform in shape and diaconal in character, is made possible (Gal. 2:20; 6:14). (4) Thus the gap between historical *is*ness and ethical *ought*ness has to be bridged and a rationale provided for the apostolic claim that the death and resurrection of Jesus impinge on human activity both as a power to break the stranglehold of evil and as an effectual summons to new life. (5) Paul's theology was bound up with his professed vocation. He was both a Christian and a missionary, charged with a mandate to proclaim and live out the saving truth he claimed to have found in Jesus Christ. Word and life for Paul go hand in hand; and missionary theology meant just as obviously both the *kerygma* and the way of life Paul exemplified and enacted in his pastoral dealings with awkward people and ugly situations.[19]

THE THEME OF RECONCILIATION

I suggest that it is the overall theme of reconciliation that meets most—if not all—of these tests. This is not to say that the word-group *katallass*—is prominent in Paul's writings; manifestly it is not. Nor is it claimed that "reconciliation" is used with the same nuance in those places where it does occur; obviously it does not.[20] But the contention stands, namely that reconciliation provides a suitable umbrella under which the main features of Paul's *kerygma* and its practical outworking may be set; and justice is done to some of the main motifs in Pauline mission theology.

The term *reconciliation* has a pre-history in the tradition Paul gladly took over, as in 2 Corinthians 5:18–21 and Colossians 1:15–20. He was not content to leave the term open to misunderstanding, and there is form-critical, linguistic, and tradition-historical evidence to show how he changed the meaning in the noun and verb by subtle editorial adaptations to the surrounding context. In particular, he has disinfected the term of its gnosticizing taint—suggested by its reference to the process of automatic fiat and physical fusion of the disparate elements in the universe—by anchoring reconciliation in the historical events of Jesus' passion and tying in the effect of reconciliation to moral transformation in human lives.

Paul's counter-arguments are always on the level of personal relationships, of which forgiveness of sins is the greatest reality shared alike by apostle and people. Regarding that experience he appeals to us through a variety of images—justification, redemption, new life, sonship, the gift of the Spirit, and the promise of resurrection.

Against those enthusiastic followers who believed that their baptism brought the completion of salvation here and now, and against the intruding teacher who discounted morality as irrelevant once the spirit had been saved, Paul entered the plea of the "eschatological proviso," the "not yet" of a reconciliation that, unlike justification, is still going on and needs to be renewed continually. Hence the call to Christians at Corinth, "Be reconciled to God" (2 Cor. 5:20), lest they receive God's grace to no purpose (2 Cor. 2:5–11; 6:11–13). Reconciliation is thus admirably suited to express and safeguard the existential element in Paul's moral theology. God has achieved a final reconciliation of the world, but men and women need to live with moral sensitivity and vigilance—until the end comes.

The blend of God's deed and Paul's role as a reconciling agent at Corinth and in the note to Philemon illustrates how the transition from historical factuality to ethical obligation may be made. The middle term is Paul's "ministry of reconciliation" (2 Cor. 5:18)—the one clear job description Paul left on record. What God did expresses his great love, with Christ's cross at the center (Rom. 5:1–11). As he gratefully rejoiced in that love as a fact of experience, conveyed by the Spirit, Paul saw his mission as modeling what God had done in recalling the Corinthians to their true allegiance and in urging Philemon to consider the social implications of the new life on which he had embarked. The skeleton of an adequate ethical theory is seen here even though it took Christians eighteen centuries to work out the force and relevance of this admonition.

Equally, the same may be said about the teaching in Ephesians 2:11–22.[21] Here reconciliation takes on a horizontal direction. The inveterate hostility between Jew and non-Jew is overcome in the cross of Jesus, who has reconciled both groups in one body. The "one new person" in place of two suggests the vision of a "third race," a new species of humankind, who, in becoming part of the divine family, form a microcosm of that new society that is a token in God's design to place all of conscious life under the headship of the cosmic Christ (Eph. 1:10).

SUMMARY

These far-ranging and distinctive ideas—covering cosmic, personal, societal and ethnic areas of our human story—are nevertheless part of a pattern, whose picture fills the tapestry. The various strands are closely textured and intricately woven together. There is an emerging design and a coherent picture. We conclude that the most adequate and meaningful title for it is "Reconciliation."

SOME RESPONSES TO REVIEWERS

The elements in recent discussion, drawn from reviews, that seem to be worth a mention are as follows:

First, several writers have queried whether it is proper to speak at all of the "center" of Paul's theology, let alone propose that it has been accurately located and identified as reconciliation. The grounds for such a denial are diverse. For some reviewers such as the editor of the *Expository Times*,[22] Paul's thought cannot be captured in a single term; J. C. Beker agrees (in the preface to his 1984 edition, p. xvii) and opts for "coherence" over "core." But this preference raises the question, Coherent with what? C. F. D. Moule[23] rightly regards Paul's epistolary materials as polemically slanted, with changing targets in his sights. But his deduction—that as "the foreground of his concern changes, (so) with it, perhaps, the centre of his picture" shifts—leaves open the question, How did Paul know how to make the appropriate response in any given situation? So, in my judgment, both Beker and Moule are left with the lingering issue of what to do with a phrase such as "*my* gospel" (Rom. 2:16; Gal. 2:2).

More reasonably Moule and others have indicted the thesis of reconciliation as the Pauline center by saying that it expresses a truism, though I should reject the inference drawn by Jeffrey W. Gillette[24] that this exposition of Paul's gospel as intimately bound up with personal relationship is an "anthropocentric formulation." Quite the opposite. The thesis repeatedly states that God's deed is the foundation, and from it Paul reasons back to human need. The cosmic setting of Paul's teaching, noted by Robin Barbour,[25] provides the backdrop and whatever we do with the hermeneutical problem of the "principalities and powers" we must take them seriously in any understanding of the apostle's gospel.[26] But when all is said and done, the question remains: How does Christ's death and triumph over these powers impinge on our lives today? This issue lies unresolved in J. C. Beker's work on Paul,[27] though he seeks indirectly and obliquely to meet the challenge in a later, semi-popular study.[28]

Second, a telling criticism by William S. Campbell[29] asks whether the proposition that reconciliation is the *Pauli theologiae proprium*, especially in regard to the letter to the Romans, should in effect be recast. "Perhaps a modified form of [Martin's thesis] would gain wide assent, i.e. not that reconciliation *was* but that reconciliation *became* the way Paul formulated his gospel in communicating it to the Gentiles. This in turn would imply some process of development in Paul's thought so that reconciliation eventually came to stand at the apex of that development toward the end of his life." This suggestion seems eminently reasonable, and I accept it.[30] Indeed, I thought I had said as much (see p. 153). But perhaps the thought needed spelling out, and Dr. Campbell has rightly done that.

Third, more than one reviewer has seen the relevance of reconciliation to both Paul's self-understanding as a missionary pastor and the present-day tasks of ministry. The study leads to a "contextualizing (of) the theology of Paul." Much to be welcomed is the practical bearing of a reconciliation for the ministry of the church today. One merit of this approach to Paul's preaching is to see "how the horizontal aspect of reconciliation flows out of the vertical, the human from the divine."[31] These points of recognition and appraisal are in line with the author's intention in offering, not simply a textbook for students, but an exposition of Paul's teaching, which at its heart has value to us because it can assist us in the ongoing tasks and opportunities of service in the church and the world. Whether the thesis stands or falls, I am content to have raised the issue and have had a hearing. If J. A. Ziesler's summary—i.e., that the author (Martin) "may well be right"—speaks for several reviewers,[32] that is perhaps all I may hope for, given the wide and conflicting range of ways of interpreting Paul to our generation. At least one good result follows: we are faced with a continuing responsibility to make Paul's essential witness intelligible and applicable to our day. Maybe "reconciliation in Christ" will point the way.

NOTES

CHAPTER ONE (pp. 1-5)

1. G. F. Hasel, *New Testament Theology: Basic Issues in the Current Debate* (Grand Rapids, 1978), pp. 216, 218f.

2. A *tour de force* in this area is J. D. G. Dunn, *Unity and Diversity in the New Testament* (London, 1977). His book reveals more of the diversity than the unity which is reduced to some bare essentials (e.g. the link between the historical Jesus and the exalted Christ, or even simply, 'Jesus himself', pp. 369f.), as hostile critics have remarked (see the review in *Themelios* 5 [1979], pp. 30f.).

3. U. Luz, '*Theologia Crucis* als Mitte der Theologie im Neuen Testament', *Evangelische Theologie* 34 (1974), pp. 116-41.

4. See the various ways of treating the matter in H. Ridderbos, *Paul and Jesus* (Philadelphia, ET 1958); V. P. Furnish, 'The Jesus-Paul Debate: From Baur to Bultmann', *Bulletin of the John Rylands Library* 47 (1964-5), pp. 342-81; E. Jüngel, *Paulus und Jesus* (Tübingen, 2nd ed., 1964); W. G. Kümmel, 'Jesus und Paulus', *New Testament Studies* 10 (1963-4), pp. 163-81; F. F. Bruce, *Paul and Jesus* (Grand Rapids, 1974); G. N. Stanton, *Jesus of Nazareth in New Testament Preaching* (Cambridge, 1974); F. F. Bruce, 'Paul and the Historical Jesus', *Bulletin of the John Rylands Library of Manchester* 56 (1974), pp. 317-35.

5. P. Stuhlmacher, *Historical Criticism and Theological Interpretation of Scripture* (Philadelphia, ET 1977), pp. 90f. See his 'Jesus als Versöhner', in *Jesus Christus in Historie und Theologie*. Festschrift H. Conzelmann, ed. G. Strecker (Tübingen, 1975), pp. 87-104.

6. T. W. Manson, *On Paul and Jesus*, ed. M. Black (London, 1963), p. 50.

7. J. Weiss, *Earliest Christianity. A History of the Period A.D. 30-150*, vol. 2 (New York, 1959 ed.), p. 498: 'One perceives therefore that "reconciliation" or "atonement" is the comprehensive expression for the whole work of salvation'. On p. 497 Weiss had remarked that 'the most common and comprehensive expression for the event which Paul had experienced, and which all Christians must experience, is undoubtedly "reconciliation".' H. Ridderbos, 'The Biblical Message of Reconciliation', in his *Studies in Scripture and its Authority* (Grand Rapids, 1978), pp. 72-90, compresses his larger treatment in *Paul: An Outline of his Theology* (Grand Rapids, ET 1975).

8. As we can see by looking at the chapter titles of *Reconciliation in Today's World*, ed. A. O. Miller (Grand Rapids, 1969) which is a document prepared for the joint discussions of the Reformed and Presbyterian Council and the International Congregational Council held in Nairobi in August 1970 under the theme, 'God Reconciles and Makes Free'. See too D. Wiederkehr, *Glaube an Erlösung* (Freiburg, 1976). An ET is promised.

9. J. B. Lightfoot, *Saint Paul's Epistle to the Philippians* (London, 1896), preface.

CHAPTER TWO (pp. 9-31)

1. W. D. Davies, *Paul and Rabbinic Judaism* (London, 1948, 2nd ed. 1955), p. 1.

2. See Josephus, *Antiquities* 5.112: 'the knowledge of the one God is

common property among the Hebrews'; cf. E. Stauffer, *New Testament Theology* (London, ET 1955), p. 323 n. 786.

3. M. Hengel, *Judaism and Hellenism. Studies in their Encounter in Palestine during the Early Hellenistic Period*, vol. 1 (London, ET 1974), p. 312.

4. For one readable treatment of Paul's social position, see Λ. J. Malherbe, *Social Aspects of Early Christianity* (Baton Rouge, 1977). R. F. Hock, *The Social Context of Paul's Ministry* (Philadelphia, 1980) offers a corrective to Judge's position (see n. 6).

5. Quoted by F. F. Bruce, *Paul. Apostle of the Free Spirit* (Exeter, 1977), p. 15.

6. E. A. Judge, *The Social Pattern of Christian Groups in the First Century* (London, 1960), p. 58. See too his article , 'St Paul and Classical Society', *Jahrbuch für Antike und Christentum* 15 (1972), pp. 19-36.

7. A. M. Hunter, *Paul and his Predecessors* (London, 2nd ed. 1961), p. 9. Later discussions have built on the thesis of a pre-Pauline Christianity already suggested by A. Seeberg, *Der Katechismus der Urchristenheit* (Leipzig, 1903). See in particular, B. Rigaux, *The Letters of St Paul* (Chicago, ET 1968); K. Wegenast, *Das Verständnis der Tradition bei Paulus und in den Deuteropaulinen* (Göttingen, 1962); P. Fannon, 'The Influence of Tradition in St Paul', *SE* 4 (TU 102) (1968), pp. 292-307; J. W. Fraser, *Jesus and Paul: Paul as an Interpreter of Jesus from Harnack to Kümmel* (Abingdon, 1974), ch. 5.

8. M. Hengel, *The Son of God. The Origin of Christology and the History of Jewish-Hellenistic Religion* (London, ET 1976), p. 2.

9. E. P. Sanders, *Paul and Palestinian Judaism* (London, 1977), pp. 433f.

10. W. C. van Unnik, *Tarsus or Jerusalem* (London, ET 1962) = *Sparsa Collecta*. The Collected Essays of W. C. van Unnik (Leiden, 1973), pp. 259-320.

11. N. Turner, 'Where was Saul brought up?', in his *Grammatical Insights into the New Testament* (Edinburgh, 1965), pp. 83-5.

12. C. G. Montefiore, 'Rabbinic Judaism and the Epistles of St Paul', *Jewish Quarterly Review* 13 (1901), pp. 161-217, concluding that Paul 'was never a Rabbinic Jew at all, or he has quite forgotten what Rabbinic Judaism was and is'; idem, *Judaism and St Paul* (London, 1914); E. R. Goodenough, 'Paul and the Hellenisation of Christianity', in *Religions in Antiquity* (ed. J. Neusner) (Leiden, 1968), pp. 23-68; S. Sandmel, *The Genius of Paul* (New York, 1958).

13. W. D. Davies, *Paul and Rabbinic Judaism*, ch. 1.

14. W. L. Knox, *Some Hellenistic Elements in Primitive Christianity* (London, 1944), p. 33.

15. E. P. Sanders, *Paul and Palestinian Judaism*, pp. 6ff.

16. A. J. Festugière, *Personal Religion among the Greeks* (Berkeley/Los Angeles, 1960), p.41. See G. H. C. MacGregor and A. C. Purdy, *Jew and Greek: Tutors unto Christ* (London, 1936), p. 232.

17. H. Jonas, *The Gnostic Religion* (Boston, 1958). For what Gnosticism means as a rival to Pauline Christianity, see W. Schmithals, *Gnosticism in Corinth* (Nashville, ET 1971), pp. 30f.

18. P. Wendland, 'Hellenistic Ideas of Salvation in the Light of Anthropology', *American Journal of Theology* 17 (1913), pp. 345-51.

19. R. Reitzenstein, *Hellenistic Mystery-Religions* (Pittsburgh, ET 1978), p. 372; cf. H. J. Schoeps, *Paul. The Theology of the Apostle in the Light of Jewish Religious History* (London, ET 1961), p. 16.

20. W. Bousset, *Kyrios Christos* (Göttingen, 3rd ed. 1926); ET *Kyrios Christos* (New York/Nashville, 1970).

21. R. Bultmann, *Theology of the New Testament*, vol. 1 (London, ET 1952), pp. 181-3.

22. G. H. C. Macgregor in Macgregor and A. C. Purdy, *Jew and Greek: Tutors unto Christ* (as in n. 16), p. 236.

23. See, for example, W. Wrede, *Paul* (London, ET 1907), pp. 151f. There is a robust rejoinder to these ideas in J. G. Machen, *The Origin of Paul's Religion* (New York, 1925).

24. K. Stendahl, *Paul among Jews and Gentiles* (Philadelphia, 1977), pp. 1-77.

25. W. G. Kümmel, *Römer 7 und die Bekehrung des Paulus* (Leipzig, 1929). There is an account of Kümmel's position in his *Man in the New Testament* (London, ET 1963). See too J. D. G. Dunn, 'Romans 7:14-25 in the Theology of Paul', *Theologische Zeitschrift* 31 (1975), pp. 257-73.

26. J. Dupont, 'The Conversion of Paul, and its Influence on his Understanding of Salvation by Faith', in *Apostolic History and the Gospel*. Biblical and Historical Essays presented to F. F. Bruce, edd. W. W. Gasque and R. P. Martin (Exeter, 1970), pp. 176-94; see too G. Bornkamm, 'The Revelation of Christ to Paul on the Damascus Road and Paul's Doctrine of Justification and Revelation. A Study in Galatians 1', in *Reconciliation and Hope*. New Testament Essays on Atonement and Eschatology Presented to L. L. Morris, ed. R. J. Banks (Exeter, 1974), pp. 90-103.

27. E. Käsemann, 'Paul and Israel', *New Testament Questions of Today* (London, ET 1969), p. 185.

28. T. W. Manson, *On Paul and John* (as in chapter one, n. 6), p. 45.

29. K. Stendahl (as in n. 24), p. 7.

30. L. Baeck, 'The Faith of Paul', *Journal of Jewish Studies* 3 (1952), pp. 93-110.

31. W. Klassen, *The Forgiving Community* (Philadelphia, 1966), pp. 136f.

CHAPTER THREE (pp. 32-47)

1. W. Wrede, *Paul* (as in chapter two, n. 23), p. 123 (his italics); cf. p. 127. On the significance of Wrede's regarding Paul's teaching on justification as a *Kampfeslehre*, see E. Jüngel, *Paulus und Jesus* (Tübingen, 2nd ed. 1964), pp. 18ff.

2. A. Deissmann, *St Paul. A Study in Social and Religious History* (London, 1925), p. 271.

3. Wrede, *Paul*, p. 139f.

4. D. Hill, *Greek Words and Hebrew Meanings* (Cambridge, 1967), p. 98. See too J. A. Ziesler, *The Meaning of Righteousness in Paul* (Cambridge, 1972).

5. E. P. Sanders, *Paul and Palestinian Judaism* (as in chapter two, n. 9), pp. 442-7.

6. V. Taylor, *Forgiveness and Reconciliation* (London, 2nd ed. 1946), p. 48.

7. A. B. Crabtree, *The Restored Relationship. A Study in Justification and Reconciliation* (London, 1963), p. 40; cf. L. E. Keck, *Paul and his Letters* (Philadelphia, 1979), pp. 118-20: 'To justify is to rectify the relation to the norm; justification is rectification'.

8. T. W. Manson, *On Paul and John* (as in chapter one, n. 6), p. 56.

9. M. Barth, *Justification* (Grand Rapids, 1971), p.31.

10. A. B. Crabtree, *The Restored Relationship*, p. 41.

11. E. Käsemann, '"The Righteousness of God" in Paul', *New Testament*

Questions of Today (as in chapter two, n. 27), pp. 168-82; 'Justification and Salvation History in the Epistle to the Romans', *Perspectives on Paul* (London, ET 1971), pp. 60-78.

On the current debate there is a useful summary of the leading positions in M. T. Brauch's essay, 'Perspectives on "God's Righteousness" in Recent German Discussion', in E. P. Sanders, *Paul and Palestinian Judaism*. pp. 523-42.

12. W. Sanday and A. C. Headlam, *A Critical and Exegetical Commentary on St Paul's Epistle to the Romans* (Edinburgh, 1902), p. 36.

13. E. R. Bevan, *Hellenism and Christianity* (London, 1921), p. 92.

14. C. A. A. Scott, *Christianity according to St Paul* (Cambridge, 1927), pp. 17f.

15. A. Deissmann, *Light from the Ancient East* (London, ET 1927), pp. 318-31.

16. The reason for this lies in Paul's pragmatism as an evangelist and pastor. He warns against any move to break down the conventional hierarchy of the household, since it was a sociological factor to retain the support and sponsorship of such patronal heads of households that enabled their dependants to maintain the cohesion of a social group. See E. A. Judge, *The Social Patterns of Christian Groups in the First Century* (as in chapter 2, n. 6), pp. 60, 75f.

17. C. K. Barrett, *The Epistle to the Romans* (London, 1957), p. 76.

18. On the precise meaning of the sexual terms used in these verses, see V. P. Furnish, *The Moral Teaching of Paul* (Nashville, 1979), pp. 67-73.

19. J. B. Lightfoot, *The Epistles to the Colossians and Philemon* (London, 1890), p. 190.

20. W. Kramer, *Christ, Lord, Son of God* (London, ET 1966), pp. 169ff., sec. 47.

21. A. Deissmann, *Paul*, pp. 186ff.; cf. p. 271 for the phrase 'communion with Christ'.

22. C. A. A. Scott, *Christianity according to St. Paul* (as in n. 14), p. 28.

23. A. Schweitzer, *The Mysticism of the Apostle Paul* (London, ET 1931), p. 225. On this book, see A. C. Thiselton, 'Schweitzer's Interpretation of Paul', *The Expository Times* 90 (1978-9), pp. 132-7, and E. Jüngel's discussion of Schweitzer, *Paulus und Jesus* (as in n. 1), pp. 20-5. Quotations that follow in the text are from Schweitzer's *Mysticism*, pp. 225, 96, 109, 124, 123, in that order.

24. A. Schweitzer, *The Quest of the Historical Jesus* (London, ET 1910), p. 391.

25. C. F. D. Moule, *The Origin of Christology* (Cambridge, 1977), pp. 60-3. These pages contain the full bibliographical references to various suggestions made regarding the formula 'in Christ'.

26. Théo Preiss, *Life in Christ* (London, ET 1954), pp. 41f., referring to Deissmann's *The Religion of Jesus and the Faith of Paul* (London, ET 1923), p. 171.

27. Théo Preiss, *Life in Christ*, p. 42.

CHAPTER FOUR (pp. 48-67)

1. G. S. Hendry, 'Reveal, Revelation', in *A Theological Word Book of the Bible*, ed. A. Richardson (London, 1950), p. 198; cf. G. Bornkamm, 'The Revelation of God's Wrath', in his *Early Christian Experience* (London, ET 1969), pp. 47-70.

2. M. D. Hooker, 'Adam in Rom. 1', *New Testament Studies* 6 (1959-60). pp.

296-306; idem, 'A Further Note on Romans 1', *New Testament Studies* 13 (1966-67), pp. 181-3.

3.   R. Scroggs, *The Last Adam* (Oxford, 1966), pp. 64f.; idem, *Paul for a New Day* (Philadelphia, 1977), ch. 1; cf. C. K. Barrett, *From First Adam to Last* (London, 1962), ch. 1, and an earlier study, M. Black, 'The Pauline Doctrine of the Second Adam', *Scottish Journal of Theology* 7 (1954), pp. 170-9.

4.   J. Jervell, *Imago Dei: Gen. i. 26f. im Spätjudentum, in der Gnosis und in den paulinischen Briefen* (Göttingen, 1960), pp. 276f.

5.   E. Stauffer, *New Testament Theology* (as in chapter two, n. 2), pp. 64f.; cf. Strack-Billerbeck, *Kommentar zum Neuen Testament aus Talmud und Midrasch* (Munich, ed. 1956) vol. I, pp. 137ff.; vol. II, p. 167.

6.   K. Heim, *The World. Its Creation and Consummation* (Philadelphia, ET 1962), pp. 124-9.

7.   F. F. Bruce, *The Epistle to the Romans* (London, 1963), p. 173.

8.   C. K. Barrett, *From First Adam to Last* (as in n. 3), p. 86.

9.   J. Weiss, *Earliest Christianity* (as in chapter one, n. 7), vol. 2, p. 602, n. 14.

10.   T. W. Manson, *On Paul and Jesus* (as in chapter one, n. 6), p. 22.

11.   E. P. Sanders, *Paul and Palestinian Judaism* (as in chapter two, n. 9), p. 499.

12.   For this translation of Colossians 2:20, see J. A. T. Robinson, *The Body. A Study in Pauline Theology* (London, 1952), p. 43.

13.   W. O. E. Oesterley and T. H. Robinson, *Hebrew Religion* (London, 1930), pp. 116f. For sin likened to 'a demon that dwells within man', see M. Dibelius, *Die Geisterwelt im Glauben des Paulus* (Göttingen, 1909), p. 123.

14.   F. J. Leenhardt, *The Epistle to the Romans* (London, ET 1960), p. 184-91. C. K. Barrett, *The Epistle to the Romans*, p. 143, is the source of this quotation.

15.   Helpful studies on this puzzling term in Paul's anthropology and ethical vocabulary are: W. Barclay, *Flesh and Spirit* (London, 1962); W. D. Stacey, *The Pauline View of Man* (London, 1956); R. Jewett, *Paul's Anthropological Terms* (Leiden, 1971), pp. 49-166; W. G. Kümmel, *Man in the New Testament* (London, 1963); E. Brandenburger, *Fleisch und Geist: Paulus und die dualistische Weisheit* (Neukirchen, 1968).

16.   R. Bultmann, *TDNT*, vol. 3, pp. 645-54.

17.   K. Stendahl, *Paul among Jews and Gentiles* (as in chapter two, n. 24), p. 21.

18.   A. T. Hanson, *Paul's Understanding of Jesus* (Hull, 1963), pp. 4-10; cf. his *Studies in Paul's Technique and Theology* (London, 1974), pp. 13-51.

19.   See J. Denney, *Studies in Theology* (London, 1895), pp. 97-9.

20.   C. K. Barrett, *The Epistle to the Romans* (as in chapter three, n. 17), p. 108.

21.   A. Deissmann, *Light from the Ancient East* (as in chapter three, n. 15), p. 316.

22.   E. Lohmeyer, *Die Brief an die Philipper* (Meyer Kommentar) (Göttingen, 1930), p. 96. Cf. his *Kyrios Jesus: Eine Untersuchung zu Phil. 2.5-11* (Heidelberg, 1928; 2nd ed. 1961), pp. 41-3.

23.   E. Käsemann, 'A Critical Analysis of Philippians 2.5-11', *God and Christ*, ed. R. W. Funk, *Journal for Theology and the Church* 5 (Tübingen, ET 1968), pp. 45-88 (72-4).

CHAPTER FIVE (pp. 71-89)

1. E. Käsemann, 'Some Thoughts on the Theme "The Doctrine of Reconciliation in the New Testament"', in *The Future of our Religious Past*, ed. J. M. Robinson (London/New York, ET 1971), pp. 49-64. The occasion and background of this essay in the Montreal consultation of 1963 are well described by A. N. Wilder's contribution, 'Reconciliation — New Testament Scholarship and Confessional Differences: Part one', *Interpretation* 19 (1965), pp. 203-16: Part two, pp. 312-27.

2. E. Käsemann, 'A Critical Analysis of Philippians 2:5-11' (as in chapter four, n. 23), p. 46 (translation amended).

3. J. A. Fitzmyer, 'Reconciliation in Pauline Theology', in *No Famine in the Land*. Studies in Honor of John L. Mackenzie, edd. J. W. Flanagan and A. W. Robinson (Missoula, 1975), pp. 155-77 (175). Fitzmyer's critique of Käsemann's essay also provides a full bibliography of recent studies.

4. E. Käsemann, 'Some Thoughts', p. 64.

5. See earlier, p. 33. Cf. J. Jeremias, *The Central Message of the New Testament* (London, ET 1965), p. 59.

6. E. P. Sanders, *Paul and Palestinian Judaism* (as in chapter two, n. 9), pp. 463-72, referring to D. E. H. Whiteley, *The Theology of St. Paul* (Oxford, 2nd ed. 1974), p. 130.

7. A. Feuillet, 'Le plan salvifique de Dieu d'après l'épître aux Romains: essais sur la structure littéraire de l'épître et sa signification théologique', *Revue Biblique* 57 (1950), pp. 336-87, 489-529.

8. J. A. Fitzmyer, 'Reconciliation', p. 165.

9. J. A. Fitzmyer, 'Reconciliation', p. 165.

10. A. N. Wilder, 'Reconciliation' (as in n. 1), pp. 315f., effectively comments that 'the personal and mutual force of the image of reconciliation in its human depth is disclosed in the pastoral situation', and appeals to Paul's handling of the situation in Philemon as an illustration of a concrete application, even if *katallagē* is not mentioned. 'The main point is that the doctrine of the work of Christ is opened up here again by a life context in the Pauline correspondence.' He concludes: 'None of the main images for the work of Christ have the poignant personal character that reconciliation has' (p. 317).

11. R. Bultmann, *Theology of the New Testament* (as in chapter two, n. 21), vol. 1, p. 46.

12. E. Käsemann, 'Zum Verständnis von Römer 3, 24-26', in his *Exegetische Versuche und Besinnungen*, vol. 1 (Göttingen, 1960), pp. 96-100; A. M. Hunter, *Paul and his Predecessors* (as in chapter two, n. 7), pp. 120-2.

13. C. H. Talbert, 'A Non-Pauline Fragment at Rom. 3:24-26', *Journal of Biblical Literature* 85 (1966), pp. 287-96; N. H. Young, 'Did St. Paul compose Rom. iii. 24f?', *Australian Biblical Review* 22 (1974), pp. 23-32. Further bibliography in D. Zeller, 'Sühne und Langmut', *Theologie und Philosophie* 43 (1968), pp. 51-75; P. Stuhlmacher, 'Zur neueren Exegese von Röm. 3, 24-26', in *Jesus und Paulus*, edd. E. E. Ellis and E. Grässer (Göttingen, 1975), pp. 315-33; and U. Wilckens, *Der Brief an die Römer* (Zurich/Köln, 1978), pp. 182-202.

14. J. Reumann, 'The Gospel of the Righteousness of God: Pauline Reinterpretation in Rom. 3:21-31', *Interpretation* 20 (1966), pp. 432-52 (p. 436, n. 10).

15. E. Lohse, *Märtyrer und Gottesknecht* (Göttingen, 2nd ed. 1963), pp. 149f.

16. W. G. Kümmel, '*Paresis* and *Endeixis*: a Contribution to the Understanding of the Pauline Doctrine of Justification', *Journal for Theology and the Church* 3 (Tübingen, ET 1967), pp. 1-13 (4, 11f.).

17. J. Reumann, 'The Gospel of the Righteousness' (as in n. 14), p. 439; K. Wegenast, *Das Verständnis der Tradition bei Paulus und in den Deuteropaulinen* (as in chapter two, n. 7), p. 76, n. 1.

18. W. Schrage, 'Röm. 3, 21-26 und die Bedeutung des Todes Christi bei Paulus', in *Das Kreuz Christi*, ed. P. Rieger (Forum 12: Tübingen, 1969), p. 65.

19. See A. Pluta, *Gottes Bundestreue*. Ein Schlüsselbegriff in Rom 3, 25a (Stuttgart, 1969).

20. E. Lohse, *Märtyrer* (as in n. 15), p. 152; cf. H. Kessler, *Die Theologische Bedeutung des Todes Jesu* (Düsseldorf, 2nd ed. 1971), p. 265.

21. D. Hill, *Greek Words and Hebrew Meanings* (as in chapter three, n. 4), pp. 42-7, suggests that Paul's thought of a propitiatory, atoning death was sparked by his remembrance of the Maccabean martyrs and a hanukkah celebration. P. Stuhlmacher, 'Zur neueren Exegese' (as in n. 13), pp. 318-25 has rebutted 'Lohse's four arguments for locating the setting of *hilastērion* in the world of hellenistic Jewish theology of martyrdom'.

22. J. Reumann, 'The Gospel of Righteousness' (as in n. 14), p. 443, based on T. W. Manson's initial suggestion, 'HILASTERION', *Journal of Theological Studies* 46 (1945), pp. 1-10. This requires the understanding of *hilastērion* not as the 'mercy seat' in the strict sense but 'the locality at which acts or events covered by the verb *hilaskesthai* (to expiate) take place' (Manson). Then it becomes possible to arrange a series of contrasts between the old and new place of 'atonement':

The old hilastērion	*The new* hilastērion
1.It is hidden in the Holy of Holies	1.It is displayed publicly (verb 'set forth')
2.Its benefits depend on ritual	2.Its benefits depend on faith
3.Its expiation is effective through blood	3.Its expiation is through *his* (emphatic) blood

There have been objections — none compelling — levelled at this view by L. Morris, 'The meaning of *hilastērion* in Romans III. 25', *New Testament Studies* 2 (1955-56), pp. 33-43 (36f.).

23. R. H. Fuller, *The Foundations of New Testament Christology* (London, 1965), pp. 118f.

24. K. Wegenast, *Das Verständnis* (as in chapter two, n. 7), p. 78.

25. L. Morris, *The Apostolic Preaching of the Cross* (London, 3rd ed. 1965), pp. 184-208; D. Hill, *Greek Words*, p. 39, says that in 20 out of 29 references *hilastērion* in the LXX renders *kappōret*.

26. F. F. Bruce, *The Epistle to the Romans* (as in chapter four, n. 7), pp. 105f.

27. This argument, employing the device of Paul's redaction of a Jewish cultic confessional formula, would offset L. Morris' otherwise conclusive statement: 'The Epistle to the Romans does not move in the sphere of Levitical symbolism, and a reference to the *kappōreth* here would be out of character.' G. Wiencke, *Paulus über Jesu Tod. Die Deutung des Todes Jesu bei Paulus und ihre Herkunft* (Gütersloh, 1939), pp. 69-78, surveys the main lines of Paul's teaching on atonement. He concludes that Paul is consistent in his avoidance of Day of Atonement imagery and so 'reconciliation' does not mean a cultic term but

relates to human relationships (p. 74). Paul has no polemic against the saving
significance of the Temple sacrifices (p. 185).

28. S. K. Williams, *Jesus' Death as Saving Event.* The Background and Origin
of a Concept (Missoula, 1975), pp. 17f. Paul's use of phrases to do with 'faith in
Jesus' can be flexible, as we note from Phil. 3:9, 10. Williams wishes to see the
pre-Pauline fragment preserved in verses 25, 26 *in toto.* He regards the Gentiles
as in view here — an unlikely idea.

29. H. G. Reventlow, *Rechtfertigung im Horizont des Alten Testaments* (Munich
1971), p. 146, on 'righteousness' as creating a new world order.

30. G. Klein, 'Gottes Gerechtigkeit als Thema der neuesten Paulusfors-
chung', *Rekonstruktion und Interpretation* (Göttingen, 1969), pp. 225-236: see
especially p. 229 on 'Grundstruktur des paulinischen Gerechtigkeitsbegriffes
als einer Kategorie der Relation'.

31. H. G. Reventlow, *Rechtfertigung* (n. 29), p. 120. The phrase 'sweet
exchange' comes from the *Epistle to Diognetus* (2nd cent.) 9:5. The text there uses
the very rare word *antallagē*.

32. This short note calls attention to a newly published work by P.
Stuhlmacher, *Das Evangelium von der Versöhnung in Christus* (Stuttgart, 1979),
written with Helmut Class who addresses (pp. 55-88) the social, political and
ecclesiastical dimensions of reconciliation in the light of Stuhlmacher's earlier
exposition of the biblical materials (pp. 13-54).

The latter has as its aim the demonstration that reconciliation is a
fundamental theme of the New Testament witnesses. It begins with Jesus'
ministry and proclamation, finds its clear expression in Paul and the later
'Pauline' writers and surfaces in documents such as 1 Peter and Hebrews. The
evangelists, with their varying emphases, are united by this common
announcement of God's act in the mission and accomplishment of Messiah
Jesus who is Lord. Stuhlmacher's conclusion is reached: 'The gospel of God's
reconciliation with his creation through the mission of Jesus Christ the Messiah
is the centrepiece of the New Testament' (p. 44).

At the close of our chapter on Romans 3:24-26 Stuhlmacher's pages (26-29)
are especially interesting. He reviews his earlier (see n. 13 above) defence of the
passage in Romans as a pre-Pauline confession of Christ's work as 'mercy-seat'
(against the objections raised by E. Lohse — see n. 15). Lohse wanted to
interpret *hilastērion* in the light of a Jewish theology of martyrdom, based on 4
Maccabees, a line recently followed by S. K. Williams (see n. 28). But the
difficulties with this view are so formidable that Stuhlmacher has little
hesitation in returning to the cultic setting of *hilastērion* as the vital clue. More
imaginatively he suggests that this pre-Pauline proclamation of Jesus' death
based on Leviticus 16 goes back to Stephen and his circle and represents a piece
of soteriology traceable to Jerusalem and later Antioch where the followers of
Stephen gathered (Acts 11:19ff.). There Paul and Barnabas become
acquainted with it (Acts 11:25; 13:1ff.).

One item of interesting 'speculation' invites another, though we recognise
the danger of building one theory upon another theory. The letter to the
Hebrews has been regarded as emanating from Stephen's circle on the grounds
of some common interests. It is remarkable that there are several points of
contact between the short paragraph in Romans 3:24-26 and Hebrews 9.

Romans 3:24-26	*Hebrews 9*
justified . . . as a gift (*dōrean*, v. 24)	gifts (*dōra*, v. 9)

hilastērion (v. 25)	*hilastērion* (mercy seat, v. 5)
'by his blood' (v. 25)	'his own blood' (v. 12; cf. vv. 14, 20-22)
redemption through the Messiah (v. 24) 'sins passed over' in God's forbearance (v. 25)	'eternal redemption' (v. 12) 'errors of the people' (v. 7), suggesting a forbearing attitude to human lapses in Hebrews 9:15-22, Exodus 24:
God's righteousness (v. 25), understood as his covenant-faithfulness	6-8 is appealed to as God's covenant — expressed by animal blood — which anticipates the 'new covenant' (Heb. 8:8-13, 13:20)

The eucharistic setting of Romans 3:24-26 would be further strengthened by a similar background in Hebrews 9, especially v. 20 which parallels the liturgical words of the Lord's supper institution, 'This is the blood of the covenant which God commanded you.'

CHAPTER SIX (pp. 90-110)

1. E. D. Hirsch, *Validity in Interpretation* (New Haven, 1967), pp. 222f.
2. F. F. Bruce, *1 and 2 Corinthians* (London, 1971), p. 23.
3. T. W. Manson, '2 Cor. 2.14-17; Suggestions towards an Exegesis', in *Studia Paulina in honorem J. de Zwaan*, edd. J. N. Sevenster and W. C. van Unnik (Haarlem, 1953), pp. 155ff. (161).
4. On the meaning of the verb in 6:1: 'working together with God' (the last two words are added *ad sensum*), see J. Murphy-O'Connor, *Paul on Preaching* (London, 1964), pp. 72-6. The basis for this approach has been correctly identified by V. P. Furnish, 'The Ministry of Reconciliation', *Currents in Theology and Mission* 4 (1977), pp. 204-18, as Paul's *apologia* in 2:14-7:4 for his apostleship. 'He seeks to establish, in the face of contrary views, what authentic apostleship is and involves' (206). The apostolic ministry is for him inseparable from the truth of the gospel, as is clear in 4:2 as well as 6:1f. See too J. H. Schütz, *Paul and the Anatomy of Apostolic Authority* (Cambridge, 1975), pp. 165-86.
5. I. H. Marshall, 'The Meaning of "Reconciliation"', in *Unity and Diversity in New Testament Theology. Essays in Honor of George E. Ladd.* ed. R. A. Guelich (Grand Rapids, 1978), pp. 117-32 (129). L. Goppelt, 'Versöhnung durch Christus', in *Christologie und Ethik. Aufsätze zum Neuen Testament* (Göttingen, 1968), p. 160, calls verse 20*b* one of Paul's kerygmatic 'imperatives' which are based on similar 'indicatives'. For what the correlation implies — and in answer to Käsemann — see Goppelt's essay, 'Die Herrschaft Christi und die Welt' (in volume as above), pp. 121-6.
6. C. K. Barrett, *The Second Epistle to the Corinthians* (London, 1973), p. 179. See too H. Vorländer-C. Brown in *The New International Dictionary of New Testament Theology*, vol. 3 (Exeter, 1978), p. 170.
7. C. K. Barrett, *Second Corinthians*, p. 163.
8. L. Sabourin, 'Note sur 2 Cor. 5, 21: Le Christ fait péché', *Sciences Ecclésiastiques* 11.3 (1959), pp. 419-24; S. Lyonnet, *Sin, Redemption, and Sacrifice: A Biblical and Patristic Study* (Rome, 1970), pp. 185-296, especially pp. 250-6.
9. R. H. Fuller, *The Mission and Achievement of Jesus* (London, 1954), p. 57.
10. E. Käsemann, 'The Saving Significance of the Death of Jesus in Paul', *Perspectives on Paul* (London, ET 1971), pp. 32-59 (44).

11. C. K. Barrett, *Second Corinthians*, p. 177; he gives the references to other possibilities.

12. R. H. Strachan, *The Second Epistle of Paul to the Corinthians* (London, 1935), pp. 115f.

13. J. D. G. Dunn, 'Paul's Understanding of the Death of Jesus', in *Reconciliation and Hope* (as in chapter two, n. 26), pp. 125-41 (130).

14. F. F. Bruce, *1 and 2 Corinthians*, p. 207.

15. H. Windisch, *Der zweite Korintherbrief* (Göttingen, 1924), p. 182.

16. T. W. Manson, '2 Cor. 2.14-17' (as in n. 3), p. 156.

17. R. V. G. Tasker, *The Second Epistle of Paul to the Corinthians* (London, 1958), p. 86.

18. J. Murphy-O'Connor, *Paul on Preaching* (as in n. 4), pp. 75, 92.

19. M. Hengel, *The Son of God* (as in chapter two, n. 8), pp. 12-15.

20. H. Johnson, *The Humanity of the Saviour* (London, 1962).

21. See now M. D. Hooker, *Pauline Pieces* (London, 1979), pp. 41-52; cf. her essay 'Interchange in Christ', *Journal of Theological Studies* n. s. 22 (1971), pp. 349-61.

22. C. E. B. Cranfield, *The Epistle to the Romans*, vol. 1 (Edinburgh, 1975), p. 291.

23. P. Stuhlmacher, 'Erwägungen zum ontologischen charakter der *kainē ktisis* bei Paulus', *Evangelische Theologie* 27 (1967), pp. 1-35.

24. C. K. Barrett, *Second Corinthians*, p. 175 (italics added). He does qualify the statement somewhat.

25. Notably by J. Dupont, *La réconciliation dans la théologie de saint Paul* (Bruges/Paris, 1953); cf. F. Büchsel, *TDNT*, vol. 1 (1964), pp. 251-9 and the more recent materials from the Murabba' at caves near Qumran to which J. A. Fitzmyer (chapter five, n. 3) draws attention (173).

26. J.-F. Collange, *Enigmes de la deuxième épître de Paul aux Corinthiens* (Cambridge, 1972), p. 268.

27. T. W. Manson, *On Paul and John* (as in chapter one, n. 6), p. 52.

28. F. Neugebauer, *In Christus* (Göttingen, 1961), pp. 85f.; H. Lietzmann, *An die Korinther I-II* (Tübingen, 1949), p. 125: *en Christō = dia Christou*, which he translates 'durch Christus'; J.-F. Collange, *Enigmes*, p. 272, agreeing with E. B. Allo, *Seconde Epître aux Corinthiens* (Paris, 2nd. ed. 1956), p. 170.

29. A. Plummer, *A Critical and Exegetical Commentary on the Second Epistle of St. Paul to the Corinthians* (Edinburgh, 1915), ad loc.; H. Windisch (as in n. 15), p. 193: 'eine unvollendete Handlung beschreibt'; D. von Allmen, 'Réconciliation du monde et christologie cosmique', *Revue d'Histoire et de Philosophie religieuses* 1 (1968), pp. 32-45 (37 n. 20).

30. See T. W. Manson's explanation (*On Paul and John* [as in n. 27], p. 53): 'When Paul speaks of "our" reconciliation, he uses the aorist; when he speaks of that of the world, not. It is a process which, as a whole, is still continuing though in any particular case it is complete.' But this 'simple' solution breaks down on the use of the aorist tense of Colossians 1:20 where cosmic reconciliation ('all things') is in view.

31. I. H. Marshall, 'The Meaning of "Reconciliation"', p. 123; but cf. p. 129, where the teaching of 2 Maccabees acted, it is claimed, as an antithesis to Paul whose 'teaching was formulated in conscious contrast to this Jewish attitude'.

32. J. Dupont, *La réconciliation*, p. 15.

33. J. Denney, *Second Corinthians* (London, 1894), p. 216; cf. J.-F. Collange, *Enigmes*, p. 274.

34. P. Bonnard, *L'épître de S. Paul aux Philippiens* (Paris, 1950), p. 49.

35. Calvin, 'Est hic insignis locus, si quis alius est in toto Paulo' (cited by Denney, p. 210).

36. P. E. Hughes, *Paul's Second Epistle to the Corinthians* (London, 1962), p. 211.

37. E. Käsemann, 'Some Thoughts' (as in chapter five, n. 1), p. 53, concluding as probable that 'in vv. 19-21 we have a pre-Pauline hymnic fragment', or at least that 'Paul has taken and used motifs from earlier forms of the Christian proclamation'.

38. E. Güttgemanns, *Der leidende Apostel und sein Herr. Studien zur paulinischen Christologie* (Göttingen, 1966), pp. 312-17; cf. Collange, *Enigmes*, p. 267.

39. W. Popkes, from a paper privately circulated (quoted with permission).

40. This close connection between Paul the 'apostle' (although he prefers the word 'servant' [*diakonos*, used 20 times in 2 Cor.]) and his message of reconciliation is well brought out by V. P. Furnish, 'The Ministry of Reconciliation' (as in n. 4), 216-18. He calls attention to the verb 'to entreat' (*parakalein*) which can mean in some contexts 'to seek reconciliation' — an appropriate nuance in 6:1 as well as 5:20. He concludes, in criticism of Käsemann's position which subordinates reconciliation to justification and which emphasises how seldom the actual term is used: 'Reconciliation is not an "incidental" idea in Paul's thought. When we see how he's using the term, we are brought into touch with the very heart of his gospel' (218).

CHAPTER SEVEN (pp. 111-126)

1. M. D. Hooker, 'Were there False Teachers in Colossae?', in *Christ and Spirit in the New Testament*, edd. B. Lindars and S. S. Smalley (Cambridge, 1973), pp. 315-32. On the nature of the trouble at Colossae, see now J. C. O'Neill, 'The Source of the Christology in Colossians', *New Testament Studies* 26 (1979), pp. 87-100.

2. E. Käsemann, 'A Primitive Christian Baptismal Liturgy', *Essays on New Testament Themes* (London, ET 1964), pp. 149-68 (149). The latest contribution to the discussion is Wayne McCown's essay, 'The Hymnic Structure of Colossians 1:15-20', *Evangelical Quarterly* 51 (1979), pp. 156-66.

3. E. Norden, *Agnostos Theos* (Berlin, 1913), pp. 250ff.

4. E. Schweizer, 'Die Kirche als Leib Christi in den paulinischen Antilegomena', in *Neotestamentica* (Zurich, 1953), pp. 293-316; cf. his 'The Church as the Missionary Body of Christ', *New Testament Studies* 8 (1961-2), pp. 1-11, and his more recent commentary, *Der Brief an die Kolosser* (Zurich/Köln, 1976).

5. For example, Peter T. O'Brien in the forthcoming *Word Biblical Commentary* (Waco, 1981).

6. N. Kehl, *Der Christushymnus im Kolosserbrief* (Stuttgart, 1967), p. 41.

7. C. F. D. Moule, *The Epistles of Paul the Apostle to the Colossians and to Philemon* (Cambridge, 1957), p. 71.

8. E. Lohse, *Colossians and Philemon* (Philadelphia, ET 1971), p. 57; cf. J. Ernst, *Pleroma und Pleroma Christi. Geschichte und Deutung eines Begriffes der paulinischen Antilegomena* (Regensburg, 1970), pp. 41-50.

9. See n. 5.

10. E. Käsemann, 'Some Thoughts' (as in chapter five, n. 1), p. 63.

11. M. Dibelius-H. Greeven, *An die Kolosser, Epheser, an Philemon* (Tübingen, 1953), ad loc.

12. G. Delling, *TDNT*, vol. 7, p. 670; on the meaning of *stoicheia*, see the latest contribution of H. Berkhof, *Christ and the Powers* (Scottdale, Pa., 2nd ed. 1977).

13. H. Berkhof, *Christ and the Powers*, p. 30.

14. E. Schweizer, *The Church as the Body of Christ* (London, ET 1964), p. 70.

15. E. Lohse, *Colossians and Philemon*, p. 131.

16. N. Kehl, *Der Christushymnus*, pp. 163-5; B. N. Wambacq, '"per eum reconciliare . . . quae in caelis sunt", Col. 1, 20', *Revue Biblique* 55 (1948), pp. 35-42; J. Michl, 'Die "Versöhnung" (Kol. 1, 20)', *Theologische Quartalschrift* 128 (1948), pp. 442-62; W. Michaelis, *Versöhnung des Alls. Die frohe Botschaft von der Gnade Gottes* (Berne, 1950), pp. 25-30, who argues against P. Benoit (*La sainte Bible* commentary, 1949, p. 56) that the reconciliation cannot be restricted to angels nor mean an 'involuntary submission' nor suggest only a 'collective salvation'; rather it must include the salvation of every individual. The term, he insists, must not be 'restricted' or 'weakened' (*abschwächen*). Michaelis' key-term is 'restoration' (*Herstellung*) relating to God's promises for the entire human race whose 'home-coming' (*Heimkehr*) is part of the divine plan. See above, p. 133.

Fr. Mussner, *Christus, das All und die Kirche* (Trier, 1955), p. 71, thinks the question evoked by Col. 1:20 is, Who is the mediator of reconciliation?, not who or what is reconciled. The answer is 'Christ alone'. So A. Vögtle, *Das Neue Testament und die Zukunft des Kosmos* (Düsseldorf, 1970), pp. 227-9, and E. Schweizer, 'Kolosser 1, 15-20', in *Beiträge zur Theologie des Neuen Testaments. Neutestamentliche Aufsätze (1955-1970)* (Zurich, 1970), pp. 113-45 (134).

E. Lohse, *Colossians and Philemon*, p. 59; P. T. O'Brien, 'Col. 1:20 and the Reconciliation of All Things', *Reformed Theological Review* 33 (1974), pp. 45-53, and his pages in the *Word Biblical Commentary* (as in n. 5).

17. W. Michaelis, *Versöhnung*, p. 25, makes a good point when he argues that the sense of 'all things' of Col. 1:20 must be decided by same expression in 1:16.

18. Fr. Mussner, *Theologie der Freiheit nach Paulus* (Düsseldorf, 1976), p. 52, describes the setting free of human beings to enjoy the freedom of God's children as 'the basic theme' of Paul's theology, and links it to Jesus' proclamation.

CHAPTER EIGHT (pp. 127-154)

1. M. Black, *Romans* (London, 1973), p. 18.

2. W. G. Kümmel, *Introduction to the New Testament* (London, 1st ed. ET 1966), p. 221.

3. J. Munck, *Christ and Israel. An Interpretation of Romans 9-11* (Philadelphia, ET 1967), p. 55.

4. E. Käsemann, 'Paul and Israel', *New Testament Questions of Today* (as in chapter two, n. 27), pp. 183-7 (184).

5. See in particular H. L. Ellison, *The Mystery of Israel* (Exeter, 1968); M. Barth, *Israel and the Church* (Richmond, Va., 1969); P. Richardson, *Israel in the Apostolic Church* (Cambridge, 1969); W. D. Davies, 'Paul and the People of

Israel', *New Testament Studies* 24 (1977-8), pp. 4-39; idem, 'Romans 11.13-24: a suggestion', in *Paganisme, Judaïsme, Christianisme: Mélanges offerts à Marcel Simon* (Paris, 1978), pp. 131-44.

6. F. F. Bruce, *Romans* (as in chapter four, n. 7), p. 223.

7. The discussion is well reported in C. E. B. Cranfield, *Romans*, vol. 2 (Edinburgh, 1979), pp. 562-72.

8. W. Sanday and A. C. Headlam, *Romans* (as in chapter three, n. 11), p. 335.

9. J. Munck, *Christ and Israel*, pp. 134-7.

10. C. E. B. Cranfield, *Romans*, vol. 1, p. 253.

11. F. F. Bruce, *Romans*, p. 119; C. K. Barrett, *Romans*, p. 100; C. E. B. Cranfield, *Romans*, vol. 1, p. 255; K. Barth, *A Shorter Commentary on Romans* (London, ET 1959) ad loc.

12. M. Black, *Romans*, p. 81.

13. M. Wolter, *Rechtfertigung und zukünftiges Heil. Untersuchungen zu Röm. 5. 1-11* (Berlin, 1978), ch. 1. I am indebted to this work for many of the ideas woven into the text, especially his arrangement of the argument of Rom. 5 (pp. 217-22).

14. J. A. T. Robinson, *Wrestling with Romans* (London, 1979), p. 57.

15. C. K. Barrett, *Romans*, p. 102.

16. 'As we are justified by faith, then, let us enjoy the peace we have with God through our Lord Jesus Christ.'

17. E. Käsemann, *An die Römer* (Tübingen, 3rd ed. 1974), p. 125.

18. M. Wolter, *Rechtfertigung*, p. 86.

19. E. Schweizer, 'The Church as the Missionary Body of Christ', in *Neotestamentica* (as in chapter seven, n. 4), p. 319.

20. W. G. Kümmel, 'Interpretation of Romans 5:1-11', in *Exegetical Method. A Student's Handbook*, ed. O. Kaiser and W. G. Kümmel (New York, ET 1963), pp. 49-58 (55).

21. E. Dinkler, *Eirene. Der urchristliche Friedensgedanke* (Heidelberg, 1973), pp. 34f. n. 108, citing Psalm 34:15: 'Let us seek peace and follow it'; cf. L. Goppelt, 'Versöhnung durch Christus', in his *Christologie und Ethik* (as in ch. six, n. 5), pp. 147-64 (162).

CHAPTER NINE (pp. 157-198)

1. C. F. D. Moule, *The Origin of Christology* (as in chapter three, n. 25), pp. 62f.

2. F. W. Beare, *The Epistle to the Ephesians* (The Interpreter's Bible, vol. 11) (Nashville, 1953), p. 599.

3. F. W. Beare, *Ephesians*, p. 600.

4. H. Schlier, *Christus und Kirche im Epheserbrief* (Tübingen, 1930).

5. W. Rader, *The Church and Racial Hostility. A History of Interpretation of Ephesians 2:11-22* (Tübingen, 1978), pp. 180f.

6. E. Käsemann, *Leib und Leib Christi* (Tübingen, 1933).

7. E. Käsemann, 'Ephesians and Acts', in *Studies in Luke-Acts*, ed. L. E. Keck and J. L. Martyn (London, 1968), pp. 288-97.

8. H. Merklein, *Christus und die Kirche: Die theologische Grundstruktur des Epheserbriefes nach Eph. 2:11-18* (Stuttgart, 1973): idem, *Das kirchliche Amt nach dem Epheserbrief* (Munich, 1973), pp. 118-58.

9. E. Percy, *Probleme der Kolosser- und Epheserbriefe* (Lund, 1946), p. 285; Fr.

Mussner, *Christus, das All und die Kirche* (Trier, 1968), pp. 94-6; R. J. McKelvey, *The New Temple* (Oxford, 1968), pp. 118-20; B. Gärtner, *The Temple and the Community in Qumran and the New Testament* (Cambridge, 1965), pp. 60-5; M Barth, *Ephesians* (The Anchor Bible, vol. 34) (Garden City, Ny, 1974), pp. 285f.; M. Wolter, *Rechtfertigung* (as in chapter eight, n. 13), pp. 62-73.

10. E. Schweizer, 'Die Kirche als Leib Christi', in his *Neotestamentica* (Zurich, 1963), pp. 294-316; H. Schlier, *Der Brief an die Epheser* (Düsseldorf, 1968); P. Pokorný, *Der Epheserbrief und die Gnosis* (Berlin, 1965), pp. 20f.; J. T. Sanders, *The New Testament Christological Hymns* (Cambridge, 1971), pp. 88-92; cf. J. Gnilka, *Der Epheserbrief* (Freiburg, 1971), excursus 5 (pp. 147-52).

11. G. Schille, *Frühchristliche Hymnen* (Berlin, 1965), espec. pp. 24-37.

12. R. Deichgräber, *Gotteshymnus und Christushymnus in der frühen Christenheit* (Göttingen, 1967), pp. 165-9.

13. J. T. Sanders, 'Hymnic Elements in Ephesians 1-3', *Zeitschrift für die Neutestamentliche Wissenschaft* 56 (1965-6), pp. 217f.

14. J. C. Kirby, *Ephesians; Baptism and Pentecost* (London, 1968), pp. 156f., 169, 189.

15. K. E. Bailey, *Poet and Peasant* (Grand Rapids, 1976), p. 63.

16. G. Giavini, 'La structure littéraire d'Eph. II. 11-22', *New Testament Studies* 16 (1969-70), pp. 209-11.

17. See nn. 12, 9; P. Stuhlmacher, '"Er ist unser Friede" (Eph. 2, 14)', in *Neues Testament und Kirche. Für Rudolf Schnackenburg*, ed. J. Gnilka (Freiburg, 1974), pp. 337-58.

18. See n. 6; D. Lührmann, 'Rechtfertigung und Versöhnung. Zur Geschichte der paulinischen Tradition', *Zeitschrift für Theologie und Kirche* 67 (1970), pp. 437-52 (447f.). Cf. K. Wengst, *Christologische Formeln und Lieder des Urchristentums* (Gütersloh, 1972), pp. 177f.

19. R. Deichgräber, *Gotteshymnus*, p. 166, argues against this on the ground that the 'both' in verse 16 looks back to a previous mention of the two human groups in verses 11-13. But the hymn's original form related to God and man as reconciled. Only by extension did a later hand introduce the notion of ethnic reconciliation.

20. H. Sahlin, *Die Beschneidung Christi* (Lund, 1950).

21. K. G. Kuhn, 'The Epistle to the Ephesians in the light of the Qumran Texts', in *Paul and Qumran*, ed. J. Murphy-O'Connor (London, ET 1968), pp. 115-31.

22. N. A. Dahl, 'Das Gehemnis der Kirche nach Eph. 3, 8-10', in *Zur Auferbauung des Leibes Christi*. Festschrift Peter Brunner (Kassel, 1965), p. 74, n. 45; cf. W. A. Meeks, 'In One Body: The Unity of Humankind in Colossians and Ephesians', in *God's Christ and His People*. Studies in Honor of Nils Alstrup Dahl, edd. J. Jervell and W. A. Meeks (Oslo, 1977), pp. 209-21 (215).

23. E. Testa, 'Gesù Pacificatore Universale', in *Studii Biblici Franciscani Liber Annuus* 19 (1965), pp. 5-64. I owe this reference to W. Rader, *The Church and Racial Hostility*, p. 198.

24. K. M. Fischer, *Tendenz und Absicht des Epheserbriefes* (Göttingen, 1973), p. 80.

25. W. Foerster, *TDNT*, vol. 2, p. 414.

26. P. Stuhlmacher, 'Er ist unser Friede' (as in n. 17), p. 356.

27. E. Käsemann, 'Some Thoughts', (as in chapter five, n. 1), pp. 60-1.

28. M. Wolter, *Rechtfertigung* (as in chapter eight, n. 13), p. 63, n. 127. D.

Lührmann, 'Rechtfertigung' (as in n. 18), p. 445, and V. P. Furnish, 'The Ministry of Reconciliation' (as in chapter six, n. 4), p. 211; both appeal to 2 Corinthians 5:19*b* as indicating the priority of the 'anthropological variant' to cosmic reconciliation in Paul's theology of redemption. They criticise Käsemann for his failure to observe this priority.

29. Ch. Perrot, 'La lecture synagogale d'Exode 21:1-22:23 et son influence sur la littérature néo-testamentaire', in *A La Rencontre de Dieu*. Mémorial A. Gelin (Le Puy, 1961), pp. 223-39. I owe this reference to W. Rader, *The Church and Racial Hostility*, p. 200.

30. H. Chadwick, 'Die Absicht des Epheserbriefes', *Zeitschrift für die Neutestamentliche Wissenschaft* 51 (1960), pp. 145-53 (147).

31. Ch. Masson, *L'épître de saint Paul aux Ephésiens* (Neuchâtel, 1950), p. 165, who gives the references to Dibelius, Haupt, and Schneider.

32. K. M. Fischer, *Tendenz und Absicht* (as in n. 24), pp. 131-7. The Nag Hammadi evidence is cited in translation from *The Nag Hammadi Library*, ed. J. M. Robinson (New York, 1977).

33. C. Colpe, *Die religionsgeschichtliche Schule* (Göttingen, 1961), pp. 199-208.

34. M. Hengel, *Judaism and Hellenism* (as in chapter two, n. 3), vol. 1, pp. 169f., 308f., referring to H. Braun, *Spätjüdisch-häretischer und frühchristlicher Radikalismus*, 2 vols. (Tübingen, 1957), vol. 2, pp. 29ff. See H. Conzelmann, *Jesus* (Philadelphia, ET 1973), p. 18.

35. W. Nauck, 'Eph. 2, 19-22 — ein Tauflied?', *Evangelische Theologie* 13 (1965), pp. 362-71; criticised by H. Merklein, *Die kirchliche Amt* (as in n. 8),pp. 119f.

36. W. A. Meeks, 'In One Body' (as in n. 22), p. 215.

37. I am indebted to a paper written for a New Testament seminar by Robert S. Reid for this paragraph.

38. D. C. Smith, 'The Ephesian Heresy', in *Biblical Literature: 1974 Proceedings* (Missoula, 1974), pp. 45-54, on which I have drawn for much of the above discussion. See too D. L. Balch, 'Background of I C. VII: Sayings of the Lord in Q; Moses as an Ascetic *Theios Aner*', *New Testament Studies* 18 (1971-2), pp. 351-64.

CHAPTER TEN (pp. 201-224)

1. J. W. Fraser, *Jesus and Paul* (as in chapter two, n. 7), p. 59.

2. J. Héring, *The Second Epistle of Saint Paul to the Corinthians* (London, ET 1967), p. 27, n. 21.

3. T. W. Manson, *The Sayings of Jesus* (London, 1949), p. 282.

4. See O. Hofius, *Jesu Tischgemeinschaft mit den Sündern* (Stuttgart, 1967), pp. 16-25, who has clearly shown how Jesus' practice of sharing a meal with the men and women whom official Judaism despised was tantamount to the offer and receiving of God's forgiveness and also promised an anticipation of the eschatological feast in God's kingdom (Isa. 25:6). On both counts Jesus' action was the good news not in word only but in action. This disposition provoked the fierce protest of the 'pious' ones in Israel who failed in their responsibility as faithful shepherds of the poor (Ezek. 34) and objected to Jesus' role as the messianic shepherd, sent to the 'lost sheep of the house of Israel' (Matt. 15:24).
A similar argument is found in P. Stuhlmacher, 'Jesus als Versöhner', in *Jesus Christus in Historie und Theologie*, Festschrift H. Conzelmann, ed. G. Strecker (Tübingen, 1975), pp. 96f.

5. J. Jeremias, *The Parables of Jesus* (London, 2nd ed., ET 1963), pp. 27, 108. The stress on God's goodness to all permits E. Fuchs, 'Das Zeitverständnis Jesu', *Gesammelte Aufsätze*, vol. 2 (Tübingen, 1960), p. 362, to comment that in this parable 'Matthew's gospel reaches its high point', and G. Bornkamm, 'Der Lohngedanke im NT', *Studien zu Antike und Urchristentum* (Munich, 1959), p. 83, to remark that the parable is 'the synoptic example of what is at the church's basis — its *articulus stantis et cadentis* — justification by faith alone'. On the rabbinic background with its tremendous contrast in tone and demand, see E. Jüngel, *Paulus und Jesus* (as in chapter three, n. 1), pp. 164-9.

6. See the discussion, with other views referred to, in H. Conzelmann, *Jesus* (as in chapter nine, n. 34), p. 71.

7. R. Otto, *The Kingdom of God and the Son of Man* (London, ET 1943), p. 103.

8. J. M. Hull, *Hellenistic Magic and the Synoptic Tradition* (London, 1974).

9. A. Fridrichsen, *The Problem of Miracle in Primitive Christianity* (Minneapolis, ET 1972); R. Leivestad, *Christ the Conqueror* (London, ET 1954); G. Aulén, *Christus Victor* (London, ET 1931).

10. See the reference to a discussion of Matt. 11:25-30 in R. P. Martin, *New Testament Foundations*, vol. 1 (Exeter/Grand Rapids, 1975), pp. 291-8. R. J. Bauckham, 'The Sonship of the Historical Jesus in Christology', *Scottish Journal of Theology* 31 (1978), pp. 245-60, brings the discussion up to date, concluding that 'we should regard this consciousness of unique sonship as the determinative factor in Jesus' life' (253). But 'sharing his sonship with others' seems to lessen the value of the adjective 'unique' in Bauckham's sentence.

11. Cf. D. E. Aune, 'Abba', *International Standard Bible Encyclopedia*, vol. 1 (1979 ed.), pp. 3f., based on J. Jeremias, *The Prayers of Jesus* (London, 1967), pp. 35-65; idem, *The Lord's Prayer* (Philadelphia, ET 1964).

12. See Jeremias, *The Prayers of Jesus*, p. 54; G. Vermes, *Jesus the Jew* (London, 1973), pp. 210-13, who comments on the example of the rabbinic 'holy man', Honi the Circle-Drawer.

13. I. H. Marshall, *The Gospel of Luke* (Exeter/Grand Rapids, 1978), p. 129.

14. E. Schweizer, *TDNT*, vol. 8, p. 368.

15. J. D. G. Dunn, *Jesus and the Spirit* (London, 1975), pp. 62-5.

16. E. Lohmeyer, *Der Brief an die Philipper* (as in chapter four, n. 22), p. 98. His words are: 'In order to snatch back the world from the power of Satan, and to reinstate God, he who was in the form of God took the road from heaven to earth. That he has become Lord is the sign that the victory is won, and therefore the word "Father" betokens that now God and the world are "reconciled" [*versöhnt*] and are one.'

17. Quoted by W. Barclay, *ExpT* 78 (1966-7), p. 32.

POSTSCRIPT (pp. 224-233)

1. F. F. Bruce, *Paul. Apostle of the Free Spirit*, pp. 422f. See too J. S. Stewart, 'A First-Century Heresy and its Modern Counterpart', *Scottish Journal of Theology* 23 (1970), pp. 420-36.

2. A. M. Hunter, *Interpreting Paul's Gospel* (London, 1954), pp. 104, 118.

3. C. A. A. Scott, *Saint Paul the Man and the Teacher* (Cambridge, 1936), p. 59.

4. Paul van Buren, 'On Doing Theology', in *Talk of God* (Royal Institute of Philosophy Lectures, vol. 2 [1967-8]), ed. G. N. A. Vesey (New York, 1969), p. 53 (in italics).

APPENDIX (PP. 235-42)

[1] J. C. Beker, *Paul the Apostle, The Triumph of God in Life and Thought* (Philadelphia, 1980: revised with new preface, 1984).

[2] C. Rowland, *Christian Origins* (London, 1985).

[3] R. P. Martin, *Philippians* (New Century Bible: rev. ed. Grand Rapids, 1980): *Carmen Christi: Philippians 2:5–11* (revised preface to 1983 reprint: Grand Rapids); *The Spirit and The Congregation: Studies in 1 Corinthians 12–14* (Grand Rapids, 1984); *2 Corinthians*. Word Biblical Commentary, vol. 40 (Waco, 1986), Introduction; and "Paul's Opponents" in *Tradition and Interpretation in the New Testament*. Essays in Honor of E. Earle Ellis, ed. G. F. Hawthorne & O. Betz (Grand Rapids/Tübingen, 1987), 279–89.

[4] See the bibliography in R. P. Martin, *James*. Word Biblical Commentary, vol. 48 (Waco, 1988), and now M. Hengel, "Der Jakobusbrief als anti-paulinische Polemik," 248–78, in *Tradition and Interpretation in the New Testament* (n. 3).

[5] E. P. Sanders, *Paul and Palestinian Judaism*, (London: 1977), pp. 431–42.

[6] See J. G. Gibbs, *Creation and Redemption* (Leiden, 1971); I reviewed this important book in *Journal of Biblical Literature* 91 (1972): 429–31.

[7] This is virtually the conclusion reached at the end of J. D. G. Dunn's discussion of *The Unity and Diversity in the New Testament* (Philadelphia, 1977), 369–70: "The *integrating centre* [is] Jesus himself" (author's italics).

[8] H. Chadwick, *NTS* 1 (1954–55): 261–75.

[9] Sanders, *Paul and Palestinian Judaism*, 441f.

[10] C. J. A. Hickling, "Centre and Periphery in the Thought of Paul". *Studia Biblica 1978; III*. Papers on Paul and Other NT Authors. Sixth International Congress on Biblical Studies, ed. E. A. Livingstone (Oxford, 1980) pp. 199–214.

[11] Ibid., 208f.

[12] Ibid., 214.

[13] Beker, *Paul the Apostle*, 15–19. In his revised edition (1984) Beker has restated this thesis, and nuanced his position (pp. xiii–xxi). Note too his more popular *Paul's Apocalyptic Gospel* (Philadelphia, 1982).

[14] Ibid., xix.

[15] E. F. Osborn, "The Unity of God in Pauline Thought", *Australian Biblical Review* 28 (1980): 39–56.

[16] Ibid., 54.

[17] See, on the other hand, P. Stuhlmacher's several essays on this theme of righteousness in his *Reconciliation, Law, Righteousness* (Philadelphia, ET 1986).

[18] E. Käsemann, "The Saving Significance of the Death of Jesus in Paul" *Perspectives on Paul* (ET 1971), 32–59, has argued this point with great verve by showing that Paul's twin enemies were Jewish nomism and Hellenistic enthusiasm. Käsemann's resistance to all kinds of a *theologia gloriae*, whether triumphalistic, ecclesiastical or evidential raises problems for a theology of Paul that includes the term *triumph* in its sub-title.

[19] D. S. Gilliland, *Pauline Theology and Mission Practice* (Grand Rapids, 1983), has seen and expressed this dimension of Paul's thought, which is often neglected. A. Schlatter's dictum needs to be recalled: "Paul the apostle not only proclaimed the Passion story; he also lived it out" (cited in Martin, *2 Corinthians*, 341).

[20]Cf. the observation of A. C. Thiselton, *The Anvil* 3, 2. 1986, to the effect that Jesus dit not come to preach reconciliation; he actually did reconcile persons.

[21]P. Stuhlmacher's essay, " 'Er ist unser Friede' (Eph. 2, 14)" referred to in chapter nine above is now in ET as " 'He is our Peace' (Eph. 2:14)", ch. 11, in *Reconciliation, Law, Righteousness*.

[22]Cyril S. Rodd, *ExpT* 94 (1982): 33–34.

[23]C. F. D. Moule, *Journal of Theological Studies*, 34 (1983): 559–601.

[24]Jeffrey W. Gillette, *Trinity Journal* 3 (1982): 110–11.

[25]R. S. Barbour, *Scottish Journal of Theology* 37 (1984): 118–20.

[26]See F. F. Bruce, "Paul and the Powers that Be," *Bulletin of the John Rylands Library* 66 (1984): 78–96.

[27]Beker, *Paul the Apostle* . See my review in *Journal of Biblical Interpretation* 101 (1982): 463–66. He has not directly responded to this critique in his 1984 preface.

[28]See his *Paul's Apocalyptic Gospel*, 79–121.

[29]William S. Campbell, *Theology* 86: 712 (1983): 300–302.

[30]This concession would answer D. E. H. Whiteley's question: "Is Martin right in supposing that reconciliation is central? We must ask 'central *for whom?*' " *Journal for the Study of the New Testament* 20 (1984): 124 (his italics).

[31]J. A. Ziesler, *The Epworth Review* 10 (1983): 99–100.

[32]C. H. Giblin, *Catholic Biblical Quarterly* 45 (1983): 313–14. See also F. F. Bruce, *The Churchman* 97 (1983): 60–61.

SELECT BIBLIOGRAPHY

Allmen, D. von, 'Réconciliation du monde et christologie cosmique', *Revue d'Histoire et de Philosophie religieuses* 1 (1968), Strasbourg. pp. 32-45

Barrett, C.K. *The Epistle to the Romans* (London: A. and C. Black, New York: Harper and Row, 1957)

———. *The First Epistle to the Corinthians* (London: A. and C. Black, New York: Harper and Row, 1968)

———. *From First Adam to Last* (London: A. and C. Black, 1962)

———. *The Second Epistle to the Corinthians* (London: A. and C. Black, New York: Harper and Row, 1973)

Black, M. *Romans* (London: Oliphants, 1973)

Bornkamm, G. *Paul* (New York: Harper and Row. ET 1971)

Bruce, F.F. *The Epistle of Paul to the Romans* (London: Tyndale Press, 1963)

———. *Paul and Jesus* (Grand Rapids: Baker Book House, 1974)

———. *Paul. Apostle of the Free Spirit* (Exeter: The Paternoster Press: U.S. title, *Paul: Apostle of the Heart Set Free*, Grand Rapids: Wm. B. Eerdmans, 1977)

Bultmann, R. *Theology of the New Testament*, 2 volumes (London: SCM; ET vol. 1, 1952, vol. 2, 1955)

Collange, J.-F. *Enigmes de la deuxième épître de Paul aux Corinthiens* (Cambridge: The University Press, 1972)

Crabtree, A.B. *The Restored Relationship* (London: Carey Kingsgate Press, 1963)

Cranfield, C.E.B. *The Epistle to the Romans* vol. 1 (Edinburgh: T. and T. Clark, 1975) (vol. 2, 1979)

Davies, W.D. *Paul and Rabbinic Judaism* (London: SPCK, second edit. 1955)

Deichgräber, R. *Gotteshymnus und Christushymnus in der frühen Christenheit* (Göttingen: Vandenhoeck und Ruprecht, 1967)

Deissmann, A. *The Religion of Jesus and the Faith of Paul* (London: Hodder and Stoughton, ET 1923)

———. *St. Paul. A Study in Social and Religious History* (London: Hodder and Stoughton, ET 1925)

Dunn, J.D.G. *Jesus and the Spirit* (London: SCM Press, Philadelphia: The Westminster Press, 1975)

———. 'Paul's Understanding of the Death of Jesus' in *Reconciliation and Hope*. New Testament Essays on Atonement and Eschatology. Presented to L.L. Morris on his 60th Birthday. Ed. Robert J. Banks (Exeter: The Paternoster Press, 1974), pp. 125-141

———. *Unity and Diversity in the New Testament* (London: SCM Press, Philadelphia: The Westminster Press, 1977)

Dupont, J. *La réconciliation dans la théologie de saint Paul* (Paris/Bruges: Desclée de Brouwer, Publications Universitaires de Louvain, 1953)

Eichholz, G. *Die Theologie des Paulus im Umriss* (Neukirchen-Vluyn: Neukirchener Verlag, 1972)

Fischer, K.M. *Tendenz und Absicht des Epheserbriefes* (Göttingen: Vandenhoeck und Ruprecht, 1973)

Fitzmyer, J.A. 'Reconciliation in Pauline Theology' in *No Famine in the Land*. Studies in Honor of John L. MacKenzie, edd. J.W. Flanagan and A.W. Robinson. (Missoula: The Scholars Press, 1975), pp. 155-177

Fraser, J.W. *Jesus and Paul: Paul as an Interpreter of Jesus from Harnack to Kümmel* (Abingdon: Marcham Press, 1974)

Furnish, V.P. *The Moral Teaching of Paul* (Nashville: Abingdon Press, 1979)

———. 'The Ministry of Reconciliation', *Currents in Theology and Mission* 4, St. Louis (1977), pp. 204-218.

Goppelt, L. 'Versöhnung durch Christus,' *Christologie und Ethik* (Göttingen: Vandenhoeck und Ruprecht, 1968), pp. 147-164

Hanson, A.T. *Paul's Understanding of Jesus* (Hull: The University Press, 1963)
——. *Studies in Paul's Technique and Theology* (London: SPCK, Grand Rapids: Wm. B. Eerdmans, 1974)
Hasel, G.F. *New Testament Theology: Basic Issues in the Current Debate* (Grand Rapids: Wm. B. Eerdmans, 1978)
Hill, D. *Greek Words and Hebrew Meanings* (Cambridge: The University Press, 1967)
Hunt, E.W. *Portrait of Paul* (London: A.R. Mowbray, 1968)
Hunter, A.M. *Paul and his Predecessors* (London: SCM Press, second edit., 1961)
Jüngel, E. *Paulus und Jesus. Eine Untersuchung zur Präzisierung der Frage nach dem Ursprung der Christologie* (Tübingen: J.C.B. Mohr, second edit.; 1964)
Käsemann, E. *New Testament Questions of Today* (London: SCM Press, Philadelphia: Fortress Press, ET 1969)
——. *Perspectives on Paul* (London: SCM Press, Philadelphia: Fortress Press, ET 1971)
——. 'Some Thoughts on the Theme "The Doctrine of Reconciliation in the New Testament"' in *The Future of our Religious Past*, ed. J.M. Robinson (London: SCM Press, New York: Harper and Row, 1971)
——. 'Zum Verständnis von Röm. 3:24-26' in *Exegetische Versuche und Besinnungen*, vol. 1 (Göttingen: Vandenhoeck und Ruprecht, 1960)
Keck, L.E. *Paul and His Letters* (Philadelphia: Fortress Press, 1979)
Kümmel, W.G. 'Interpretation of Romans 5:1-11' in *Exegetical Method. A Students' Handbook*, edd. O. Kaiser and W.G. Kümmel (New York: The Seabury Press, 1963), pp. 49-58
——. *Man in the New Testament* (London: The Epworth Press, ET 1963)
Lohse, E. *Colossians and Philemon* (Philadelphia: Fortress Press, ET 1971)
——. *Märtyrer und Gottesknecht* (Göttingen: Vandenhoeck und Ruprecht, second edit. 1963)
Lührmann, D. 'Rechtfertigung und Versöhnung. Zur Geschichte der paulinischen Tradition,' *Zeitschrift für Theologie und Kirche*, Tübingen, 67 (1970), pp. 437-452
Lyonnet, S. and Sabourin, L. *Sin, Redemption, and Sacrifice: A Biblical and Patristic Study* (Rome: Biblical Institute, 1970)
J.G. Machen. *The Origin of Paul's Religion* (Grand Rapids: Wm. B. Eerdmans, 1925)
Malherbe, A.J. *Social Aspects of Early Christianity* (Baton Rouge: Louisiana State University Press, 1977)
Manson, T.W. (ed. M. Black). *On Paul and John* (London: SCM Press, 1963)
——. '2 Cor. 2:14-17; Suggestions towards an Exegesis' in *Studia Paulina in honorem J. de Zwaan*, edd. J.N. Sevenster and W.C. van Unnik (Haarlem: Erven F. Bohn, 1953)
Marshall, I.H. 'The Meaning of "Reconciliation"' in *Unity and Diversity in New Testament Theology*. Essays in Honor of George E. Ladd, ed. R.A. Guelich. (Grand Rapids: Wm. B. Eerdmans, 1978), pp. 117-132
Masson, Ch. *L'épître de saint Paul aux Éphésiens* (Neuchâtel/Paris: Delachaux et Niestlé, 1950)
McKelvey, R.J. *The New Temple — The Church in the New Testament* (Oxford: The University Press, 1968)
Meeks, W.A. 'In One Body: The Unity of Humankind in Colossians and Ephesians' in *God's Christ and His People. Studies in Honor of Nils Alstrup Dahl*, edd. J. Jervell and W.A. Meeks (Oslo: Universitets forlaget, 1977)
Morris, L. *The Apostolic Preaching of the Cross* (London: Tyndale Press, third edit. 1965)
Moule, C.F.D. *The Origin of Christology* (Cambridge: The University Press, 1977)
Munck, J. *Christ and Israel. An Interpretation of Romans 9-11* (Philadelphia: Fortress Press, ET 1967)
O'Brien, P.T. 'Col. 1:20 and the Reconciliation of All Things,' *Reformed Theological Review*, Melbourne, Victoria 33 (1974), pp. 45-53
Otto, R. *The Kingdom of God and the Son of Man.* (London: Lutterworth Press, ET 1943)
Rader, W. *The Church and Racial Hostility. A History of Interpretation of Ephesians 2:11-22* (Tübingen: J.C.B. Mohr, 1978)
Reitzenstein, R. *Hellenistic Mystery-Religions* (Pittsburgh: Pickwick Press, ET 1978)
Ridderbos, H. *Paul and Jesus. The Origin and General Character of Paul's Preaching of Christ* (Grand Rapids: Baker Book House, ET 1958)
——. *Paul: An Outline of his Theology* (Grand Rapids: Wm. B. Eerdmans, ET 1975)

Robinson, J.M. (ed.) *The Nag Hammadi Library* (New York: Harper and Row, 1977)
Robinson, J.A.T. *The Body. A Study in Pauline Theology* (London: SCM Press, 1952)
———. *Wrestling with Romans* (London: SCM Press, 1979)
Sanders, E.P. *Paul and Palestinian Judaism* (Philadelphia: Fortress Press, London: SCM Press, 1977)
Schmithals, W. *Gnosticism at Corinth* (Nashville: Abingdon Press, ET 1971)
Schoeps, H.J. *Paul. The Theology of the Apostle in the Light of Jewish Religious History* (London: Lutterworth Press, Philadelphia: The Westminster Press, ET 1961)
Schweitzer, A. *The Mysticism of the Apostle Paul* (London: A. and C. Black, ET 1931)
Schweizer, E. 'The Church as the Missionary Body of Christ,' *New Testament Studies*, Cambridge, 8 (1961-62), pp. 1-11
———. 'Kolosser 1, 15-20' in *Beiträge zur Theologie des Neuen Testaments, Neutestamentliche Aufsätze (1955-1970)* (Zurich, 1970), pp. 113-145
Scott, C.A.A. *Christianity according to St. Paul* (Cambridge: The University Press, 1927)
Scroggs, R. *The Last Adam* (Oxford: Blackwell, 1966)
———. *Paul for a New Day* (Philadelphia: Fortress Press, 1977)
Smith, Derwood C. 'The Ephesian Heresy' in *Biblical Literature: 1974 Proceedings* (Missoula: The Scholars Press, 1974), pp. 45-54
Stendahl, K. *Paul among Jews and Gentiles* (Philadelphia: Fortress Press, 1977)
Stuhlmacher, P. *Das Evangelium von der Versöhnung in Christus* (Stuttgart: Calwer Verlag, 1979)
———. '"Er ist unser Friede" (Eph. 2, 14)' in *Neues Testament und Kirche. Für Rudolf Schnackenburg*, ed. J. Gnilka (Freiburg: Herder, 1974), pp. 337-358
———. 'Jesus als Versöhner' in *Jesus Christus in Historie und Theologie. Festschrift H. Conzelmann*, ed. G. Strecker (Tübingen: J.C.B. Mohr, 1975), pp. 87-104
Taylor, V. *Forgiveness and Reconciliation* (London: MacMillan, second edit. 1946)
Unnik, W.C. van, *Tarsus or Jerusalem: The City of Paul's Youth* (London: The Epworth Press, ET 1962)
Weiss, J. *Earliest Christianity. A History of the Period A.D. 30-150*, vols. 1, 2 (New York: Harper and Row, ET 1959)
Whiteley, D.E.H. *The Theology of St. Paul* (Oxford: Blackwell, second edit. 1974)
Williams, S.K. *Jesus' Death as Saving Event. The Background and Origin of a Concept* (Missoula: The Scholars Press, 1975)
Wolter, M. *Rechtfertigung und zukünftiges Heil. Untersuchungen zu Röm. 5:1-11* (Berlin: de Gruyter, 1978)
Wrede, W. *Paul* (London: P. Green, ET 1907).
Ziesler, J.A. *The Meaning of Righteousness in Paul* (Cambridge: The University Press, 1972)

INDEX OF SUBJECTS

INDEX OF MODERN AUTHORS

INDEX OF PRINCIPAL SCRIPTURAL PASSAGES AND OTHER WRITINGS

INTER-TESTAMENTAL AND OTHER JEWISH LITERATURE

OTHER ANCIENT AUTHORS AND WRITINGS